Blind Evolution?

The Creation of Adam,
Sistine Chapel fresco by Michelangelo, c.1508-12.

BLIND EVOLUTION?

The Nature of Humanity and the Origin of Life

David Frost

Ⓒ
James Clarke & Co

James Clarke & Co

P.O. Box 60
Cambridge
CB1 2NT
United Kingdom

www.jamesclarke.co
publishing@jamesclarke.co

Hardback ISBN: 978 0 227 17696 2
Paperback ISBN: 978 0 227 17711 2
PDF ISBN: 978 0 227 90691 0
ePub ISBN: 978 0 227 90692 7

British Library Cataloguing in Publication Data
A record is available from the British Library

First published by James Clarke & Co, 2020
Copyright © David Frost, 2020

To my grandchildren,
Daniel, Matthew, Natasha, Tiffany and Sebastian,
whose delightful reality lured me to explore again
the whole question of origins

CONTENTS

List of Illustrations

Preface

It is now more than fifty years since the events that occasioned the writing of this book. I was then a Fellow of St John's College, Cambridge and had just been appointed to a lectureship in the English Faculty of the University. As a specialist in English Renaissance drama who was about to publish a study of the interaction of Shakespeare with his contemporaries, *The School of Shakespeare* (1968), and also as a member of a Church of England Liturgical Commission charged with devising an *Alternative Service Book* in acceptable modern English for the Anglican Church (my special responsibility, with a panel of Hebraists, being a modern English translation of the Book of Psalms), I must have seemed a godsend to my Faculty colleagues as supervisor for a newly arrived student from India, Mangala Nilakantan, in 1968 the first woman to win the Nehru Memorial Scholarship. She (though a Hindu from a Brahmin family distinguished by many generations of scholarly pundits) had offered a research topic that spanned both Christian theology and literature: 'The Problem of Evil in Jacobean Drama'.

Recent research directed by the University of Kent into beliefs currently prevalent in five different countries indicates that a large proportion of any population, whether they be atheists, agnostics or followers of an established religion, hold that some things 'are just meant to be'. But however appropriate the arrangements made by the Cambridge English Faculty, after what was only a year of supervision I felt obliged, by what

I still hold to be a proper if unwritten code of conduct, to inform the Chairman of the Faculty that I and my pupil had developed a more than academic interest in each other and hence she should be directed to another supervisor.

We are now two years away from celebrating fifty years of marriage and if 'By their fruits shall you know them' be an acceptable test, our meeting was providential for the fulfilment of what we both felt ourselves, as individuals, required to do. Together we have brought up four children, all of whom have experience of differing cultures. We have five grandchildren, to whom I have dedicated this current book, because their existence has confronted me with the basic questions that I wrestle with daily and which are the subject of this present study. Christine Mangala, who before our marriage was baptised into the Christian faith, has fulfilled the aim of the Nehru Memorial Trust to encourage understanding between members of the Commonwealth of nations, by, first of all, publishing a series of novels in English set mainly in India and drawing on her knowledge and experience of the culture into which she was born. Her first volume, *The Firewalkers* (1991), was shortlisted for the Commonwealth Best First Book Prize and the London *Deo Gloria* award. Though she currently has a fourth novel, *Shalimar Gardens*, forthcoming, its narrative set in an India now convulsed by Hindu and Muslim conflict, her fundamental concern for reconciling competing religions, which has been her interest in inter-faith dialogue, has been maintained by teaching comparative religion in the University of Newcastle, New South Wales, Australia (where I was for twenty-one years a Professor of English Literature and for part of that time also Chairman of Religious Studies), and then subsequently back in Cambridge, where for eleven years I held an honorary post as Principal and Administrator of the Institute for Orthodox Christian Studies, part of the Cambridge Theological Federation, where Christine Mangala could further her research interests as an invited lecturer. Finally, by publication of *The Human Icon: A Comparative Study of Hindu and Orthodox Christian Beliefs* (Cambridge: James Clarke & Co., 2017), she has discharged her obligation both to her Hindu past and her Christian faith.

From all this, one duty remains, which springs from the days of our first meeting and which my own book is designed to fulfil. Our developing personal relationship meant that Mangala had to be directed to a new Faculty supervisor, Wilbur Sanders, who, though eminently qualified, expressed some unease lest her evident religious concerns might dominate what, by its nature, he felt should be a more dispassionate intellectual pursuit.

Then occurred one of those catastrophic irruptions of evil into everyday life that brings everything we have believed about our situation and our very existence into question. The young daughter of Mangala's new supervisor, crossing the road outside their home in Grange Road, was knocked down by a passing car and killed outright.

We both felt, I as a colleague of Wilbur Sanders in the Faculty and Mangala as his current research student, an obligation to call on the family and, as the conventional term is, 'to convey our sympathies'.

The memory of that visit has stayed with us for all of the intervening years. We found ourselves, like Job's comforters in the Old Testament, unable to do more than sit on the ground with him and weep. What else was there to say?

Discovering what more there might be to say has been my recurring preoccupation for almost half a century: I am no longer content to sit on the ground and weep, and would rather try to explore and reconcile what seem our contradictory human experiences as a race or species. Hence, my original title for what was initially a proposed series of lectures for the Antiochian Orthodox Church of Australasia, 'The Goodness of God and the Problem of Evil', which the President of the Cambridge Institute, Metropolitan Kallistos Ware, suggested might be emended to 'The Goodness of God and the *Challenge* of Evil', since I might otherwise be read as claiming to have entirely solved the problem! Being myself an incompetent mathematician, my retort to him was that for me a 'problem' signified something that you were always unable fully to resolve. But I am especially grateful to my then editor at James Clarke & Co., Frazer Merritt, for perceiving that the immediate interest of my writing for today's public was likely to be my 'boots-and-all' attack on atheistic neo-Darwinism, countering its assertion that evolution had occurred solely by chance and is essentially without direction or meaning. Hence, the stark and questioning title, '**BLIND EVOLUTION?**', for which my own subtitle, 'The Nature of Humanity and the Origin of Life', gives some indication of the range of discussion made possible by a more discriminating approach to scientific evidence. However, I cannot neglect mentioning Frazer's successor as Production Editor at James Clarke & Co., Debora Nicosia, who achieved that writer's dream: of giving the author exactly what he or she wanted, without compromising the book-designer's craft.

It is usual in a Preface to thank those who have contributed to the book – but with the exception of Christine Mangala, who should by rights be credited as co-author – it turns out that, when you reach beyond an eightieth year, most of those who were formative in your life and work have passed on and will now have, if our shared beliefs were correct, a better appreciation of just how I much owe them – a 'great cloud of witnesses'. Nevertheless, among my family support team, I owe a special debt to son Mark, his wife Fong and children Matthew and Daniel, who have endured living daily with a work in progress, to son Kim, who advised on content and how to make stills, to daughters Juliet and Meera and her husband Dan Juncu, who gathered the illustrations so essential to my argument, and who have also kept me in touch with the likely preoccupations of readers of their generation. But above all, I'd like to thank two pair of longstanding friends who have been with us from the outset, Dr Robert Cockcroft and his wife, Susan, and the Revd Dr Andrew Macintosh, formerly Dean of Chapel of St John's College, Cambridge and his wife Mary, all of whom stood by us from our first meeting to the present day, and in counselling us both have invariably got their advice precisely right, if judged by its outcome. Andrew has a preferred method for ending a letter, which is an appropriate conclusion to my own Preface: '*Onward – and Upward!*'

David Frost,
Christmas Eve, 2019

CHAPTER ONE

The Answers of the Book of Job and the Experience of Mankind

In one sense, all that could helpfully be said on the problem that my proposed course of lectures was to face – 'The Goodness of God and the Challenge of Evil' – is already there in the Old Testament, in the Book of Job, written sometime in the first millennium before Christ. I hardly need to remind you of what it contains but I shall be interested to see if I can get through even a private rehearsal of its conclusion without breaking down in tears – something which I have never achieved when reading in public.

The story opens with Satan (whose name means 'the Accuser') suggesting to God that his servant Job, a man to all appearances entirely good and upright, is only so because of the rewards that he gets out of his righteousness: 'But stretch out your hand and strike everything he has, and he will surely curse you to your face' (Job 1: 11). So, God allows Satan to do to Job whatever Satan fancies – provided he leaves Job's person alone. So Job's work-animals, his oxen and his donkeys, are stolen by the Sabeans, who kill the servants looking after them. Then Job's sheep, together with their shepherds, are struck by lightning and his camels are taken by raiding Chaldeans. Finally, a desert wind collapses the house where Job's sons and daughters are feasting and all his offspring are killed (Job 1: 13-19).

But Job refuses to charge God with wrongdoing (Job 1: 22), so that when the angels (in Hebrew, 'the sons of God') next assemble before God, God is able to point out to Satan that Job (and I quote the words given to God) 'still maintains his integrity, though you incited me against him to ruin him without any reason' (Job 2: 3). Satan is then permitted to inflict what illnesses he pleases on Job, short of killing him: so Job receives 'painful sores from the soles of his feet to the top of his head' (Job 2: 7). His wife is exasperated by Job's claim not to have deserved all this: 'Are you still holding on to your integrity? Curse God and die!' (Job 2: 9) but she rightly gets slapped down by him: 'You are talking like a foolish woman. Shall we accept good from God, and not trouble?' (Job 2: 15).

Then three friends arrive, trying (much as we moderns would) to help by giving Job their company.

> But when they saw him from a distance, they could hardly recognize him; they began to weep aloud, and they tore their robes and sprinkled dust on their heads. Then they sat on the ground with him for seven days and seven nights. No one said a word to him, because they saw how great his suffering was.
> (Job 2: 12-13)

If any of us have had to visit a couple whose child has been knocked down and killed by a passing car, could we do anything more than Job's friends – sit on the ground and weep with them?

At the outset of Chapter 3 of the Old Testament account, Job opens his mouth and curses the day of his birth. He asks, 'Why is light given to those in misery, and life to the bitter of soul, to those who long for death that does not come' (Job 3: 20-21). That finally pushes Job's guests to the point where they feel that have to say *something*.

'Job's Comforters' are notorious as an instance of the kind of people who offer comfort that is no comfort at all. But, in a way, they have had a bad press. Eliphaz the Temanite is the first to be moved to say something – and his attempt to help chimes in with a great deal of human experience. He argues that God is just – and if Job is entirely innocent, he will eventually be vindicated: 'As I have observed, those who plough evil and those who sow trouble reap it. At the breath of God they are destroyed; at the blast of his anger they perish' (Job 4: 8-9).

The comfort that Eliphaz the Temanite offers Job is something that appeals to unbelievers and Christians alike: the assertion that there is, eventually, some justice in the world is based on widespread experience. Since I want throughout this discussion to tie matters to what we actually feel, I am prepared to testify that, when I think of the wrongs done to me in the course of a lengthy career, those cases where I know I had not been at fault have sooner or later been exposed, and the eventual consequences have been (at least so far) much to my benefit. The problem then seems to be, as the proverb puts it, that 'The mills of God grind slow' – vindication is late in coming.

The pagan Plutarch in the first century AD, in his *Moralia*, writing 'On the Delay in Divine Vengeance', sees the idea as one so widespread that even a sceptic must take some notice – although he adds: 'I do not see what use there is in those mills of the gods said to grind so late as to render punishment hard to be recognized, and to make wickedness to be fearless.'

However, that isn't exactly what we see happening, for sometimes things seem better than that – and again I am going to venture into personal experience. When I first arrived in Newcastle, New South Wales, Australia, for an interview for the Professorship of English at the University, I was met by an Anglican priest, the Revd. Lance Johnston, Principal of the Anglican training college of St John's, Morpeth. He was representing the Anglican Newcastle Diocese, since I was an Anglican of some reputation in the Old Country. But he and his wife Jenny went far beyond the call of duty in helping my young family to accommodate to a new country, and we became lifelong friends.

Now jump thirty-nine years, from early 1977 to mid-2016, when I received a phone call across the world from Newcastle, Australia, requiring me to give evidence to the Australian Royal Commission into Institutional Responses to Child Sexual Abuse, which was then investigating charges against a ring of senior homosexual clergy in the Newcastle diocese, who were alleged to have grossly, even blasphemously, abused young boys. A former mature student of mine had given evidence to the Commission that she had reported to me after a class that her adolescent son had been violated at a diocesan youth camp run by certain clergy, and I had undertaken to take up the matter with the then Bishop, Alfred Holland. I could not recall the name of the student after a gap of at least three decades but I did recall the incident, because it was unique. I could testify that I had informed the Bishop in confidence and that he later rang me to say he had contacted the boy's mother. If I suspected that not much might have been done, or that the boy's mother might have exaggerated, I had alerted the proper authority and had to leave matters there.

But my evidence thirty or so years later supported the mother's account and Bishop Holland was forced to fall back on the defence that he recalled nothing of the alleged episode – but that answer – 'I can't remember' – was a defence which a letter from the diocesan solicitor had advised the Bishop to make to all awkward questions – and it had been shown to the Commission. The charges of grossly improper behaviour by clergy were supported by a mass of testimony, and the bishop who had done nothing about it was now, in advanced old age, exposed and disgraced.

However, 'the slow mills of God' had not done yet. My lifelong friend, Lance Johnston, had been Principal of the theological college where many of the offending clergy had trained and he was at risk of being held responsible for a corrupt clique, or for turning a blind-eye. I was able, thanks to our long friendship that had sprung from Lance's initial care of my family, to testify that, as a Member of the St John's College, Morpeth, Board of Management and because our intimate family connection was so close, it was unbelievable that we would have not known of any problem that the Principal had with a paedophile ring.

That friendship led to some further evidence from me to the Commission and to the eventual humiliation of the next Bishop of Newcastle, Roger Herft, who by the time the Commission met had gone on to be Archbishop of Perth. It had been alleged before the Commission that the senior priest, who was a ringleader of the homosexual predators (though now dead) had been cross-examined by Bishop Herft, but the priest had managed to intimidate the Bishop by threatening legal action if any move were made against him. The excuse made for the Bishop doing nothing was that he had insufficient evidence to hand. However, I recalled one visit to my Newcastle home by my friend Lance Johnston, in great distress because he had just been told, immediately after confiding some intimate personal matters to the Bishop in an interview, that 'You do realize, Lance, that I record all conversations with my clergy, and the tapes are kept in the cellar at Bishopsthorpe'. We were therefore able to point to the likelihood of tapes being made and probably still existing of the Bishop's discussions with the offending priest, and we could substantiate our allegations as to the Bishop's practice, since we had been so outraged by it that we had later written jointly to a Committee considering appointments to the Archbishopric of Canterbury, suggesting that Archbishop Herft's violation of clergy trust made him unsuitable to be a candidate for that high office – and an acknowledgement of our objection was on record from the then Prime Minister's Secretary. In response to the Commission's criticisms of his inaction whilst Bishop of Newcastle, Roger Herft felt obliged to resign as Archbishop of Perth.

The problem with Eliphaz's consolations is that they are true to experience but they don't go far enough. He asks the protesting Job to 'Consider now: Who, being innocent, has ever perished? Where were the upright ever destroyed?' (Job, 4: 7). But take the instance of the Hillsborough disaster in England in 1989, where a football-stand collapsed and the ensuing panic cost the lives of ninety-six people. Responsibility was finally laid at the door of those who had been at fault, even if it took twenty-seven years to do it. Those who covered up what had happened were exposed, and *The Sun* newspaper, which had spread lies about allegedly irresponsible crowd behaviour, had its reporters banned from the premises of Liverpool Football Club. The bereaved who had campaigned for justice at last had closure and expressed an enormous sense of relief – but nothing could bring back their loved ones, killed for no crime but only because someone had been negligent or incompetent. However, exact justice did not stop there, for in November 2019 the police officer who had responded to pressure to admit insistent fans to stands he knew were already overloaded, and who had admitted to his shame that he had to an earlier enquiry denied his action, was acquitted of manslaughter. Strict justice required that he not be held guilty for more than an accidental, if admittedly negligent slaying, whilst those remaining of the bereaved who had demanded 'an eye for an eye and a tooth for a tooth' were deprived of what would only have been a pointless multiplication of evil.

But even that problem is resolved in the Hebrew version of the Book of Job, which has what Christians are bound to see as an extraordinary prophecy of Christ's coming, which took place at least half a millennium after the writing of the Book of Job. The prophecy is known internationally through Handel's *Messiah* and I'll quote it from the *New International Version* of the Bible, because it is a passage in the Hebrew scriptures which for reasons unknown was never reproduced in the much later translation of the Hebrew text into Greek for the Septuagint version of the Old Testament, made for Jews who could no longer read Hebrew. Many Orthodox Christians still take the Septuagint as their version of the Old Testament, even though it is at many other points seriously defective. It is probable that the Orthodox adopted the Septuagint version of the Old Testament because that was the Bible translation known to most early Christians, especially the writers of the New Testament – but in so doing, they have deprived themselves of a passage of extraordinary and crucial comfort:

I know that my Redeemer lives,
and that in the end he will stand upon the earth.
And after my skin has been destroyed,

yet in my flesh I will see God;
I myself will see him with my own eyes – I, and not another.
How my heart yearns within me!
(Job 19: 25-27)

That reads like a prophecy of the God/Man, Jesus Christ, who by his voluntary and innocent sacrifice, a death entirely undeserved, has conquered death itself and promises resurrection to all who have died and forgiveness for any wrongdoing, if only they will accept his gift of himself. How the prophecy got there in the Book of Job, or how it was omitted from the Septuagint translation, are both a mystery. But its promise is the full and complete answer to the problem of evil. And even if it is not in the Bibles of Orthodox Christians, the truth has somehow filtered into Orthodox thinking, for Righteous Job is celebrated as a 'type' of Christ, a forerunner of the one wholly righteous God/Man who 'by death trampled down death' and by his and our resurrection offers a complete justification of God's goodness and a total solution to the 'Challenge of Evil'. If we follow Christ, it will lead to the cross and we are likely in the world's eyes to be crushed; but our destruction, like his, is not final: justice and restoration await us.

Meanwhile, in the story, Job's Comforters persist with their insistence that, somewhere, somehow, God being just, Job must have gone off the rails. Job longs for a chance to have it out with God, face to face. 'So these three men stopped answering Job, because he was righteous in his own eyes' (Job 32: 1). The last person to speak to Job is the young man Elihu – and he dismisses the arguments of the Comforters altogether: 'I gave you my full attention. But not one of you has proved Job wrong; none of you has answered his arguments' (Job 32: 12). Elihu claims to be fired by 'the spirit within me' (Job 32: 18) and he argues that only God can refute Job's charge of injustice: once one fully appreciates what God is, what he has done, the mystery, glory and complexity of all his creation, his ways of communicating with individuals and his care for all things, and how man alone has been equipped to appreciate and reverence his wonders, then all questioning and protest will seem blasphemous. That theme is common throughout the Book of Psalms: God's nature is revealed in all that he has made. Take the opening of Psalm 19, vv.1-6, which I'll cite from *The Cambridge Liturgical Psalter*:[1]

---

1. *The Cambridge Liturgical Psalter (with Notes)* (Cambridge: Aquila, 2012), first published as *The Psalms: A New Translation for Worship* (London: William Collins, 1976, 1977), used in and bound up with *The Alternative Service Book 1980* as *The Liturgical Psalter*.

The heavens declare the glory of God:
and the firmament proclaims his handiwork;
One day tells it to another:
and night to night communicates knowledge.
There is no speech or language:
nor are their voices heard;
Yet their sound has gone out through all the world:
and their words to the ends of the earth.

You may remember how in the Book of Job God eventually does speak in answer to Job's complaining – and how God silences him by what God's modern and hostile critics have called a display of overweening power, an appeal to superior divine knowledge and might, a list of his spectacular achievements in creation, even (it is said) by a kind of fireworks display – to the point where Job's doubts and protests are simply overwhelmed.

I shall quote this time from the King James Authorized Version, for that is where I first met the words that I have never been able to read in public without breaking down:

Then the Lord answered Job out of the whirlwind, and said,
Who is this that darkeneth counsel by words without knowledge?
Gird up now thy loins like a man: for I will demand of thee;
and answer thou me.
Where wast thou when I laid the foundations of the earth?
declare, if thou hast understanding.
Who hath laid the measures thereof, if thou knowest?
or who hath stretched the line upon it?
Whereupon are the foundations thereof fastened?
or who laid the corner stone thereof;
When the morning stars sang together,
And all the sons of God shouted for joy?
(Job 38: 1-7, Authorized Version)

After four chapters of this, in which God appeals to the glory, beauty and complexity of the natural world that he has created, Job cracks:

Then Job answered the Lord, and said,
I know that thou canst do every *thing*,
and that no thought can be withholden from thee.
Who *is* he that hideth counsel without knowledge?
therefore have I uttered that I understood not;

things too wonderful for me, which I knew not.
Hear, I beseech thee, and I will speak:
I will demand of thee, and declare thou unto me.
I have heard of thee by the hearing of the ear:
but now mine eye seeth thee.
Wherefore I abhor myself, and repent in dust and ashes.
(Job 42: 1-6, *AV*) (my emphasis)

This is the point where I too crack – and, whatever the cynics may say – it is not at the display of some almighty power: it is the experience of God as he is, first-hand experience, face to face, that blows away all doubt as to the goodness of God and whether or not he is (as the ancient Orthodox liturgies keep reminding us) 'the Lover of Mankind'. My doubts then feel like a betrayal of that love and, like Job, I am moved to 'repent in dust and ashes'.

If direct experience of God is what blows away all doubt, then it follows that an experience of God as he is, as a God in reality both just and loving, must be open to every man, woman and child. We can as Christian counsellors, whether clergy or laity, point to the blocks to faith, and so to the barriers to direct experience of God that are a consequence of human wrong attitudes and human wrongdoing. But when it comes to the apparently meaningless, inexplicable evils that permeate the world around us, we will need to bring to sufferers some explanations that can satisfy both head and heart – and the evil suffered by ourselves and our fellow human beings cannot always be explained by the suspicion that we or they have done something wrong.

Evil extends throughout creation – and Australia forces the fact on newcomers such as my wife and myself when we first arrived to teach at the University of Newcastle in early 1977. Someone in our early weeks presented us with a book entitled *The Venomous Beasts of Australia*, and I would regale my Indian wife by sitting up in bed at night reading titbits – such as the news that the taipan is *sixty times* more deadly than the Indian cobra. (How that is measured I cannot fathom: – was it done by lining up 60 persons to be bitten – and then noting that they all died?) The next Sunday we went to Newcastle Cathedral, where the first hymn was Mrs C.F. Alexander's '*All things bright and beautiful, All creatures great and small, All things wise and wonderful: The Lord God made them all*'. That night I wrote back to 'England's green and pleasant land', to the Dean of Chapel of my Cambridge college, sending a parody that may still exist: '*All things vile and horrible, All creatures great and small, All things inexplicable – the Lord God made them all!*'

These realities touch the lives of Australians more than those in the 'Old Country'. We were befriended when we first arrived in New South Wales by the much-loved Dean of Newcastle, Robert Beal (later Bishop of Ballarat) and his wife Valerie – and he once told me of an incident in the early days of his ministry when he was called to help a parishioner who had stepped on a stonefish when paddling off the beach in Townsville and who then spent nine hours dying in excruciating agony. What could one do? What could one say?

And yet we must say something to those whose experiences are a barrier to any belief or trust in a good and loving God. That is the whole purpose of *theodicy*, the attempt to argue that God is good, just and also loving – and it will be the core of everything I have to say.

But because I am not so much concerned with any *technical* problem in theodicy, with any *intellectual* enquiry into God's goodness, I now want once more to get 'up close and personal' and try, by showing you two contrasting photographs, to make clear just what the problem is for me.

The first photograph is of two of my grandsons, who live with us and their parents in a joint family:

Daniel and Matthew Frost.

Whenever I am sunk under reports of the wickedness of the world or am swamped by what appears to be its meaninglessness, I sit quietly in a corner of the living-room and contemplate Daniel and Matthew. Eight years ago Daniel did not exist; eleven years ago, neither did Matthew. They came into my life out of nothing. Yet they are so beautiful, so amazing in their skills, in their movement, their intelligence, their ability to communicate and their capacity to give and receive affection, that the only appropriate reaction is reverent and astounded silence. And that is what is due to each one of us, and has been due to each of our ancestors, for thousands of years.

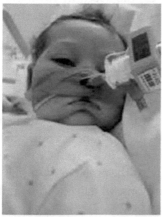

Charlie Gard and his parents.

The second couple of photographs have gone around the world, fed by a media that keeps its audience by trading in vicarious suffering and stirring anger at distant sorrows. Nevertheless, the pictures of Charlie Gard and of his grieving parents bring us up short.

Charlie Gard suffered from a rare inherited disease: *infantile onset encephalomyopathy mitochondrial DNA depletion syndrome* (MDOS for short). Our genes give the instructions for the growth and maintenance of our bodies, and Charlie had inherited through his parents a faulty RRM2B gene. This defect, which affects the development of the body cells responsible for energy production and respiration, left Charlie able only to move and breathe with the aid of a ventilator, and he had to be fed through a tube. It also causes multiple damage to the organs of the body, including irreparable damage to the brain. On 8 June 2017, after a succession of court judgements had determined there was no hope of a cure, the British Supreme Court decided Charlie's doctors could cease providing artificial life-support.

The passionate rage that gripped people worldwide was not, I believe, so much against the doctors or the judges, or in sympathy with parents who were determined never to give up the hope that their child might live: the anger was primarily that such things could be. Whether you believed the world was the result of meaningless chance and purposeless evolution, or even if you thought a supposedly loving God had created or permitted such a horror, the protest was against the stark facts of existence as we experience them: against the reality of things as they are.

But I want straight away to warn against one immediate explanation for Charlie Gard's situation: an explanation so immediate and obvious that one might almost call it 'natural': the idea that someone, somewhere, somehow, must have done something *wrong*. Whether we are believers or unbelievers, our first instinct when confronted by disaster is to ask 'Where did I – or maybe, where did *someone else* – go off the rails?' And in much of our experience, that proves to be the right question to ask. Such an explanation is already creeping into analyses of illness that we might expect to be purely rational and scientific. I have noticed a number of medical papers recently that hint at a possible link between acute anxiety-states and the development of those cancerous cells whereby the human body starts to destroy itself. Further studies may well provide further evidence of such a link. And in the same way it might be argued that, at some time in the life of Charlie Gard's parents – or of their parents or grandparents - someone did or experienced something that had the effect of interfering with the correct copying of DNA instructions, so that Charlie had before birth the faulty directions for growth and development that would kill him before he had completed his first year of life.

Of course, that's tough on Charlie and on those who loved him! But aren't we warned by the Old Testament itself – and in the Ten Commandments, no less – that 'I, the Lord your God, am a jealous God, punishing the children for the sin of the fathers to the third and fourth generation of those who hate me'? (Exodus 20: 5). And doesn't experience confirm that children do often suffer because their parents did wrong and through no fault of their own?

BUT HOLD BACK FOR A MOMENT: for orthodox Christians of every denomination are taught that everything in the Old Testament must be read in the light of the revelation of Jesus Christ – and we have in the Gospel according to St John an account of Jesus dealing directly with a case of congenital defect and refusing absolutely to attribute it to any human wrongdoing. In the account of 'the man born blind' (The Gospel according to John: 9. v.1 and following), Jesus is asked by his own disciples, 'Rabbi, who sinned, this man or his parents?' Jesus replies (v.3) 'Neither this man nor his parents sinned . . . but this happened so that the work of God might be displayed in his life'. Jesus then mixes his saliva with earth, anoints the eyes of the man born blind – and for the first time in his life, the blind man sees. (I can't resist enjoying over again the blind man's reply to the Jews, who first asked his parents and then him directly, how it was that he had been healed, given that this Jesus was a known sinner: 'Whether he is a sinner or not, I don't know.

One thing I do know. I was blind but now I see' (v.25). But the key point for our discussion here is that Jesus, in the case of the man born blind, denies that human suffering is always the result of human wrongdoing.

Chapter Two

Has Modern Science Proved
There Is No Creator God?

Before I can go further into a discussion as to whether God can be good, given the nature of the world as we experience it, I need to deal with the argument that God does not exist, that there is no need for the time-honoured belief in a Creator, if we follow the evidence that modern evolutionary science puts before us.

The neo-Darwinist (new Darwinist) account of the emergence of all we know in the world is that it occurred by blind chance, without any direction or meaning, with the survival of life-forms governed by 'natural selection': that is what is taught in our schools throughout the western world and especially in English-speaking countries. And since I want our discussions to relate to the realities of our experience, I'm going to start with a health warning: I have never encountered such a tide of evil oppression as when I attempted to do justice to the Darwinian position and to consider the arguments for and against it. There was a weight on my forehead, my brain felt as if it was mined by worms, I couldn't sleep for the pain, I was prone to sudden bursts of black depression, and my wife couldn't bear any further talk about my struggles with neo-Darwinian theory. And yet I have been a convinced Christian believer for over sixty years. I have always believed in the truth of Christ's saying of people and their ideas: 'By their *fruits* you shall know them' and I find the fruits of even considering the Darwinist creed to be dangerously destructive.

So if you have a firm faith in the rational presumption that, if a thing looks to be made, it must have had a maker, you might consider leaving the discussion at this point and coming back a chapter or so later, when I examine the evidence for design in the world that would support that faith. However, there is one good reason for staying with us: however robust your own faith may be, are you likely to have to deal with someone entangled in the consequences of Darwinian belief or in what is called 'scientism': a belief that science has supplied or can supply the answers to everything?

In September of 2017, A.N. Wilson published an honest, workman-like account of Charles Darwin's biography in *Charles Darwin: Victorian Mythmaker*,[1] paying special attention to the origin and development of Darwin's ideas and summarizing criticisms of Darwin's theories as he put them over in his *Origin of Species* (1859) – criticisms that were made after its publication and continuously up to the present day. Wilson repeated the conclusions of previous biographers and claimed to say little that was new. Yet his study was met with savage reviews, and one comment in a supposedly highbrow newspaper in the United Kingdom, *The Guardian*, suggested that the only way now to deal with these constant snipings at the great man was simply not to argue back but to ignore them. In 2006 an Oxford Professor, Richard Dawkins, then holder of a Chair for Public Understanding of Science, had published a study entitled *The God Delusion*,[2] where, as an evolutionary biologist of Darwinist persuasion, he attacked religious belief as the pursuit of fools and as dangerous to human stability and happiness. The level of bad argument and of gross abuse in Dawkins' book gives me, as a product of 'the Other Place' (as they call Cambridge), a degree of glee that Oxford should be so humiliated as to have him as a luminary – but what gives me no pleasure whatever is that the book has been an international best-seller: on 3 September 2014 Dawkins tweeted to say that sales 'have topped three million'. My son-in-law, whilst working for a technology company in Cambridge, reported that many of his science-trained colleagues were persuaded by Dawkins and had no interest whatever in religious discussion.

Small wonder, then, that on 4 September 2017 *The Guardian* newspaper reported a British Social Attitudes Survey as showing that 'for the first time, more than half the population say they have no religion' – the decline being 'driven by the young'. Two days earlier, on 2 September 2017, the same newspaper reported that suicides of students

1. A.N. Wilson, *Charles Darwin: Victorian Mythmaker* (London: John Murray, 2017).
2. Richard Dawkins, *The God Delusion* (London: Bantam Press, 2006).

had been at a record level in U.K. universities in 2015, having 'nearly doubled in the last decade' and that 'mental problems reported by students rose fivefold' in the same period.

Another report in *The Guardian*, on 20 September 2017, pointed to a nationwide problem, in that a government-funded study of more than ten thousand 14 year-old girls showed a quarter of them as suffering from depression, reporting that their lives felt meaningless and without direction – a conclusion confirmed by reports right up to the present time.

Of course, Dawkins and his followers would be outraged at any suggestion that the teaching of the neo-Darwinist view of creation as being by blind and directionless chance, and the fact that it is taught throughout the educational systems of the English-speaking world, had *anything* to do with the attitude to life of the young – any more than the neo-Darwinists are willing to accept that Darwin's doctrine of 'survival of the fittest' in any way encouraged those developments in eugenics that were held to justify the extermination of the Jews in Nazi Germany as a defective people who ought be prevented from polluting the bloodline of the master-race.

But 'by their fruit you will recognize them' (Matthew 7: 16, 20) – and it is small wonder the youth become depressed if they are taught as established scientific truth the account of our world as propagandized by Professor Dawkins. I quote from page 133 of his book *River out of Eden: A Darwinian View of Life.*[3] 'The universe we observe has precisely the properties we should expect if there is, at bottom, no design, no purpose, no evil and no good, nothing but blind pitiless indifference.'

I can best explain what is so wrong with the neo-Darwinist approach and what is so destructive of right-thinking about our own human nature and our position in the universe by asking you to imagine that you are invited to visit a famous glove factory, which supplies gloves in various shapes and sizes, for a whole variety of purposes, and sells them worldwide.

Some are of heat-resistant material and are obviously suited for work around ovens and blast furnaces. Others appear to have their fingers cut short, presumably to allow finger-ends to handle delicate work, without some covering material blunting their sensitivity. Some gloves are made of thick wool to give protection against the cold; others are of fine silk, which is cooling – but these are clearly intended more for decoration

---

3. Richard Dawkins, *River out of Eden: A Darwinian View of Life* (Basic Books, a division of Harper Collins, New York NY, 1995 and Orion, an imprint of Weidenfeld & Nicholson, London, 1995).

than protection. There is even a company museum, where you can study the evolution of gloves and see some historical throwbacks – such as armoured gloves for knights who fought with swords in medieval battles.

Looking at all the variety of gloves produced by the factory, you notice that, despite their great variety and their differing materials, they have a certain basic and repeated shape and pattern: they are of a size to go over a hand, and (with certain exceptions such as mittens) they have five-finger offshoots. But they also have extra features: some have laces to tie them to the wrist, some have air-holes to allow the skin underneath to breathe. Some features look as though they once had a purpose but are now simply decorative: fake jewels have been sewn into the holes in the back of the glove, so as to look elegant when you place your delicate hand over the shoulder of your dance-partner.

When we look at all this variety, we make certain elementary assumptions, based on experience. We know that nothing we see in the factory is accidental: somebody *made* everything we see. Gloves, often looking rather different, follow a basic design and are variations on a pattern drawn up by human intelligence at a point in the past: the variations are *purposive*, to meet somewhat different needs as they emerged over time.

HOWEVER, when Charles Darwin in the middle of the nineteenth century looked at the variety of creatures in the Great Factory of Life and studied some of the available evidence in the Earth's museum as to its past products, as seen in the fossil-record, he began with an arbitrary and unexplained premise: despite the wisdom of generations and our automatic assumption that everything we see, if it looks designed, probably *is* designed, Darwin ruled out any need for a world-designer. Life in all its variety and its astonishing beauty and complexity had for him no origin and no design in its development. There was no pattern behind the variety of life-forms: it just looked like that to the uninitiated.

Instead, Darwin suggested that everything was caused by a process of small changes over millions and millions of years, a succession of small, undesigned and quite accidental variations that produced the enormous variety of life-forms that we see today. Each tiny change, however slight, survived because in some way it made its possessor a shade more of a winner in the pitiless battle for life. Darwin accepted to name this mechanism for change and development '**the survival of the fittest**': if the change in you helped you somehow to survive against your competitors, you would probably live to pass on that change to your offspring.

Just *why* Darwin chose to begin from this unargued premise – that no design and hence no Designer can exist – is hard to explain: I'm tempted to exclaim 'God only knows!' But if Darwin's current followers among evolutionary biologists are anything to go by, the virulence of the prime exponents – the arrogant, self-aggrandizing and irrational arguments, for instance, of a Richard Dawkins in *The God Delusion* (2006), his abusive detestation of believers and his resort to the doing-down of his professional opponents, however unfair the means – suggests an enormous need to convince oneself that no God is there, and a strong corporate desire in modern society to escape from any notion of an Originator to whom we might perhaps be held accountable. As compared to the civility and sad regret of an older generation of unbelievers, who were all too aware of what consolations they might be taking away both from themselves and their fellow human beings, Dawkins and his disciples flail about with the desperation of people who feel they can only survive among the fittest if they can kill off the notion of a God altogether.

I will begin by setting out the objections to what is presently the dominant theory of all life, the neo-Darwinian account of origins, promoted aggressively by the New Atheists, where everything emerges by blind chance; and I will then put up against it the arguments of a younger scientific movement, that which is labelled 'Intelligent Design', which sees a complexity even in the earliest and simplest forms of life – one that cannot be explained without positing the existence of a designer. To revert to my image of the glove factory, neither side denies the similarities we observe in the varieties of glove or that one thing looks to have led on to another – it is just that one side suggests that everything looks designed because a glove-maker designed and supervised the surprising developments in usefulness, adaptability and even beauty over time; whereas the other side asserts that, never having observed the glove-maker at work or even having had the pleasure of meeting him, it is really a question of whether he exists at all: it is daft to presume he is around the factory just from what we see in front of us.

But before I leave the issue of chance evolution or 'intelligent design' till later in my discussion, I will bring before you once more the case of Charlie Gard.

The distinguished scientist, Francis Collins, headed the Human Genome Project which in April 2003 completed mapping of the human DNA that gives instructions for the building of every human being. If he is right in his book, *The Language of God: A Scientist Provides Evidence for Belief* (2006),[4] to suggest that his Christian faith is compatible with

---

4. Francis Collins, *The Language of God: A Scientist Provides Evidence for Belief* (New York, NY: Free Press, 2006).

modern evolutionary theory, there seems no way in which the notion of a loving and all-knowing and all-powerful God can be reconciled with what went wrong with Charlie Gard. It is true that the disaster of mis-copied genetic information started Francis Collins on the road to mapping genes, so as to be able eventually to correct genetic defects before they could wreak havoc: but are we prepared to say that a loving God created a system capable of gross malfunction so that people like Francis would have the privilege of putting God's work to rights? Late twentieth-century theologians in the United States toyed with the idea of a Learner God, not always getting it right first time, and perhaps glad of a helping hand – but no explanation of that kind has satisfied those who from scripture or from their experience encounter a good and loving Creator.

I put my problems in a letter to Francis Collins in March 2017, and his very gracious reply to 'my thoughtful and provocative letter' (as he put it) made clear that he believes not in a version of atheist neo-Darwinism but in something he calls 'theistic evolution' or 'BioLogos'. He was as perturbed as I am by any suggestion that God might have set a system up, then jumped ship, leaving everything to blind chance. Nonetheless, he was clear as to the problems modern science creates for theodicy – which is the attempt to defend God's goodness and justice – and says 'I don't have ready answers for that'. So the journey of trying to find reasons for what some of us may be fortunate enough to know by faith to be true still lies ahead of us.

CHAPTER THREE

The Assault of Modern Atheism
on Religious Faith

When, some years back, I proposed to give a course of lectures on 'The Goodness of God and the Challenge of Evil', I intended to point to that extraordinary prophecy in the Hebrew version of the Book of Job, which gives the ultimate solution both to our questionings as to the nature of this world in which we find ourselves and to our doubts about the goodness or otherwise of its Creator.

Approximately six hundred years before the advent of Jesus Christ, in an ancient story which I would suggest has visionary meaning rather than being a simple, factual narrative, Job the innocent sufferer is brought to assert his belief in the ultimate blessing that awaits us all, if we choose to accept it:

> I know that my Redeemer lives,
> and that in the end he will stand upon the earth.
> And after my skin has been destroyed,
> yet in my flesh I will see God;
> I myself will see him with my own eyes – I and not another.
> How my heart yearns within me!
> (Job 19:25-27)

St Paul, anything up to a thousand years later, proclaims in his Letters his belief, based on the eye-witness of the apostles he had talked to but also on his own 'vision' of the living Christ, that the Redeemer has come: that Christ's death and his resurrection after three days give grounds on which all who believe in him can expect their hopes to be fulfilled: that their own death and the death of those whom they have loved is not the end, that they will be resurrected to enjoy the vision of God, the end of all suffering and the putting to rights of all wrong. What clinched that faith in me as a young man was Paul's honesty, his realism. We have very early copies of two of his actual letters to the Corinthians: in the first he writes: 'if Christ has not been raised, your faith is futile; you are still in your sins . . . If only for this life we have hope in Christ, we are to be pitied more than all men!' But he goes on to say: 'But Christ has indeed been raised from the dead, the firstfruits of those who have fallen asleep' (1 Corinthians 15: 17-20).

However, in the Biblical story of Job, it was not faith in a future resurrection that convinced Job of the goodness of God. Rather, it was his meeting with God through the glory of God's creation that brought Job to his exclamation at last of comprehending love:

> I have heard of thee by the hearing of the ear:
> but now mine eye seeth thee.
> Wherefore I abhor myself,
> and repent in dust and ashes.
> (Job 42: 5-6, Authorized Version)

We shouldn't deny ourselves the possibility of an encounter with God through his creation. So in this chapter I want to place side by side two accounts of how the world is and how it came to be – and then ask which one looks to be most likely. I will put the neo-Darwinist account of the origin of all things, the devaluing view that everything arose by meaningless chance (something which is taught in our Western schools and universities as if it were scientific truth); and then, against that, I'll put the more recent suggestion of certain modern biologists, that the deeper we explore into the nature of all living things, the more we see evidence for what has been called 'Intelligent Design' – we find signs of there being a creative and directing agent.[1]

But before I take you into the intricacies of life as increasingly revealed by modern scientific enquiry, I want first to confront you with an experience that is both a puzzle and a wonder.

---

1. See J.P. Moreland, Stephen C. Meyer, Christopher Shaw, Ann K. Gauger and Wayne Grudem (eds), *Theistic Evolution: A Scientific, Philosophical, and Theological Critique* (Wheaton, IL: Crossway Books, 2017).

In 1995 divers began to report seeing some extraordinary and complex designs underwater in the sands off the coast of Japan. They turned out to be the work of a male Japanese Puffer Fish; and what appeared to be an elaborate artwork was intended to lure a female to a central platform in his design, where she could lay her eggs and he could fertilize them.[2]

Underwater design by a male Japanese pufferfish.

What can we say? By what process did so tiny and simple a creature, as compared with ourselves, learn and store in its memory so complex and beautiful a design? What drove it into persistent activity over a whole week to execute such an artwork? Why should creating something so beautiful be part of its wooing of a female to mate with? And how can it be that, if I were to weave such a design into a shawl for a lady friend, the similar pattern, not in sand this time but in fabric, could also be taken as a gesture of affection? And how strange but how appropriate it is that a Japanese Puffer Fish should produce such a sophisticated design in sands just offshore from a Japanese nation which shows a particular passion for complex and beautiful decoration! And how could the same thing be beautiful enough to attract the attention of a tiny fish yet also be able to delight us humans, whether we are Japanese or Australians or Europeans or Americans or of any other nation? I've drawn attention

2. See 'Pufferfish Love Explains Mysterious Underwater Circles', via Netflix, from BBC Four, 'Life Story', Episode 5.

to this extraordinary phenomenon so as to demonstrate, despite the remarkable developments of modern science, how little we really understand.

Now I want to confront you with a second baffling wonder that is also part of the world in which we find ourselves. The Book of Proverbs 6: 6-8 advises us:

> Go to the ant, you sluggard;
> consider its ways and be wise!
> It has no commander,
> no overseer or ruler,
> yet it stores its provisions in summer
> and gathers its food at harvest.

St John Chrysostom, who died more than sixteen hundred years ago, invited us to 'master the handiwork of the ant' – so let us try, and see what the latest research can tell us, when hidden cameras allow us to view the creatures of the ant factory, uninfluenced by any human presence:[3]

What can we say about this ant factory?

First, it is a complex operation by which reeds inedible to ants are converted into something they can digest, a process in which each ant knows its own particular role. The ants with the most powerful jaws climb up the reed and cut it down into manageable sections, and do nothing else. The porter ants in hundreds if not thousands carry the reed cuttings a distance

Ant carrying a reed for processing as food.

3. See BBC Two, 'Natural World: The Ant Factory'; also BBC Nature's 'Miniature Miracles', Episode 5, 'The Ant Factory'.

to the ant mound, and there the reed sections are fed to a fungus that will grow on them and then become food that the ants can absorb. (It used to be thought that the number of ants standing on the touchline, as it seemed, of the procession were simply idling: but further research has shown them to be reserves, programmed to take the place of any ant eaten by a predator and then to take over its work of transportation.)

Second, note that the whole activity is organized and each ant knows exactly its role and place – but where is there an organizer or any sign of one?

Third, the successful operation of the ant factory depends on prior knowledge. Somewhere, somehow, information necessary to the successful production of food is stored away: it is not known, presumably, to each individual ant, and wherever the information may be stored, it cannot be kept just to, say, the queen ant, because she does not survive indefinitely. Yet that knowledge is governing what happens. Reeds are not digestible by ants but a fungus grows on them that ants can eat: some intelligence has to put this information to work.

Finally, something has to know that the fungus which converts the reeds into ant-food produces toxic gas during the process that will kill the occupants of the anthill. So something instructs the ants to open ventilation-holes in the factory mound to let fresh air blow through.

When we come to talk about rival accounts of how our world and all things in it came to be, it would be wise to bear in mind St John Chrysostom's comment on our limitations in understanding and the need for a proper response to 'things too wonderful for me':

> Tell me, how does the bee frame her comb, and then you shall speak about God as well. Master the handiwork of the ant, the spider and the swallow, and then you shall speak about God as well . . . He indeed who says he is ignorant knows something. And what is that? That it is incomprehensible to man . . . God has marked out limits to our knowledge, and has laid them deep in nature. He assigns the whole to His will. So let us only 'give thanks for all things'.
> (*Homily XIX on Ephesians V*)

Now that we are in an appropriate state of humility about our ability to understand the world around us, let us turn to that still dominant account of how all things are – the theories of Charles Darwin in his book *On the Origin of Species by Means of Natural Selection, or the Preservation of Favoured Races in the Struggle for Life,* first published in 1859 (and note the significance of the full title and – especially – the subtitle).

After over 150 years, that account is looking decidedly shaky: one recent critic, Tom Bethell, has called his study *Darwin's House of Cards* (2017)[9] – the point being that, if you pull away one prop of Darwin's argument, the whole structure collapses. But I am inclined to use a less kind image: Darwin's work is more like an ancient building with serious cracks appearing in its structure, which the landlords are desperately seeking to paper over, whilst at the same time assuring prospective tenants that builders will shortly come to make good any defect. The owners of any property (and that includes an intellectual property) fear the very considerable loss to them in money and status that will result from that property being devalued.

Let's begin by pulling out a few cards from Darwin's structure. Darwin attempted to explain how it could be that lifeforms on the earth have certain obvious similarities and yet also demonstrate enormous differences in structure, size, complexity and function. He constructed an imaginary 'tree of life', starting from one original lifeform that had developed into others by the process of what he called 'Natural Selection':

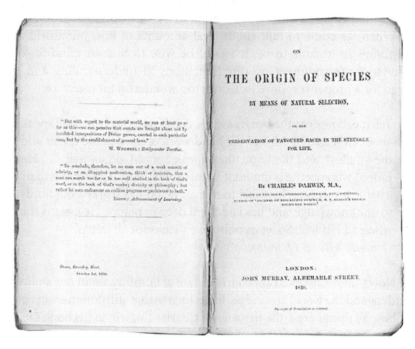

Title and last page of Charles Darwin,
On the Origin of Species.

the idea was that a tiny change in a single creature might aid its chances of surviving in the battle of life and so the creature would pass on that beneficial change to its offspring. What is more, he argued that a series of these small changes over a vast tract of time – taking, literally, millions upon millions of years – would eventually result in a variety of creatures. To quote one of Darwin's own more extreme examples, he suggested that a land animal such as a black bear would, over the ages, change step by step (each step being a different living creature) into an ocean-going, legless but air-breathing whale. (He obviously thought himself that this particular example sounded a bit far-fetched, for he dropped it from later editions of his book.) A point to note is that each minor change can only be perpetuated if every change gives the slightly modified creature an advantage in the battle for survival over other life-forms that were alive at the same time. Only so is it likely to live and pass on any changes to its offspring.

We now have a better understanding of how the instructions for the creation of living matter – and, in our case, for a human being – are encoded in the DNA of the male sperm cell and of the female egg cell, which when united create a new individual. This process explains why we inherit characteristics from both of our parents. The problem for Darwinian theory is that almost all major changes in the DNA instructions we can observe have disastrous consequences for the newly developed creature – take the early death caused by a genetic defect in Charlie Gard, which I pointed to in my first chapter. An enormous stretch of time is required for it even to be remotely possible that a sufficient number of beneficial small changes could happen by chance: my former colleague as a Fellow of St John's College, Cambridge, the astronomer Fred Hoyle, calculated, with a mathematician Chandra Wickramasinghe, that the likelihood of a coming together by chance of the required set of enzymes to make even the simplest living cell was one in $10^{40,000}$. In consequence, dedicated Darwinians have shown great anxiety to argue that the earth may be even older than we currently think, for fear the time available might not prove to be enough for everything to evolve.

A request to the mathematicians in my acquaintance to gloss this estimate as to the likelihood of life emerging on earth by chance produced odds against of such magnitude as to be well-nigh unintelligible – yet Fred Hoyle went on to supposedly increase the chances by arguing for life developing elsewhere in a vast and ancient universe and then travelling to earth as spores on the back of a meteor. He later suggested that plagues and diseases on earth such as caused by the corona virus were similarly transported by meteors from other worlds. Both he and Darwin appear merely to have laughed off the improbability of spontaneous generation of life on earth, as though the notoriety of their opinions mattered more to them than their truth.[4]

But for those of us who are not smart enough to calculate betting-odds, there is a much easier way to pull down the Darwinian house of cards. The whole theory depends on each of a thousand small changes aiding the survival of a creature *at exactly the time they happened* – otherwise, the changes won't be handed on. It has been suggested that the giraffe developed its enormously long neck because fires and drought destroyed the grass and all the lower vegetation in its habitat, with the result that only the leaves of the highest trees remained for fodder. The giraffe's long neck is not formed by adding extra vertebrae but by lengthening each one to about 11 inches long – almost double the length of those in its nearest relative, the okāpi. 'The giraffe's head and neck are held up by larger muscles and a strengthened nuchal ligament [which runs from the back of the head to a point on the seventh ligament of the spine], and muscles and ligament are anchored to long dorsal spines on the anterior thoracic vertebrae, giving the animal a hump' (so says *Wikipedia*) – which means, of course, that there have to be yet more simultaneous supporting changes at the right time, both to make the neck work and also to give the creature that necessary advantage in life. Moreover, somehow, the system also makes sure that giraffes don't develop their long necks till after birth – presumably so as not to make things more difficult for the unfortunate mother. It is very difficult to explain how all this could happen by accidental but beneficial mutation – and just as difficult to explain why the related okāpi didn't automatically develop the same neck-stretching ploy for obtaining food.

It does, of course, make better sense to presume that some designing power or intention, whether from within the creature or without, set going a series of interlocking changes in the structure of an animal so as to enable it to survive better in changed conditions. Only if you have decided to exclude from the outset the most plausible explanation – the presence of intention – are you forced to fall back on a mechanism of blind chance operating over eons of time, and to assert that a series of

---

4. For a more up-to-date and scientific explanation of the odds against life emerging anywhere by chance see the paper by microbiologist Professor Olen R. Brown, Professor Emeritus at the University of Missouri, 'Enzymes Are Essential for Life; Did They Evolve?', Olen. R. Brown (https://evolutionnews.org/author/olenbrown/), August 22, 2018.

accidental changes, each of them beneficial when they occurred, did at all times support a fully functioning creature which by stages became very different from what it was when the process began.

The improbability of what Darwin proposed was evident to his very first critics, and up until the present day their objections remain unanswered. Darwin's friend and fellow-naturalist, St George Jackson Mivart FRS, though initially attracted to Darwin's account of evolution, published his doubts in his own book, *On the Genesis of Species*, in 1871, twelve years after Darwin's *Origin of Species*, and found himself thereafter treated as a lifelong enemy. Mivart pointed to the widespread occurrence in the natural world of protective imitation and cited as his prime example the astonishing leaf insect, which avoids being eaten by predators by looking like a piece of vegetation.

Think of yourself as a hungry sparrow hunting grasshoppers, to which family the leaf insect was initially thought to belong. You won't pass over a juicy insect if just bits of it look like a dead leaf: for the deception to succeed, the disguise has to be thorough-going. If the neo-Darwinists try to argue that it is Darwin's mechanism of 'natural selection' operating by blind chance that has been at work, the theory requires them also to assert that the grasshopper's successful deception resulted from a progressive accumulation of tiny changes over eons of time, with every small

The leaf insect.

change increasing the grasshopper's chances of survival. Unfortunately for neo-Darwinist explanations, the mechanism of 'natural selection' is held to operate universally: if chance mutations make a grasshopper look progressively more like a leaf over eons of time and so enhance its survival, the same process of 'natural selection' favours those sparrows who by mutation become more capable of detecting that what appears to be a tatty leaf is in fact a grasshopper: the deception is rumbled and the mutation-bearing grasshopper killed off. Note also that in talking of 'deception', 'disguise', both sides of the debate are already resorting to the language of intention, as if the creature itself or some power governing its development had designed its changed appearance.

One of the oddest things about Charles Darwin is that he seems to have been so intoxicated by his theory of how one living creature might develop into another of a different form that he gave little or no consideration to the question of how all things began. He said in the autobiography he wrote for his children before his death that at time of writing *The Origin of Species* he was a theist, and occasionally in the book he would guard himself by slipping in a remark suggesting God might somehow be behind the processes of creation. However, when asked by a friend for his thoughts on the origin of life itself, Darwin almost made a joke of it:

> It is often said that all the conditions for the first production of a living organism are now present, which could ever have been present. But if (& oh what a big if) we could conceive in some warm little pond with all sort of ammonia and phosphoric salts, – light, heat, electricity &c present, that a protein compound was chemically formed, ready to undergo still more complex changes, at the present such matter w^d be instantly devoured, or absorbed, which would not have been the case before living creatures were formed.
> (Charles Darwin, in a letter to Joseph Hooker (1 February, 1871))[5]

You might have thought that, since Darwin was constructing a theory as to how all life had developed through unguided chance, he would also have been interested in experiments in creating life by bombarding his 'warm little pond' and its chemical soup with forces such as light or electricity. It is, after all, axiomatic in science that unassailable scientific truth should be established by repeatable experiment. Yet from Darwin's day to the present, all attempts to develop the basic constituent of life, the simplest cell, out its chemical constituents have failed.

---

5. See Darwin-Hooker Letters, Cambridge University Library, cudl.lib.cam.ac.uk/collections/darwinhooker.

In 2011 certain semi-scientific journals and the BBC reported on the rediscovery of experiments in the creation of life conducted by Stanley Miller and Harold Urey in the 1950s: 'By passing sparks through a brew of methane, ammonia, water vapour and hydrogen – a mixture thought at the time to be similar to earth's primordial atmosphere – Miller and his collaborator created amino-acids, the building blocks of proteins.'

Further experiments in 2011 attempted again to create amino-acids, the building-blocks of life – and this time with a more probable guess at the chemicals that would have been present in that early period of the earth's formation. But as a report put it, 'They're a long way from actual life-forms'.

Then in 2016, a Nobel Laureate, Jack Szostak of the Harvard Medical School, published in the journal *Nature Chemistry* a claim to have achieved in the laboratory the non-enzymatic replication of RNA (one of the two informational sets of instructions for creating and directing life) as evidence that chemicals could have assembled by chance to generate living things – only to have his post-doctoral assistant, Tivoli Olsen, discover that their results couldn't be repeated. Szostak said candidly that he had been 'incredibly excited' by the work, but 'the team had misinterpreted the initial data . . . we were totally blinded by our belief' – his 'belief' being that life emerged by chance from an assembly of chemicals. Since then, things have gone very quiet. It seems that, as was always the case, we can reduce our black cat to her constituent chemicals by dropping her into the fire – but to bring Cinders back to life again is quite another matter!

In late 2017, two highly eminent practitioners of biotechnology, Matti Leisola (currently professor in bioprocess engineering at Aalto University, Finland, and previously director of research for Cultor Ltd, an international biotech company), and James M. Tour (an expert in synthetic organic chemistry and a professor of chemistry, computer science and nano-engineering at Rice University) both contributed chapters to a volume challenging Darwinian theory as unsubstantiated bunkum.[6]

From their wealth of experience, they conclude that several different lines of experiment have shown that it is simply not possible to produce new functioning genes or proteins just by chance. What is possible is to manipulate in the laboratory already existing genes, proteins and micro-organisms, which can be modified to a considerable extent. But such elaborate manipulations require human intelligence and skill and the employment of complex technology that has been designed for a

6.   J.P. Moreland et al. (eds), *Theistic Evolution*, pp. 139-192.

purpose. In other words, the whole operation requires designers, and it is impossible to conceive of such changes happening without direction, whatever the length of time available for accidents to occur.

They comment with some exasperation that the practitioners of so-called 'pre-biotic research', which speculates on those changes in circumstances that may have encouraged the emergence of life on earth, seem largely ignorant of just what constitutes an existing life-form and what human effort is required to modify it, let alone to maintain any change that has been achieved and prevent the modified life-form from deteriorating.

Darwin's attempts to explain the development of all forms of life on earth without considering origins or producing believable processes is as absurd as it would be to explain how a mode of transport like the ancient chariot or a modern two-wheeled bicycle could evolve over time by a succession of small changes into a two-section 'bendy-bus' – and yet remain at every stage of development a fully operational mode of transport. Moreover, to tactfully accommodate the Darwinians, we would have to overlook the necessity of having an engineer to provide an initial plan and to make each small modification along the way.

If I myself were to write a history of human transportation from, say, the horse and cart through cars and lorries, trains and bendy-buses, reaching eventually to aeroplanes and even to space rockets, my first port of call would be a transport museum. Darwin was well aware that the rock sediments of the earth could serve as a museum for different life-forms over millions of years. But it was already apparent by 1859 that what should have been evidence for step-by-step evolution of one life-form into another simply wasn't there in the fossil record: Darwin admitted that any continuing absence of intermediate forms would destroy his theory, but set an example to all his followers by hoping that, given time and further exploration, something would show up.

But after a hundred and fifty years and an estimated discovery of as many as 250,000 fossil species, there is still no convincing evidence of this gradual, step-by-step change. A desperate search for the missing intermediaries continues: museums have been shown to 'doctor' or dress up fossils so as to promote a particular theory of a connection between two different creatures, and there is in fossil-rich northern China a highly lucrative and very skilled industry in the manufacture of so-called 'missing links' – which are then exported illegally to the United States where they fetch millions of dollars.[7]

7.   See, for instance, Carl Werner, EVOLUTION: The Grand Experiment – The Quest for an Answer (Green Forest, AR, New Leaf Press, third edition 2014).

In contrast, the record seems to show species emerging from nowhere, as in the so-called 'Cambrian explosion' (dated to around 541 million years ago), with no discernible predecessors to be found in earlier rock layers: the new species survive largely unaltered for millions of years and then (like the dinosaurs) they suddenly drop out of the fossil record. It has been suggested that these apparent 'jumps' into new life-forms – the so-called 'saltations' – (and also the equally sudden disappearances) were stimulated by sudden dramatic changes in the circumstances of life – a phoney 'explanation' at least for completely new life-forms that my former colleague, Fred Hoyle, famously mocked, by describing the notion as akin to suggesting that an electrical storm might hit a scrap-metal yard and leave behind it a fully-operational Boeing 747. Fred was a determined unbeliever but an honest man!

How could a competent biologist like Darwin be so daft? Whenever you see an explanation that seems not be an explanation and is riddled with holes, the first question to ask is 'Who benefits from it?' Whether it is theories in economics or politics, history or science, if in doubt the cry should be 'Follow the money!' A.N. Wilson, in his 2017 biography *Charles Darwin, Victorian Mythmaker*, argues that Darwin's doctrine of 'the survival of the fittest' suited the capitalism of nineteenth century Europeans, with their neglect of the poor and their ruthless exploitation of the weak, whether at home or among the 'inferior' races that populated their overseas empires. Inhumanity to one's fellowmen could be seen as 'only natural', 'how things are'.

But the greatest apparent benefit of neo-Darwinism, at least as promoted in the twenty-first century by the New Atheists, is that it allows you to dispense altogether with the idea of a creator God to whom you might feel yourself responsible for your actions. The evolutionary biologist and Oxford University professor, Richard Dawkins, used the millions derived from sales of his book *The God Delusion* to sponsor atheist propaganda – including a London bus in 2009 which carried the slogan 'There's Probably No God – Now Stop Worrying and Enjoy Your Life'. Attempts were made to promote a similar message in fourteen other countries, including Australia. Never has atheistic evolutionary theory had such a boost!

Yet it may be that 2006 will be seen as the year in the history of science when Darwinism finally collapsed. In that year Dawkins, as one of the world's most prominent exponents of evolutionary theory, published *The God Delusion*. But in the same year, another even more eminent though more practical biologist, Francis Collins, published what in essence was a complete contradiction. Collins had previously been Head of the Human Genome Project which by April 2003 had mapped the whole DNA coding that gave instructions for the creation of a human being, and his book was entitled *The Language of God: A Scientist Provides Evidence for Belief.* In it, evolutionary theory was among the sources drawn on as evidence of how the Christian God operated in bringing the world into being. Since both writers drew on Darwinian theory, that might suggest that Darwin's arguments were so poorly evidenced and the inferences so vague that you could get from them quite contradictory conclusions.

In fact, what had really brought Darwinian theory to the point of collapse was the steadily increasing pressure of new information. In 2004 the lifelong atheist philosopher Antony Flew, at the age of 81, had astonished friends and foes alike by announcing what he humorously called his 'conversion' to belief in theism, in the necessity for a God to explain phenomena that seemed to require a designer – things such as our ant factory. The particular difficulty that drove him to reverse his lifelong unbelief was the problem of accounting for the existence of DNA as the code for creating all life: new observations, substantiated by evidence and tested by repeatable experiment, suggested the presence of a design and so required a designer. In 2007, at the age of 84, and following what he said had been his lifelong Socratic practice of going with the argument wherever it led, Flew published his last book: *There is a God: How the World's Most Notorious Atheist Changed his Mind.*[8]

---

8. Antony Flew, with Roy Abraham Varghese, *There Is A God: How the World's Most Notorious Atheist Changed his Mind* (New York, NY: Harper Collins, 2007).

CHAPTER FOUR

Neo-Darwinism versus Intelligent Design

In the first part of my discussion of 'Blind Evolution', which developed from what was, some years back, a proposed series of lectures on 'The Goodness of God and the Challenge of Evil', I suggested that the real selling-point of Darwinism, with its doctrine of a complex world created by a long succession of accidental and directionless changes, was that (despite the poverty of Darwin's arguments and the lack of supporting evidence) it allowed you to dispense with the awkward notion of there being any God at all. When the philosopher Antony Flew in 2004 announced that facing up to the reality of DNA as the instruction-code for all life had caused him to abandon his lifelong atheism and when in 2007 he published a book giving his reasons, 'all hell broke loose'. It was alleged that Flew was now senile, that his collaborator on the book, Roy Varghese, had foisted his own opinions on a man now too old to know what he was doing. Flew was obliged to go public and assert that he was still in his right mind, that he had authorized every word in his recantation, and the fact that he had had a helper was only because, at the age of 84, he needed some assistance in the writing.

You will find similar personal abuse employed by Dawkins and fellow neo-Darwinists to discredit a movement among younger biologists in the past twenty-five years or so, who have pointed to the same kind of evidence from observation as that which caused Antony Flew to change his mind. The movement calls itself 'Intelligent Design', and only recently it has had to make clear that it is primarily concerned with what is observed and not with any particular way in which the observations can be explained. Their position has been rejected as 'unscientific', despite the fact that Professor Dawkins, one of their most passionate and abusive critics, is (as one of his erstwhile allies put it) not a practising scientist, 'only a journalist', in that he writes up, theorizes and draws conclusions from other peoples' experimental observations. But rather than challenging 'Intelligent Design' over what it thinks it sees, Dawkins and associates prefer to blacken the movement by association: it has been lumped with fundamentalist Christianity, accused of being 'creationist', as supposedly taking the Genesis myth of the creation of all things by God in six days to be literal truth. Of late, the Intelligent Design movement has had to make clear that it is not promoting any particular candidate as designer, whether God, Allah or Mother Earth: the purpose is to point to evidence that suggests design, not who did it. But even the *possibility* that God might make a come-back as designer has reduced Dawkins and his associates in the New Atheism to what seems from the outside like panic-stations.

Developments in the last sixty years or so of research into cell biology will illustrate the problem that the 'Intelligent Design Movement' (ID) seeks to point to, if not to explain. When I was at school, all I recall being told about the cell was that it had a thin circle (the cell wall) with a black dot in the middle (the cell nucleus). We had a vague notion that all living matter, including ourselves, was made up of these cells: red or white in the case of blood cells (as you could see if you got yourself a scratch); most likely green if you were a plant – because the process by which plants used energy from sunlight to produce glucose from carbon dioxide and water seemed to turn them green.

What has made the difference in my lifetime has been the power to look within cells, thanks to the development of x-ray crystallography and of the electron microscope. What you see – and here I am indebted to descriptions by a leading cell biologist, Michael J. Behe, in his book *Darwin's Black Box: The Biochemical Challenge to Darwinism* (1998) – is not a black dot nucleus corralled within a cell wall, but a hive of activity that seems more like a miniature factory. Best to quote from Behe's summary of his observations and experiments:

> The cumulative results show with piercing clarity that life is based on *machines* – machines made of molecules! Machines haul cargo from one place in the cell to another along "highways" made of other molecules, while still others act as cables, ropes and pulleys to hold the

cell in shape. Machines turn cellular switches on and off, sometimes killing the cell or causing it to grow. Solar-powered machines capture the energy of photons and store it in chemicals. Electrical machines allow current to flow through nerves. Manufacturing machines build other molecular machines, as well as themselves. Cells swim using machines, copy themselves with machinery, ingest food with machinery. In short, highly sophisticated molecular machines control every cellular process. Thus, the details of life are finely calibrated, and the machinery of life enormously complex. [1]

Seeing is believing – so I suggest you access a computer animation of a particular molecular machine in operation.[2]

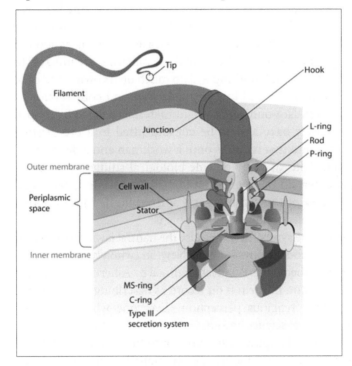

The bacterial flagellum.

This is a sketch of one example of the complex machinery within a single cell, which in this case serves to move materials about. A rotor powers the flagellum, which by spinning around imparts movement to the whole, allowing it to move rather like a boat.

1. Michael Behe, *Darwin's Black Box: The Biochemical Challenge to Evolution* (New York, NY: Simon & Schuster, 1996, second edition 2006.).

2. See 'Michael Behe and the Mystery of Molecular Machines', Discovery Science: https://www.youtube.com.watch?v=7ToSEAj2VOs.

Having registered what happens at the cell level, it is worth repeating an analogy of Michael Behe's by which he demolishes any Darwinian notion that these complex machines could have originated step by step through blind chance and natural selection. He uses the example of his family mousetrap.

A mousetrap has a wooden platform as a base and a tight central spring-mechanism, which can be pulled back and held flat, exposing a smaller platform on which you put the bait. But the bait-platform also functions as a trigger, for as soon as the mouse's weight presses down on it, it releases the spring mechanism, which swings over and pins the unfortunate creature to its dinner.

Behe makes the point that a simple machine like a mousetrap doesn't assemble itself by accident. The ingredients have to be obtained: a piece of wood to serve as platform, cut to the right size, a powerful metal spring, a smaller bait-platform, a trigger to release the spring as soon as the mouse's weight presses on the bait. All these materials are unlikely to be found together by chance, nothing will do much on its own – and each component has to be fashioned to a particular size and construction to interact with the rest. Not only do the right materials have to be shaped and assembled – they have also to be cut and fitted to a pre-existing pattern or design – and that requires both a workman and a designer.

Scientists from fields of study outside biological studies seem much more willing to entertain the suggestion that all life was designed – and that not just because of the common and age-old human presumption that, if something looks designed, it probably is.

Physicists tend to be sympathetic because the natural laws uncovered by the two founders of modern physics, Isaac Newton (who was also a highly competent Christian theologian)[3] and later refined by Albert Einstein, seem to demand an originator. Einstein is on record as describing how scientific enquiry turns into a religious perception: 'Everyone who is seriously engaged in the pursuit of science becomes convinced that the laws of nature manifest the existence of a spirit vastly superior to that of men, and one in the face of which we with our modest powers must feel humble.'[4] Hence, it is no surprise that the Nobel Prize winner Brian Josephson, Professor of

3. My generation was educated to believe that Newton's theological ramblings were something of an embarrassment. In fact, he was by modern standards a formidable theologian and also a critic of the New Testament text. See Remus Gabriel Manoila, 'Origenes est bonus Scripturarum Interpres, malus dogmatistes: Isaac Newton reading Origen', in *'That Miracle of the Christian World': Origenism and Christian Platonism in Henry Moore* (Münster: Aschendorff Verlag, 2020).

4. Max Jammer, *Einstein and Religion* (Princeton, NJ: Princeton University Press, 1999), p. 93, quoted by Antony Flew, *There Is A God*, p. 102.

Physics and Head of Department at Cambridge University in my time, said in a television interview that he was '80% confident of Intelligent Design'.[5] Still less is it a surprise that Professor Josephson has been abused in sceptic journals as having won his Nobel Prize at the age of 33 – as a mere beginner – and, since he was at the time of giving his opinion on 'Intelligent Design' 77 years old, now obviously senile.

Cosmologists tend to be receptive to notions of 'Intelligent Design' because of evidence that indicates the universe is not eternal but has had a beginning and will have an end. From a point out of nothing, time and all matter have appeared, yet the universe is expanding to a further point where it must inevitably disintegrate. The similarity of that understanding to the Genesis account of God creating all things out of nothing and to the Christian expectation of a final end to the world caused my colleague Fred Hoyle (though he seems himself to have first coined the term 'Big Bang' as a joke) to resist the actual theory until he died. Nevertheless, despite what seemed to his colleagues to be an anxiety to avoid slipping back into what we took to be his non-conformist Christian background, Fred was not oblivious to a further puzzle: the sheer unlikelihood that the carbon atom – an essential element in living things – could be created from other elements by chance:

> Would you not say to yourself, "Some super-calculating intellect must have designed the properties of the carbon atom, otherwise the chance of my finding such an atom through the blind forces of nature would be utterly minuscule". A common sense interpretation of the facts suggests that a super-intellect has monkeyed with physics, as well as with chemistry and biology, and that there are no blind forces worth speaking about in nature. The numbers one calculates from the facts seem to me so overwhelming as to put this conclusion almost beyond question.[6]

In his Omni Lecture at the Royal Institution in London on 12 January 1982 Fred Hoyle confirmed his position:

> If one proceeds directly and straightforwardly in this matter, without being deflected by a fear of incurring the wrath of scientific opinion, one arrives at the conclusion that biomaterials

---

5. See https://evolutionnews.org/2017/06/brian-josephson-nobel-laureate-in-physics-is-80-percent-confident-in-intelligent-design/
6. Fred Hoyle, 'The Universe: Past and Present Reflections', *Engineering and Science* (November 1981), pp. 8-12.

with their amazing measure of order must be the outcome of intelligent design. No other possibility I have been able to think of seems to me to have anything like as high a probability of being true. . .[7]

Hoyle's comments lead me to mention an understanding amongst cosmologists about life on earth that is charmingly characterized as 'the Goldilocks Phenomenon'. Remember the nursery story of 'Goldilocks and the Three Bears'? A hungry Goldilocks is attracted to three bowls of porridge set out in a strange house in the woods. She does not know it, but the bowls belong to three bears – Daddy Bear, Mummy Bear and Baby Bear. When she samples each, the porridge in the big bowl for Daddy is 'too hot', that for Mummy Bear is 'too cold' – but the smallest bowl, belonging to Baby Bear, is 'just right'.

Scientists in various fields of enquiry see the earth as being, like Baby Bear's porridge, exactly right for sustaining life. Our distance from the sun is precisely what is needed so as not to freeze or to fry us, and the earth's angled orbit around the sun allows us to have both day and night and the bearable variations of winter and summer. The formation of the earth from its basic materials allowed for precisely those chemical constituents in the right proportions that are necessary for life: if there were not enough oxygen we couldn't breathe or fuel our bodies and if there were a little more carbon dioxide in the atmosphere we would die. Water is necessary to all life: so it is essential that enough of two hydrogen atoms and one oxygen atom can combine to form H_2O, water. Neighbouring planets like Venus, which is too hot and has no water, or Mars where any water is probably frozen, give as yet no convincing sign of living things (NASA has recently announced that its evidence for water flowing on Mars was mistaken – and then still more recently it has announced that there seems to be a substantial frozen lake beneath a polar cap. [8]) It is argued that it is mathematically improbable that the necessary elements for life could have assembled elsewhere in the universe by chance – and so far, the best efforts of scientists and astronomers have discovered no evidence of life or of man-like intelligence anywhere else in the universe. So at present, we're fine here – but 'Baby, it's cold outside!'

---

7. The text can be found in Fred Hoyle and Chandra Wickramasinghe, *Evolution from Space: A Theory of Cosmic Creationism* (New York, NY: Simon & Schuster, 1982), pp. 27-28.
8. "Liquid water 'lake' revealed on Mars", – BBC News, 27 July 2018, at: https:// www.bbc.co.uk/news/science-environment-44952710.

HOWEVER – it's not so fine even here on earth. Belief in the goodness of God, and that he is not only 'the Lover of Mankind' but of each and every one of us in particular, is the essential gift that we as Christians can offer to the suffering, the wronged, the sick and the dying. That is why I have spent and will spend so long rebutting the neo-Darwinist, New Atheist view that all life is accidental and meaningless, the product of blind chance. Not only does that view abolish all hope: it reduces Good and Evil to meaningless terms. Human behaviour would then have nothing to guide it but personal whim: as Dostoevsky put into the mouth of Ivan in his novel *The Brothers Karamazov*: "If there is no God – then everything is permitted". The unbelief promoted by a Richard Dawkins as if it were scientific truth is in its human results fundamentally evil.

And yet, even for the proponents of 'Intelligent Design', there remains the problem that much of what we experience in the natural world seems not good but evil, however much we may recognize the astonishing complexity, mystery and even beauty of life's designs. Darwin himself moved steadily away from any belief in a benign Creator: and the cause was not only the early and painful death of three of his ten children, the first, Anna, his favourite, aged eleven, from tuberculosis, the second, Mary, after twenty-three days, and the youngest, Charles, from scarlet fever at eighteen months. Moreover, like his contemporary Alfred Lord Tennyson, who wrote of 'Nature red in tooth and claw'[9], Darwin was also rather endearingly troubled by the evil he saw even at the level of the insect – and of the cat playing with its prey.

He wrote in a letter to a botanist, Asa Gray, on 22 May 1860, in defence of his *Origin of Species* a year after publication:

> With respect to the theological view of the question; this is always painful to me. – I am bewildered. – I had no intention to write atheistically. But I own that I cannot see, as plainly as others do, & as I shd wish to do, evidence of design & beneficence on all sides of us. There seems to me too much misery in the world. I cannot persuade myself that a beneficent & omnipotent God would have designedly created the Ichneumonidæ [parasitic wasps] with the express intention of their feeding within the living bodies of caterpillars, or that a cat should play with mice. Not believing this, I see no necessity in the belief that the eye was expressly designed. On the other hand I cannot anyhow be contented to view this wonderful universe & especially the nature of man, & to conclude that everything is the result of brute force. I am inclined to look

---

9. Alfred, Lord Tennyson, *In Memoriam A.H.H.* [Arthur Henry Hallam], canto 56.

at everything as resulting from designed laws, with the details, whether good or bad, left to the working out of what we may call chance. Not that this notion at all satisfies me. I feel most deeply that the whole subject is too profound for the human intellect. A dog might as well speculate on the mind of Newton.[10]

A prime instance of a believer who accepts the Darwinian doctrine of evolution but gives it a theistic slant is Francis Collins. Early on in Francis' university studies, an inspired teacher presented the class with someone suffering from a genetic defect. That set Francis on a path of study that led eventually to the mapping of the human genome: the hope was that by such mapping it might eventually be possible to identify and repair defective human genes, such as those that brought Charlie Gard to an early death – and recent work seems to be justifying such hopes.

So when I wrote to Francis Collins in March 2017, (relying on the fact that we had both been brought from an unbelieving background to Christian belief by the writings of C.S. Lewis, one of my Cambridge lecturers), I asked Francis, since he seemed to accept Darwin's view of everything as 'resulting from designed laws, with the details, whether good or bad, left to the working out of what we may call chance', how he could defend the goodness of a God who set in motion, and left to run on its own, a system that produced such mishaps as condemned Charlie Gard and his parents to such suffering. Francis would, I was sure, reject the view of my school chaplain, that life was like the school's hundred yards hurdles race, where God put obstacles in our path to see how high our faith could leap, and just how much we could get over!

Francis' reply seemed to be that he had no answers. He was not, I think, attracted to a view put about in the late twentieth century amongst certain theologians (chiefly in the United States) that God could best be thought of as some kind of well-meaning 'Learner God', not able at first to get everything right and so leaving us with a margin of error to correct and the privilege of assisting in divine improvement. As far as I know, that solution has faded away!

So there remains still a need to argue for the 'Goodness of God' and to give some kind of reply to the 'Challenge of Evil'. In the course of my discussion, I will look at filmed evidence as to behaviour in the animal kingdom and what forces might seem to be at work there, and I will also draw on modern studies of human interaction. But I will also turn from modern scientific enquiries into animal and human behaviour

---

10. Charles Darwin Letters to Asa Gray, at: https: Biodiversitylibrary.org/ bibliography/130912#/summary.

to consider the visionary witness of ancient scripture and see what the Old and New Testaments have to say; I will draw on the Fathers of the Church and orthodox Christian tradition as being still relevant and I shall also treat the insights of poets, dramatists, novelists and creative artists generally as giving plausible indications as to who and what we are. Finally, I shall make a historian's assessment of the reliability of New Testament evidence, before arriving at what I believe to be a satisfying solution.

But I would like to conclude this present chapter with a treat. We have deserved, I think, to be cheered by one clear example of evil being put down. So I'll conclude my discussion here by drawing your attention to a video clip of dangerous micro-organisms invading the human body,[11] so as to show the way our human immune-system identifies an intruding pathogen, sends forces to deal with it, with the result that it is finally trapped, zapped and destroyed. We may not know by what power or agency the predatory microbe is produced but something has created a defence mechanism that also needs explaining. It seems that good (our good) and evil are in constant conflict, without and within – but sometimes, at least, evil is put down. The video shows – and I am inclined to say by God's beneficent design – how our bodies are equipped to defend us from invading illness.

But before launching into a commentary on this particular piece of evidence, I need to make a point that applies to all the video evidence that follows. When you are viewing those videos whose salient features I will describe verbally, it is crucial to realize that, as with our understanding of human existence and of every instance of what is presented as animal behaviour, what we believe to be true is ultimately a question of *who* rather than *what* we trust. Film evidence can be faked. In this first sequence, which I have labelled 'Zapping the Enemy', we trust that modern cameras are now capable of filming the smallest elements that together make up the human immune system and so allow us to watch that system in action. We trust that the prime researcher, Professor Daniel Davis of the University of Manchester, has done no more than colour cells differently so we may distinguish them as we watch them perform their differing functions.

The video introduces us to two female researchers whose work regularly takes them to a cave in New Mexico where bugs that breed in the droppings of thousands of bats condemn them to an invasion of deadly pathogens with every breath they take. In consequence, they have suffered a succession of major illnesses. Their ability to keep working in

---

11. BBC One, 'The Human Body', Episode 2, www.bbc.co.uk/programmes/b096slbg.

such dangerous conditions is because we all have, in each of our bodies, a complex immune system that can identify previous invaders and destroy them.

We are shown in the video a lung that has, when expanded, a surface area as large as a tennis-court, on which pathogens land with every intake of breath. But once a pathogen has landed, we see how a specialized white blood-cell from the immune system of the person invaded latches itself on to the invader – not to kill it but to take a sample. We then see that sample taken to a node in the human immune system, which seems to house a library which stores what appear to be samples of previous invaders. If the sample is identified as from a known enemy, killer-cells are generated to scour the bloodstream for any further instances of the identified intruder that may be on the loose. Once a further instance of the now recognized intruder is identified, the killer-cell will envelop it in a mesh that resembles the strings of a tennis racquet. Once the intruder is enmeshed, the killer-cell seems to transmit some kind of toxic poison that causes the pathogen to explode – whereupon the killer-cell will move to take on the next identifiable example of the invader.

Sampling the invader.

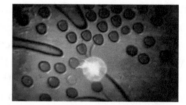

Identifying the invader.

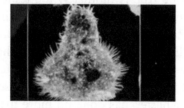

A killer cell ready for action.

A diseased cell surrounded and destroyed.

No doubt the specialists will tell us that this exposition on video for the general public grossly simplifies the variety and complexity of immune systems in the various forms of life so far examined. However, to multiply complexities does nothing to solve what would seem to be a simple but insurmountable problem for the neo-Darwinist: that any immune system that helps a creature to survive must have all its interacting components functioning effectively from the outset. The survival of that creature depends on a complex interactive system that cannot arise by slow accretions over eons of time; it has to be purpose-built. To survive as the fittest, you have to be protected by a complex and well-functioning system from the start. The Enigma Code worked from the outset because it was designed by human intelligence to be too complex to fathom: only human intelligence could solve it, not a succession of mindless accidents.

CHAPTER FIVE

The Prestige of Scientific Knowledge and Other Approaches to Truth

We began our consideration of 'The Nature of Humanity and the Origin of Life' with a very practical need in mind: our necessity as human beings to find something to say to those suffering the evils that assail us all: the wrongdoing of others and of ourselves, injustice, cruelty, lovelessness, indifference, hunger, want, natural disaster, pain, illness, bereavement and death.

The only sure and final consolation that can be offered is a belief in the Christian God, who suffered on our behalf and who is, as the ancient liturgies of the Christian Church assure us, 'the Lover of Mankind', of each and every one of us, and who eventually will put all things to right.

Yet immediately, almost at first setting out, our undertaking hit a rock. For the first time in human history, our schools and universities teach, as a truth supposedly uncovered by scientific study, that our human existence is the consequence of blind chance: that we and everything in our world evolved without purpose, by accident, through an endless process of directionless mutations. Such is the theory of Darwinian evolution as promoted by the New Atheists: any notion of a creator God who made us for a purpose is dismissed as a self-harming and dangerous delusion, an obstacle to whatever crumb of comfort or pleasure we might snatch from life before our certain extinction.

Such a cheerless view of our origins and of our existence as human beings wins acceptance because of the enormous (and deserved) prestige of the natural sciences. Over the last century and a half since Darwin first developed his theory of 'natural selection', scientific knowledge has made possible the further development of steam power, of petrol engines, of motorized transport, of machinery of all kinds to replace manual labour, of gas and electric lighting and heating, of the distance-defying transmission of messages by telephone and telegraph, by radio and television, and now the internet – and all because, through science, we have understood the physical and chemical processes underlying our existence. My own lifetime has seen the development of nuclear power, of computers and smart phones, of international air travel, of space exploration and moon landings. In addition, and of particular relevance to human survival, science has given us the power to understand and predict the weather, to make more secure the provision of adequate food and shelter, and through medical knowledge to live longer and healthier lives and – most impressive of all – to ameliorate and even eliminate some of those fearful diseases that have been the scourge of human existence for many thousands of years.

However, there is a darker side to the achievements of science. The same scientific culture that wins our gratitude and respect has in my lifetime created a 'Challenge of Evil' of a greater magnitude and extent than anything since the world began. World War II ended in August 1945 with the dropping of two atomic bombs on Japan. From that moment the human race has had the power by nuclear fission or fusion to destroy not just itself but the whole natural world and even the planet that has supported our life. Science knows so little about our aggressive impulses and how to control them that it is a wonder that we do not descend into mass anxiety and paralysis. Given the ancient prophecies (both from the Prophets and from Christ himself) about a catastrophic ending for our world, a final conflict and conflagration, leading to a Second Coming and a Last Judgement, you might expect a revival of old beliefs – yet almost no one now seems to take such doctrines seriously. The Dean of Chapel of my Cambridge College, Stephen Sykes, later Bishop of Ely, once described to me Christ's warnings of an end to this world as 'part of the baggage of a Jewish wonder-worker' – and so, not acceptable to the modern mind even though we have now given ourselves the means to usher in Armageddon.

But the chief tragedy at present for ourselves and our children is that science appears to be robbing us of any ultimate meaning to our lives – and that because of an unscientific assertion, chiefly from influential figures in the biological sciences, that they have achieved a certainty about the non-existence of God. I say it is 'unscientific', because no plausible method has been devised to test such an assertion. The proponents of 'Intelligent Design' can point only to what seems to them to require a Designer, whilst Darwin's defenders are reduced to asserting that the supposed evidence is bunkum. Similarly, in other branches of science where researchers think they see signs of apparent design – the cosmologists (for example) arguing for some 'Big Bang' that brought an ever-expanding universe into being out of nothing, or those who believe in a 'Goldilocks Phenomenon' by which a whole range of requirements for life on earth seems miraculously to be 'just right' – on such matters, it remains impossible, simply as a scientist, to decide what is true.

So, how do we know what is true? And is there anything that you know *for certain*? I would suggest that there is one thing you know for sure, and it is a knowledge that is not acquired by scientific study. You know that you *are*, that you exist. *(At this point, when I am lecturing, I usually ask anyone who is not sure who they are to stay behind – so we can arrange for some urgent help!)* You are self-conscious, and though you also know other people, you know you are not your neighbour or your spouse, or your dog or cat – and because you are not them, you always run the risk of misunderstanding them. The seventeenth century philosopher René Descartes, thought of as one of the founders of scientific method, expressed our experience of ourselves in the phrase 'Cogito, ergo sum', 'I think, therefore I am': my family know me as a dreadful grunter and groaner, so I prefer a slightly different formulation: 'Patior, ergo sum', 'I *suffer* therefore I am'. You know from observation that there are other human beings like yourself and you presume (usually rightly) that they think, or grunt and groan, roughly like you do. You also know from observation that your dog or cat, however much you might like sometimes to think of them as 'almost human', are still very different to you in their degree of self-consciousness, even if they also have affections, likes and dislikes, appear to suffer and at other times to be at ease.

However, if you want a theory as to what your knowledge of yourself is, or where a sense of yourself might lodge in your brain or your body, if you ask where your mind is among the enormous number of the brain's interacting neurons – in other words, if you look to science for answers to the one thing that you know for certain, that you **are** – you will find that you enter a 'Cloud of Unknowing'. There is a mass of confused, confusing and contradictory theory, many puzzles, and little in the way of hard evidence. When I was a postgraduate in Cambridge, I had a philosopher friend, Sandy McMullen, who claimed at that time to believe that mind, and our sense that we choose with our minds between alternative actions, was simply a mistake: chemical changes took place in our brain that gave us the illusion of choosing. I offered to test his hypothesis by sticking him with my penknife to see if he would hold me or my brain chemicals responsible for what happened: but he declined to make the experiment.

Up until quite recent times, the human race has got its view of what was true not just by observation of life and reflection on it, but also through dreams, trances, visions and prophecies. So it is appropriate – just when I was cogitating on why the Darwinian theory of mindless, chance evolution of all things seemed so terribly wrong – that I fell asleep: and behold, I dreamed a dream! And it was the most fearful dream of my life.

My origin in my dream (though, of course, I was not then consciously aware of any origins) was according to the strictest Darwinian principles. I had evolved over time and through a succession of directionless and unintended mutations, my nearest living relatives now being the higher apes. The climate over many eons had been changing and in our part of the world it had become increasingly hot, so the more hairy among my chimp-like ancestors died early from heat-stroke. That happened more and more as the temperature rose, until only those like me with little body hair survived into adulthood, mated, and so passed on a largely hairless skin to our offspring.

The heat had also killed off those large trees from which my ancestors swung by their hands and feet, so circumstances favoured other chance adaptations. A more upright gait made it easier to see further, to run faster, and at the same time to throw clubs and spears: so my lot did better in the hunt, survived, multiplied and became eventually what you would think of as having many of the characteristics of modern man.

But then something appalling happened, again by a random, unplanned and directionless genetic change. It happened to me alone – and though it could (by current scientific understanding) have happened at the same time to a group of brothers who were identical twins through the splitting of a single human egg, it couldn't occur at the same time to someone of another sex, except by a coincidence of massive mathematical improbability.

I woke up, by a slight but momentous genetic change, to realize that I was *me*: I was the first person since the beginning of time to be a self-conscious human being. I looked at my mate – and saw immediately that she was no more conscious of herself than was our dog. I could share with her nothing of what I thought or felt about anything – except by a grunt to indicate approval or a snarl to signal dislike. She had no sense of herself, no capacity for self-reflective thought, so she could not share the fearful state in which I found myself. We had developed no language except simple signs, so what I wanted to tell her couldn't be told: when I heard a most beautiful birdsong and nudged her, she fetched my spear, thinking I wanted to hunt the creature and eat it. I pointed to her and said, 'You', and then to myself and said, 'Me' – and she just looked at me goggle-eyed.

When I eventually faced my absolute loneliness and isolation, the feeling was so dreadful as to be unbearable. I walked to the top of a cliff, decided I would no longer be the one and only Darwinian Man – and jumped off into the ravine below.

If my dream of the first Darwinian Man does not terrify me when awake, it is because I do not believe that so solitary and fearful an anguish could ever have existed. We know enough, from scientific studies of modern human beings in enforced isolation or in solitary confinement, to predict that the first emergence of so singular a creature would have resulted in mental collapse and probably in self-destruction. If we were to adjust our evolutionary theory enough to admit the likelihood of a Designer, it is highly improbable that any even partly competent designer would permit self-consciousness to arise just in a single individual and so condemn that person to appalling isolation.

The Creator-God of the Judaeo-Christian tradition knew that 'It is not good for the man to be alone' (Genesis 2: 18) and so he created human beings to be companionate, with each other and with himself. Admittedly, that is religious story, myth. Yet myth and story belong with visions, revelation, dreams, intuition and insight: a whole category of human understanding that is at least as ancient and revered as that of empirical enquiry. That visionary mode of understanding has been the foundation of theology, of the knowledge of God and of what he requires of us; and as late as the mid-nineteenth century, theology could still be regarded as 'the Queen of the Sciences'. Only when science and religion began to part company and the differing modes of understanding were divorced, did each begin to talk impoverished nonsense.

But to return for a moment to my dream of the first emergent Man. According to all we now know about the earliest human beings – from the sciences of archaeology and anthropology, from sociology, history and geography – that first Man, wherever he was in the world, confronted by his terrible aloneness, and before throwing himself into the abyss – would have fallen to his knees and committed himself to his God.

I want now to show you an image from nearer that beginning in time when we estimate that the first true human beings first emerged into their fearful self-consciousness. They knew that they *were*, that they were the

The Lion Man (from three aspects).

The Lion Man's head (detail).

same if separate from those other human beings like themselves – and because they all had that same self-consciousness, they knew also that all humans were radically different to every other living creature on the earth.

This photograph gives three aspects of a carving in mammoth-ivory, 'the Lion Man', pieced together from fragments found in the Stadel Cave, Baden-Württemberg, Germany, just before the Second World War, and by carbon-dating dated to around forty thousand years ago – nearer the time when the fossil record suggests that human beings first emerged. It was found at the back of a cave that had some signs of human use, in a smaller cave that seems to have been kept unoccupied, and was presumably reserved for special ceremonies, since the surface of the carving was worn smooth as if it had been passed from hand to hand and over many years. The carving suggests that these early human beings made images of a Being who was like them but not like, in some way greater than themselves: Someone or Something with whom or with which they felt impelled to make contact, something that was Other, Outside, beyond the world of mundane experience.

Here now is an image of the Lion Man's head, and I'll give you the comments of Jill Cook, a Keeper at the British Museum, about it [10 October 2017]:

> The Lion Man is a masterpiece. Sculpted with great originality, virtuosity and technical skill from mammoth ivory, this 40,000-year-old image is 31 centimetres tall. It has the head of a cave lion with a partly human body. He stands upright, perhaps on tiptoes, legs apart and arms to the sides of a slender, cat-like body with strong shoulders like the hips and thighs of a lion. His gaze, like his stance, is powerful and directed at the viewer. The details of his face show he is attentive, he is watching and he is listening. He is powerful, mysterious and from a world beyond ordinary nature. He is the oldest known representation of a being that does not exist in physical form but symbolises ideas about the supernatural.

To continue with Jill Cook's account:

> Found in a cave in what is now southern Germany in 1939, the Lion Man makes sense as part of a story that might now be called a myth. The wear on his body caused by handling suggests that he was passed around and rubbed as part of a narrative or ritual that would explain his appearance and meaning. It is impossible to know what that story was about or whether he was [a] deity, an avatar to the spirit world, part of a creation story or a human whose experiences on a journey through the cosmos to communicate with spirits caused this transformation.
> Obviously, the story involved humans and animals. Lion Man is made from a mammoth tusk, the largest animal in the environment of that time and depicts the fiercest predator, a lion, now extinct,

that was about 30 centimetres taller than a modern African lion and had no mane. Distinct from other animals through their use of tools and fire, humans were nonetheless dependent on some animals for food while needing to protect themselves from predators. Perhaps this hybrid helped people to come to terms with their place in nature on a deeper, religious level or in some way to transcend or reshape it.

An experiment by Wulf Hein[1] using the same sort of stone tools available in the Ice Age indicates that the Lion Man took more than 400 hours to make.

This was a lot of time for a small community living in difficult conditions to invest in a sculpture that was useless for their physical survival. Allowing this to be done might suggest that the purpose of the image was about strengthening common bonds and group awareness to overcome dangers and difficulties. Some support for this exists at the cave itself.

Archaeological discoveries in other caves in this region include small sculptures as shown in the British Museum's 2013 exhibition *Ice Age art: arrival of the modern mind*. They were found in caves with large quantities of stone tools and animal bones that indicate people lived in the shelter of the daylight areas of these sites for repeated periods of time.

Stadel Cave, where the Lion Man was found, is different. It faces north and does not get the sun. It is cold and the density of debris accumulated by human activities is much less than at other sites. This was not a good place to live. Lion Man was found in a dark inner chamber, carefully put away in the darkness with only a few perforated arctic fox teeth and a cache of reindeer antlers nearby. These characteristics suggest that Stadel Cave was only used occasionally as a place where people would come together around a fire to share a particular understanding of the world articulated through beliefs, symbolised in sculpture and acted out in rituals.'

The Lion Man featured prominently in an exhibition at the British Museum from 2 November 2017 to 8 April 2018 that was designed to illustrate – by displaying a variety of religious artefacts, from earliest beginnings and from every time up until the present, from every religion and every race of human kind, and in every corner of the known world – that our species, *homo sapiens*, has not only been conscious of itself

1. See: https: exarc.net/individual-members/wulf-hein.

and of knowing people like itself but has reached out to beings *beyond* itself, has seen itself (to quote the title of the exhibition) as '**Living with Gods: Peoples, Places and Worlds Beyond**'. Worship of 'the Other', seeking contact with the world of the Spirit, has been a feature of every human society of which we have scientific knowledge. The phenomenon of worship has been so ubiquitous, so everywhere present in the history of our race, that the organizers of the London exhibition suggested that it might be appropriate to re-class our species, *homo sapiens*, thinking man, as *homo religiosus*, man that worships.

One purpose, I suspect, of the British Museum exhibition was to be a reminder, from sciences outside the narrow world of evolutionary biology, that there has always been another way of understanding our human life which runs in tandem with empirical enquiry: knowledge by the power of the spirit, the realms of intuition, inspiration, vision, of reaching out toward something greater than ourselves, to the Unknown Other. If Professor Richard Dawkins, on the basis of a rickety Darwinian theory of life's origins, is prepared to assert that 'God is a Delusion', he is condemning as self-deceived idiots not just the believers of his own day but also believers over eons of time, in every branch and tribe of the human race.

When we prayed to our Gods, sang hymns to them, made images of them, gave them our devotion, offered sacrifices to them for ourselves and for others, when we asked blessings for ourselves and for our loved ones, at birth, at marriage and at crises in our lives, before battles, ordeals, journeys – and when after their death we committed those same loved ones to the care of spirits in some after-life – were we, all of us, over thousands upon thousands of years, simply off our heads?

I guess that, even if it were possible to submit belief in God over the ages to a majority vote, Professor Dawkins would not be persuaded. Still less would he accept what I shall argue next: that the Christian faith, of all the world religions, is the only one where God, the Other, the Unknown, has consented to expose himself to empirical, scientific enquiry in the person of Jesus Christ.

CHAPTER SIX

The Evidence for a New Species, *Homo Theos*, the 'God-Man', Unifies Our Understanding

At the close of my previous discussion of those two apparently quite different ways of understanding who, what and where we human beings are – the path of scientific enquiry as against that apparently quite opposed mode of knowledge by inspiration, through vision, by reaching out to the world of the spirit – I concluded with a startling assertion: that, alone among the world religions, Christianity believes that its Unseen God offered himself for scientific scrutiny in the person of Jesus Christ. So doing, God united our modes of perception, allowing each to balance and correct the other.

John, the son of Zebedee and first cousin of Jesus, sums up in his Gospel what he had experienced and now offers as an eyewitness account:

In the beginning was the Word *[by which he means the organizing Intelligence],* and the Word was with God, and the Word was God. He was with God in the beginning. Through him all things were made; without him nothing was made that has been made.

The Word became flesh and made his dwelling among us. We have seen his glory, the glory of the One and Only, who came from the Father, full of grace and truth.
(John 1: 1-14)

We would expect a reliable witness to tell much the same story, even after a considerable lapse of time. Here is John again, now an old man, putting the same experience in a letter and even more touchingly:

> That which was from the beginning, which we have heard, which we have seen with our eyes, which we have looked at and our hands have touched – this we proclaim concerning the Word of life. The life appeared; we have seen it and testify to it, and we proclaim to you the eternal life, which was with the Father and has appeared to us. We proclaim to you what we have seen and heard . . .
> (1 John 1: 1-3a)

Two thoughts occur to me at this point – the first a very personal one. I also have a 'cousin-brother' (as my Indian wife would put it in English), we also are sons of two sisters, and are very close. His name also happens to be John, and I am Professor David: but the likelihood of him experiencing me as the Word of God is *nil*.[1] My second thought is that John among the disciples has all the characteristics that we would look for in a good scientific witness: the ability to observe closely and accurately, and then to produce a plausible theory which accords with the best of previous hypotheses.

But before we talk further about the unseen God opening himself to scientific scrutiny in the person of Jesus Christ, we need to be clear how scientific knowledge is gathered. How does empirical enquiry work? It depends, first, on the perceptiveness and capacity of the individual enquirer or enquirers: they need training in the techniques of observation, in the skills and accuracy required for measuring, weighing, assessing, testing and analysing what they see, hear, taste and smell. An essential quality is honesty, in reporting what they observe without distortion or inaccuracy, and in not allowing any pre-existent theory to dictate what is observed. They must consider any rival explanations of what they report, they must submit their results where possible to repeated observation and experiment – and finally, they must undergo critical examination by other scientists experienced in similar or related studies. Then – and even then only conditionally and subject to further enquiry – do their results become accepted scientific truth.

I want now to subject to scientific scrutiny a phenomenon which is reported to have occurred in ancient Israel when it was under Roman rule, approximately two thousand years ago. It is alleged that there were numerous sightings of an apparently new species of *homo sapiens* or *homo religiosus*, a species which we will name provisionally *homo theos* – 'God Man'.

---

1. See NIV footnote to Mark 15: 40: 'Salome. Probably the wife of Zebedee and the mother of James and John (see NIV note to Mt 27:56)'.

Professor Dawkins and his ilk would of course object that such an enquiry can't, mustn't, shouldn't be made: that it would be as irrational as to as look for evidence of 'Big Foot' or of the 'Abominable Snowman', the Himalayan yeti. It is certainly unfortunate that the first reported specimen of *homo theos* was killed off by human beings around the thirtieth year of the Christian Era and that no physical evidence of it seems to have survived, though there were further alleged sightings of such a being immediately after that initial slaying. Nonetheless, there have been persistent reports of humans encountering *homo theos* throughout two millennia, either individually or in groups, right up until the present day.

You might object that it is 'unscientific' to look into matters that we can no longer directly observe. Yet scientists are quite willing – even if, like my former colleague Fred Hoyle, they may personally regret the conclusions – they are quite willing to accept that an event such as the emergence of the universe from nothing at the 'Big Bang' actually occurred, even though no human being was present to observe it – and though it cannot, of course, be validated by any repeatable experiment. Wikipedia currently reports the estimated age of the earth from its inception to be 4.54 ± 0.05 billion years, though again there was, of course, no human observer present to attest that it actually happened at that time. Similarly, the whole story of the earth's development is not something that has been observed: its fiery origin and rapid expansion, its gradual cooling, the creation of tectonic plates in its outer crust that have subsequently moved and overlapped, those intense pressures beneath the earth's crust that have thrown up mountain ranges, the occurrence of the ice age, the development and shifting of oceans as the ice melted – all those established 'conclusions' are scientific conjectures deduced by the power of human intelligence from observations of layers of rock which we believe were laid down and then displaced over millions of years. We also construct from traces of living organisms preserved as fossils in the rock a history of how life on earth originated and developed into a myriad of forms – but only a tiny fraction of what has been now survives for us to observe, and the bulk of our thinking is reasonable conjecture based on imperfect evidence.

When it comes to creatures from the recent past who no longer survive, we can usually establish their characteristics from better remains but also from human records: for the recently extinct Dodo, we have both stuffed specimens of the creature and sailors' accounts of what the Dodo was like, how it behaved and moved. But as much here as with the dinosaurs, of which in the main only bones survive, we need the assistance of other branches of science to determine how exactly these creatures were and what they were like. We need the anatomists and the experts in aerodynamics and hydrodynamics to determine how they moved, how they flew or swam, and how they might possibly have developed into something new. We need such specialists to advise when it comes to the question of whether a feathered dinosaur might evolve by tiny mutations into a creature that could possibly glide and then fly.

When it comes to the pre-history of our own human race, we rely on the anthropologist and the archaeologist to reconstruct the lives of past civilisations from scrappy relics, from destroyed buildings, remnants of stone walls, brick edifices, caves with signs of human occupation, refuse, artefacts, bits of pottery, remainders, sticks and stones. But once we get to recent times, to that relatively short period during which beings like ourselves left records of themselves, we enter the realm where history is the appropriate scientific discipline, though it needs also the assistance of other branches of knowledge: of geography, mathematics, physics, astronomy, of anatomy, psychology, sociology, socio-biology, socio-economics, the behavioural sciences and studies of politics and religion – all this if historians are to accurately place and evaluate what they study. And as with every other branch of science, the accuracy of their observations as scientists, seekers of knowledge, depends on appropriate training and experience, precise observation, informed interpretation, honesty and reliability, and the willingness to distinguish good evidence from what is less certain. And finally, they must accept that the most certain of conclusions will be provisional, always subject to modification in the light of fresh information and fresh thought.

For our particular purpose, that of establishing the existence and characteristics of a species *homo theos*, the 'God-Man', of which Jesus Christ is said to be the first example, the most immediately appropriate scientific method would seem to be that of the historian. When we look for apparently reliable and contemporary evidence of Jesus Christ, we are extraordinarily well-provided with information. It is often said that we know more about him, from a range of documents, than about any other figure in the ancient world. From a variety of sources, from those claiming to be first-hand witnesses and from those summarizing information from people close to Jesus but written down at a somewhat later date, we appear to have accurate information as to what he was like, how he conducted himself, what he said about himself, what he taught, how he was viewed, both by those who knew him intimately, family and friends, and by the public at large, and also what was thought about him by the critics amongst his followers and elsewhere, and by the religious and political authorities of his day.

At this point, I was about to say that Jesus Christ was, in almost every respect, a biographer's dream!

He came, mysteriously, from out from nowhere – one of his early followers is reported as saying, 'Can there any good thing come out of Nazareth?' (John 1: 46, Authorized Version). But there were also intriguing stories that he had some aristocratic background, that he was born in Bethlehem, of which city the prophet Micah, seven hundred years or so before, had predicted that 'out of you will come for me one who will be ruler over Israel, whose origins are from of old, from ancient times' (Micah 5: 2b). It did appear that this Jesus came from good stock, and two of the major witnesses, Matthew and Luke, report that he was, through his adopted father Joseph, a descendent of King David himself – though there were also rumours circulating that he might have been born 'on the wrong side of the blanket'.

Whatever his origins, he burst on the public scene at about the age of thirty, attracting vast audiences to his public preaching and healing rallies, but outside the major cities: some of these gatherings, as is reported in all four of the major accounts, the Gospels, numbered four to five thousand people at one time, not counting women and children – who were all then miraculously fed (Mark 6: 35-44; Matthew 15: 32-38, 16: 1-12; Luke 9: 12-17; John 6: 5-13).

Reports of extraordinary insights and spectacular healings both by Jesus himself and by his followers were rife – even though there were major accusations – not of fraud, for it seems no one accused Jesus of trickery – but a more scandalous charge: that what he did, though it could not be denied, was done through some evil power.

As a public speaker, in a career that lasted no more than three years, Jesus was charismatic: to vast crowds or to only to a handful of disciples, he was a master of the memorable phrase. He is reported as covering those aspects of human life that most matter, making his point with sayings, parables and stories, with open and sometimes hidden meanings that you had to watch out for, and which for that reason stuck in the memory like nothing else. He was a master of the quick retort: I confess that when I leave a meeting having got nowhere with the point I was trying to make and am then chewing things over for fear I have made a fool of myself, I hear a voice at my ear saying 'Leave the dead to bury their dead!' After two thousand years his utterances provide proverbs and sayings in pretty well every language under the sun. In the English-speaking world, it is said that the sign of a really good education is to know whether a particular saying comes out of Shakespeare or from Jesus Christ!

Despite Jesus' enormous popularity, it seems from the record that he did not aim at political power: 'My kingdom is not of this world' he is reported as telling his Roman interrogator, Pontius Pilate (John 18: 36). Nevertheless, he did enter Jerusalem at the major Jewish festival of liberation, the Passover, as if he were the promised King or anointed Messiah prophesied by the prophet Zechariah, 'gentle and riding on a donkey' (Zechariah 9: 9), and he was accompanied by a vast crowd of supporters, who waved palm branches and who gave what sounds like a royal salutation: 'Hosanna to the Son of David!' All four Gospel writers report the formal Entry into Jerusalem (Mark 11: 9-10; Matthew 21: 1-11, Luke 19: 28-40, and John 12: 12-19) – and all the Gospel writers also record that by hints or explicit warnings Jesus told his followers that it would all, from a human point of view, turn out badly (Mark 10: 32-34, 17: 25; Matthew 16: 21-28, 20: 17-19, 26: 2; Luke 18: 31-34; John 12: 23-36).

Both the Romans as the occupying power, and the Jewish priestly elite trying to preserve their own authority and to keep the peace, were sufficiently worried to have Jesus arrested, to put him through two trials, to try and convict him on charges of stirring civil and religious rebellion – and then to get rid of him by a particularly excruciating and prolonged method of public execution.

HOWEVER, after putting together what I had to say about Jesus Christ as being ideal material for a biography, I dried up, had a sleepless night, everything went dead, and I felt as though I had rammed into a brick wall.

I should have remembered that in the nineteenth century eminent people attempted a life of Jesus – but no one can be said to have made a hit of it. David Friedrich Strauss in 1835 produced in German a three-volume *Life of Jesus, Critically Examined*, which the subsequently famous English novelist George Eliot thought enough of to make a translation into English as her first major literary work. The Frenchman Ernest Renan produced his *Vie de Jésus* (*The Life of Jesus*) in 1863, presenting 'a mythical account of the making of Christianity by the popular imagination', to quote from the *Encyclopedia Britannica* – in other words, the book was not a biography but an attempted explanation of how a popular yarn grew up and spread. An even more successful English novelist than George Eliot, Charles Dickens, wrote between 1846 and 1849 *The Life of Our Lord* for his children, but he would not allow what was a fairly simple re-telling of the story to be published in his lifetime: it didn't appear in print till 1934 and cannot as a narrative stand up against his masterpieces such as *David Copperfield* or *Bleak House*. There have been many 'Lives of Jesus' written since – but none of them have made much of a splash.

One problem that faces any biographer of Jesus Christ is not just that you have to beat four Gospels that for two thousand years have done rather well. If you want to write about the man Jesus as just a man, you would have to treat him as someone suffering from a severe psychiatric illness. We had someone like that at the top of my cousin-brother's street, Malham Road in Forest Hill, south-east London. As boys – and sometimes my uncle would join the fun – we would amuse ourselves on a Saturday afternoon by arguing with the man that he was not, as he thought himself to be, the Emperor Napoleon. But we soon got bored by the ingenious ways he found to prove that he was really French though he couldn't speak a word of the language, and we grew tired of his accounts of how he had survived for almost two hundred years, even though he didn't look his age.

The writers of the four Gospels, the Evangelists or 'Messengers of Good News', Matthew, Mark, Luke and John (the same Luke who was later author of 'The Acts of the Apostles', a history of Christ's immediate followers after his death) and the other writers of those twenty-one often lengthy Letters about Jesus that came from people who had known him or his associates – from Peter, his closest confidante and successor as leader, from James who was probably Christ's brother and eventually leader of the Christians in Jerusalem, from Jude, who says he was a 'brother of James', from John who was called Jesus' 'beloved disciple', from Paul, who had checked the accuracy of his information with Peter and James and others of Jesus' immediate circle and then wrote at least nine detailed letters, and, finally, from the author of the Letter to the Hebrews, whom Tertullian said (around 200 A.D. was Barnabas, a co-worker with Paul (though I myself favour Apollos, another associate of Paul mentioned in Acts 18: 24) – not a single one of these writers is much interested in Jesus the man in the way that a biographer might be: none of them describe what he looked like, how tall he was, if he had ginger hair, whether perhaps he had one brown and one hazel eye, if he had a crooked finger or walked with a limp, if his trade as a carpenter had left him with any work-related injuries, if he spoke high or low or with a stammer, whether he ever smiled or cracked a joke, whether he was in general rather dour or occasionally a bit short-tempered.

I want now to show you another artefact from the religious history of *homo sapiens*, otherwise known as *homo religiosus* – not this time a sculpture of the 'Lion Man' from Germany about forty thousand years before the birth of Jesus Christ, but a painting done a mere six hundred years or so after the death of Jesus, and demonstrating what the writers of the New Testament were chiefly interested in. It is an inspirational

Christos Pantocrator.

image from the Monastery of St Catherine on Mount Sinai – but of that new type of being, a hybrid of the human and the divine, the 'God-Man', *homo theos.*

Placed against a background that seems to span the heavenly bodies and some buildings of earth, Christ's halo might suggest that he is a ruler both of the present and of some uncharted realm beyond. In his left hand he holds what appears to be, from its bejewelled cover, a special book: perhaps, from the cross on the outside, a Christian gospel, though it may also be a book of record and of instructions, the Book of Life. The darker expression on the side of Christ's face above the book is severe, that of an all-seeing Judge; the expression on the side of his face that is above his right hand raised in blessing is compassionate and serene, the gaze of one who is a Saviour.

What you are seeing is an image of that new species of being – if you like, that new hybrid: the God-Man, *homo theos*, whose emergence has reconciled earth and heaven, conquered evil and death, and united what had seemed the two opposed methods of human understanding, the way of empirical science and the way of inspiration. His eyes interrogate the viewer, face on, his look is challenging, he assumes a posture of command but also of understanding, his right hand is raised in power but also in blessing. His question is not so much, 'What do you make of my life?' but 'What do you make of *me*?'

That is why the four books written about Jesus Christ known as the Gospels, together with that account of the subsequent actions of Jesus' followers, called the Acts of the Apostles and put together by one of the Gospel writers, Luke, and also all those further twenty-one Letters about Jesus by associates, relatives, disciples and friends, all seem to be not much interested in writing about another example of *homo sapiens* – even if he was (as the author of the Letter to the Hebrews puts it) fully human, 'tempted in every way, just as we are – yet was without sin' (Hebrews 4: 15). They are concerned to report as accurately and therefore as scientifically as possible what appeared to them to be the emergence of a new kind of being, a hybrid (if you care to put it that way) between God and Man, something never before seen: *homo theos*, the 'God-Man'.

They report what this supposed 'God-Man' said and what he presumably thought about himself: 'Anyone who has seen me has seen the Father' (John 14: 9; cf. Matthew 11: 27) – or again: 'I and the Father are one' (John 10: 30; cf. John 10: 34-38, 11: 25-26, 14: 9-11, 17: 1-26). They document what they had observed or had heard told about his actions and attitudes, they note anything in the way of unusual knowledge or unexpected powers that might support the view that he was something unique – perhaps a new species. We are told that he terrified his disciples by walking on water (Mark 6: 47-51; Matthew 14: 25-32; John 6: 19-20), that he calmed storms at sea so that they asked 'Who is this, that even the winds and the waves obey him!' (Matthew 8: 27). He claimed like God to forgive sins (Matthew 9: 2-7) and is reported as healing all manner of illnesses and fearful diseases, as driving out demons, even as raising the dead (Mark 5: 22-43, Luke 7: 11-15 John 11: 1-44). But like good researchers, some at least of the reporters record the negative evidence: that his own mother and brothers thought at one time that Jesus was 'out of his mind', and wanted to take him back home for safe keeping (Mark 3: 21, 31-34). They also note that Jesus couldn't do his healing miracles all the time and that his performances in his home area were rather a flop – the reason he gave being that those who had known him as a local boy lacked faith: 'Only in his home-town among his relatives and in his own house is a prophet without honour' (Mark 6: 4, cf. Matthew 13: 54-58; Luke 4: 24).

The witnesses record also that he seemed – as we might put it today – to 'have done his homework': he had boned up on that other type of knowledge, the world of vision and prophecy, announcing to a synagogue congregation at the beginning of his ministry that the prophecies of Isaiah about the One who was to come had come true: 'Today this scripture is fulfilled in your hearing' (Luke 4: 21). At the end of his career, he entered Jerusalem like the promised Messiah, the ruler 'gentle and riding on a donkey' as prophesied by the prophet Zechariah (Zechariah 9: 9).

What finally convinced all the contemporary witnesses who have left a record that here was a new species of being, *homo theos*, God-Man, was that he survived death. No one doubted that Jesus had died horribly on the Cross, and two of the major witnesses report his terrible cry of agony and despair: 'My God, my God, why have you forsaken me?' (Mark 15: 34; Matthew 27: 46) – and at the time, no one is reported as having thought that Jesus was anything but finished for good. Yet after three days his tomb was empty, the authorities could not produce a dead body, and relatives, disciples, and even women from Christ's entourage, women who because of their sex would at that time not normally have been cited as reliable witnesses, encountered Jesus as being alive. Somehow – and in the twenty-first century we have for the first time an idea of how it might be done – the human/divine genome had formed itself again from its elements into a visible and touchable body – but one that, by all reports, could pass into enclosed spaces through locked doors (Luke 24: 36-49; John 20: 19-28; 1 Corinthians 15: 5) and yet could also eat and drink like a human being (Acts 1: 4) and who, to prove he was not a ghost, would ask for 'a piece of broiled fish' and eat it in front of witnesses (Luke 24: 40-43). To make clear to his friends and followers that he remained the person they had known, he still bore the marks of his terrible death, so that Thomas was able to thrust his hand into Christ's wounded side (John 20: 24-29). In terms of anything that the ancient world might have anticipated, the disciples should either have seen a ghost or a spirit, or a re-animated corpse, a zombie: it was unimaginable to be able to experience all of this re-combined into a living Man.

Furthermore, we have at least eight different, well-attested sightings from multiple witnesses: an appearance first to two women, Mary Magdalene and 'the other Mary', who (as we've noted) would neither of them at that time have been regarded as suitable witnesses in a court of law (Matthew 28: 9-10). Then there were individual appearances to relatives and close friends such as James and Peter (Luke 24: 34, 1 Corinthians 15: 5-8), then to the eleven remaining disciples together (Luke 24: 36-49, John 20: 19-23, 1 Corinthians 15: 5), also to two disciples on the road to Emmaus (Luke 24: 13-32); later to seven disciples at the Sea of Galilee (John 21: 1-24); to the disciples and 500 brethren at one time (Matthew 28: 16-20; 1 Corinthians 15 :6); and, finally, forty days after the Resurrection, to the Apostles and a large number whom they had led to Bethany as witnesses to the Ascension (Luke 24: 50-53, Acts 1: 4-9).

The resurrection of Jesus Christ not only validated the claim that he was in some way a different species, *homo theos,* the God-Man. It lent substance to his claim to be 'the way, the truth and the life' (John 14: 6), able to make good on his promise to turn human beings who followed him and identified with him into that new species of *'homo theos,* God-Men, God-Women and God-Children like himself, who could surmount the miseries and evils of this life, and finally overcome 'the last enemy to be destroyed', Death itself (1 Corinthians 15: 26). They would learn both from vision and from natural science, they would be in knowledge and perception united with the Divine and with each other: they would no longer feel like wanderers and outcasts on the earth.

Those who talked and wrote about Jesus Christ in the decades immediately following his death have to be assessed by the criteria of what makes a good scientist, a competent seeker of knowledge, reporting as best he or she can on what they have observed, and comparing their results and their theoretical interpretations with others in the same field of study. Sometimes we can assess a New Testament writer's accuracy against what is only now becoming known from historical and archaeological studies: the gospel writer Luke is increasingly being proved more accurate than his critics over details he gives in the Acts of the Apostles about the Roman world, its names, positions and places. But what is immediately obvious is that, whether the reporters were close friends or even intimate family of Jesus Christ, whether they got their results by direct observation or were like Luke in his Gospel, by his own claim only collecting, summarizing and assessing the recollections of others, whether they were, some of them, alive at the time of Jesus or wrote as much as forty or so years after his death, they all make very similar reports, and they all have much the same theoretical understanding of this new species of man, *homo theos,* the God-Man. Putting matters in the most cynical of terms, they all 'sing from the same hymn sheet'. Even if they were all part of one vast national and international conspiracy and con-trick, that would have to rank as the most competent and plausible deception of all time.

One further unusual feature of this particular scientific investigation into Jesus Christ is that its most believable and coherent results come early and are the standard by which subsequent interpretations and conclusions are judged. Saul, later known as Paul, was not himself a 'hands-on' researcher. He had never met Jesus in the flesh, though in his work on behalf of the Jewish religious authorities he had persecuted, arrested and presumably interrogated early Christians, some of whom would have had personal knowledge of Jesus and his claims. Saul changed tack dramatically, no more than six years after Jesus' execution – but his conversion to being Paul, 'an ambassador of Christ' (to use his own term), was by a visionary experience of Jesus on the road to Damascus, according to his own account (1 Corinthians 9: 1, 15: 8), and that of his co-worker Luke as reported in the Acts of the Apostles (9: 3-9).

And yet Paul still did the scientific thing: no doubt he had derived information of a sort from Christian believers he had arrested, and it is probable that he had extracted some of that by intimidation, if not by torture. But he was aware that he had no first-hand observations of his own, so he took the opportunity to check his statements about Jesus by going to Jerusalem to meet eye-witnesses: he stayed fifteen days with Peter, Jesus' close friend, confidant and successor as leader (so Paul's letter to the Galatians 1: 18), and he met James, the brother of Jesus (Galatians 1: 19), who in Acts is treated as leader of the Jerusalem Christians (Acts of the Apostles 21: 18). 'Fourteen years later', again by his own account, Paul went once more to Jerusalem to check a second time what he was teaching with 'those who seemed to be leaders' (Galatians 2: 1-10), 'for fear' (as he puts it) 'that I had run or was running my race in vain'. Paul was clearly of an independent mind at times, disputing publicly with Peter in Antioch (Galatians 2: 11-21) and with conservative Jewish Christians at the First Council of the Church over appropriate Christian behaviour towards uncircumcised pagan converts (Acts 15: 1-35). So it is all the more surprising, therefore, that his understanding of the God-Man Jesus, arrived at early but then taught by him for thirty or more years all over Asia Minor, at Rome, and perhaps as far afield as Spain, should have always been accepted as the 'gold standard' by which every other account is to be judged.

As I have said earlier, it is highly unusual for the early results of any investigation to be accepted later and everywhere to be the most accurate. If Paul had successfully introduced and propagated a mass deception on this scale, he must have been a publicist with unique talents. To do it in the face of Simon Peter, who was an eye-witness and Christ's friend would have been impossible. But the accuracy of Paul's account (though he had never met Jesus in the flesh) concurs with that of Peter, who was Jesus' adviser and his appointed successor, and with that of James, Christ's own brother. And all three of them (and many more down the ages) have been prepared to attest to the accuracy of their reports by dying for them – a phenomenon not much seen even in the highest echelons of natural science!

In this part of my consideration of Origins, of our world and our human situation, I have been concerned to show how what seem two different modes of knowing – that of scientific enquiry into the things of this world, and that of divine intuition, vision, insight and prophecy, reaching out to a world beyond – have to be combined, if we are to give an accurate account of what appears to be a new species, *homo theos* – the God-Man, Jesus Christ, a being who belongs both to the human and to the divine.

When we continue further our discussion of Origins and all that that entails, I will suggest how the Old Testament explanation as to how and why evil came into the world – the Genesis account of Creation and of the Fall of Man – can in fact be reconciled with what seem very different truths uncovered by modern scientific enquiry. If we are to fully understand our own nature and that of the world in which we live, we must draw not just on scientific understanding but also on *'nous'*, on what we intuit about the divine. So I will examine the nature of our world as described by scientific enquiry, and then I will also seek to understand its nature and destiny and ours, as seen through inspired insight – and especially in those prophecies, visions and revelations that we find in the scriptures of the Church, in both the Old and the New Testaments.

CHAPTER SEVEN

Science Must Partner 'Nous':
A Necessary Marriage

In my previous discussions of the nature of humanity and the origin of life, I have talked about the two ways of understanding ourselves and our situation in the world in which we find ourselves: the method of scientific observation and enquiry – and the path of vision, intuition, insight and prayer, putting ourselves in touch with a realm beyond, the abode of the Other, the Divine. In Orthodox theology, that God-given power to tune-in to the Divine Nature and to understand what he requires from us is called '*Nous*' (in Greek νοῦς, in English pronounced 'Nows']. My schoolmaster used to explode at me with exasperation: 'For heaven's sake, Frost: show a little *nous!*' – by which I think he meant, 'Exercise some common sense!' But the word *nous* means more in the Greek: 'your God-given, intuitive understanding', which you must activate by tuning-in to the divine frequency. The much-loved twentieth-century Elder, Father Paisios, who had been a radio-operator in the Second World War, was fond of saying that God could always be heard if you tuned in at the correct point on the dial – which was labelled 'Humility'.

I also pointed out that neither method of understanding, left to itself, can be the sole guide to absolute truth. Scientific observation may be seriously at variance with spiritual insight in interpreting what is supposed to have been discovered, and each mode of enquiry requires the other to counteract the limitations of both. If it were not so, it would not have been necessary for the unseen God, hitherto only reachable through inspiration, prayer, vision, prophecy and insight, to become human in Jesus Christ, the 'God-Man', and, by so doing, to open himself to empirical study. As the Gospel of John puts it: 'No one has ever seen God, but God the One and Only, who is at the Father's side, has made him known' (John: 1: 18).

It is only that direct intervention of the divine into the world of the human in the person of Jesus Christ that can finally resolve for us any question as to the goodness of God in the face of undeniable evil. St Paul, when he begins his Letter to the Romans and is intending to summarize what is the evidential basis of the Christian faith, writes initially from the standpoint of 'nous', divinely inspired insight – but he runs the danger of appealing to 'nous' alone:

> The wrath of God is being revealed from heaven against all the godlessness and wickedness of men who suppress the truth by their wickedness, since what may be known is plain to them, because God has made it plain to them. For since the creation of the world God's invisible qualities – his eternal power and divine nature – have been clearly seen, being understood from what has been made, so that men are without excuse.
> (Romans 1: 18-20)

I enjoy Paul's stinging rebuke to those who, like the New Atheists, do not respond to the evidence of God's 'eternal power and divine nature' that is before their eyes in the natural world. However, that is not quite fair to those researchers who derive their evidence from the empirical sciences: what they see of God's 'eternal power and divine nature' as expressed in the natural world seems not always to be quite what ancient insight, vision and intuition would lead us to expect.

The dilemma was summed up by a contemporary of William Shakespeare, Fulke Greville, in a 'Chorus Sacerdotum', a 'Chorus of Priests', which he wrote for his play *Mustapha: A Tragedy* (1609). The 'priests' are, presumably, Muslim imams but they stand for all leaders of religious worship who find themselves required to proclaim an image of God, of Nature, and of what God requires from us, which seems at odds with what they as human beings actually experience:

> O wearisome condition of humanity!
> Born under one law, to another bound;
> Vainly begot and yet forbidden vanity;

Created sick, commanded to be sound.
What meaneth Nature by these diverse laws?
Passion and reason self-division cause.

Is it the mark and majesty of power
To make offences that she may forgive?
Nature herself doth her own self deflower
To hate those errors she herself doth give.
For how should man think that he may not do,
If nature did not fail and punish, too?
Tyrant to others, to herself unjust,
Only commands things difficult and hard,
Forbids us all things which it knows is lust,
Makes easy pains, unpossible reward.
If nature did not take delight in blood,
She would have made more easy ways to good.

We that are bound by vows and by promotion,
With pomp of holy sacrifice and rites,
To teach belief in good and still devotion,
To preach of heaven's wonders and delights;
Yet when each of us in his own heart looks
He finds the God there, far unlike his books.

I'd like now to invite the reader to join me in looking into our own hearts
so as to find what we understand of the nature of God, of his creation and
what he requires of us, as we confront the natural world. I'm going to begin
by asking you to follow me on my own initial path to understanding, the
path of vision as expressed in a particular artistic creation.

From my childhood I have been deeply moved and both morally and
spiritually educated by a myth, a work of the visionary imagination:
Samuel Taylor Coleridge's *The Rime of the Ancient Mariner*.

The story is told by what seems to be a guilt-obsessed old seaman
who for no obvious reason once destroyed a great seagoing bird, the
Albatross, which had followed his ship through the oceans of the south
Pacific:

God save thee, ancient Mariner,
From the fiends that plague thee thus! –
Why lookst thou so?' – 'With my crossbow
I shot the Albatross.

His shipmates feel instinctively that to destroy such a creature for no good cause was an offence against the whole order of things, even if they give an unscientific explanation:

And I had done an hellish thing,
And it would work 'em woe:
For all averr'd, I had kill'd the bird
That made the breeze to blow.
Ah wretch! said they, the bird to slay,
That made the breeze to blow!

The sailors are ignorant of meteorological science, and change their tune for a while when favourable winds blow; but as soon as they become becalmed in scorching heat, and are without drinking water, they return again to their instinctive condemnation, and by the insight of *nous*, mark the Ancient Mariner out as a criminal:

And every tongue, through utter drought,
Was withered at the root;
We could not speak, no more than if
We had been choked with soot.

Ah! well-a-day! What evil looks
Had I from old and young!
Instead of the cross, the Albatross
About my neck was hung.

Eventually, his shipmates die off one by one and the Ancient Mariner is left alone to contemplate his own self-loathing:

The many men, so beautiful,
And they all dead did lie:
And a thousand thousand slimy things
Lived on; and so did I!

What in the end releases the Ancient Mariner is the stirring in him of a previously unrecognized veneration for the wonder and beauty and life of the natural world.

Beyond the shadow of the ship
I watched the water-snakes:

They moved in tracks of shining white,
And when they reared, the elfish light
Fell off in hoary flakes.

Within the shadow of the ship
I watched their rich attire:
Blue, glossy green, and velvet black,
They coiled and swam; and every track
Was a flash of golden fire.

O happy living things! No tongue
Their beauty might declare:
A spring of love gushed from my heart,
And I blessed them unaware:
Sure my kind saint took pity on me,
And I blessed them unaware.

The selfsame moment I could pray;
And from my neck so free
The Albatross fell off, and sank
Like lead into the sea.

There is a prominent living example of that saving sensitivity to the natural world in the scientist David Attenborough, from 8 May 2020 in his ninety-fourth year – and still pursuing a lifetime's commitment to scientific observation and to reporting on those other living creatures with whom we share our current habitat, planet Earth – on their differing forms and actions, on their variety and complexity, on their striking beauty and their repellent ugliness, on their endearing qualities and also on what comes across as their appalling savagery. I have heard Attenborough's hushed, reverential tones accompanying some documentary on living creatures since I was a young man, and all our children and now our grandchildren have been brought up to share our veneration for the man my eldest son always called 'Captain'. You might call him the 'High Priest of Nature', and though I am told that Attenborough describes himself as an agnostic and subscribes to no formal religion, I am convinced that at his death he will hear the words 'Well done, thou good and faithful servant: enter thou into the joy of thy lord' (Matthew 25: 21, Authorized Version).

To venerate the natural world, to have an appreciation of it that leads to a sense of moral obligation to care for and protect it, is not something scientific observation can teach us. It comes from the realm of vision, that insight into God's nature and purposes that the Orthodox call *'nous'* and which is instinctive, intuitive: we do not feel the possible extinction of the Siberian tiger or the African rhinoceros to be a crime because we may suffer some disadvantage or material loss. Rather, we feel it would somehow be an outrage not to ensure the survival of something so awe-inspiring, so strangely beautiful or so oddly ugly, yet so wonderful *in itself*. To protect such a creature does nothing to ensure our own Darwinian 'survival of the fittest': why we feel as we do, God alone (and I mean that literally) – God alone knows.

This other way of knowing, of understanding, which leads to reverence for something quite outside ourselves, is as honourable and probably even more ancient than the scientific method. But only if those two different approaches to reality come together and are reconciled can they lead us to the whole truth. The world of scientific enquiry and rational analysis of data needs validation from the world of vision, prophecy, and insight – and the converse is equally true.

When we come to examine the 'Challenge of Evil', the need for science to refine our visionary understanding is particularly acute. In the Judaeo-Christian tradition we have two myths that explain, first, the Creation of the World and next, the Fall of Man. At the outset of the Book of Genesis ('The Book of Beginnings'), the myth presents God as originator of everything, the Great Designer – thus settling an issue on which modern science has been unable to reach an agreed conclusion. The statement that God made the world 'in six days', if interpreted as an insight expressed through myth, is a claim that everything in the world had the same originator: it is not a scientific calculation about the precise number of God-hours that went into creation! Estimates as to the probable age of the earth and the extent of time it took for all life-forms to emerge are more properly the province of rational scientific enquiry.

It so happens that the details of the story of Creation in the myth – beginning from an initial nothingness and formlessness, then the emergence of light and darkness, the creation of an atmosphere, then the addition of an essential ingredient, water, then vegetable life, the emergence of living creatures – first, in the waters, then on the earth – and finally, the emergence of Man – all of that accords roughly with the sequence of events as established by scientific enquiry. The Sun and moon in the myth are formed somewhat later in the process than science would accept. Nevertheless, even if aspects of the story were much more contrary to scientific inference, induction and deduction, it would not contradict the truth that the myth was intended to communicate: that God originated everything.

However, when we get to the second Genesis myth, that of the Fall of Man, to treat the story as a record of historical events rather than as visionary insight can lead us into very serious error. If we accept it simply as a story that conveys spiritual truth, very few Christians (if any) would deny that it records what we feel to be a painful reality of our experience: which is that everything wrong that we have ever done has been, either intentionally or thoughtlessly, a turning-away from God, from what we knew instinctively to be his will for us. What is more, even if Satan may be currently keeping a low profile, quite a few of us would admit that we were well aware of something nasty persuading us that what we were tempted to do could perhaps be rather delightful: 'Forbidden fruits? – Oh yes, *please!*'

The story also rings true over our eagerness to shift the blame for wrongdoing to someone else, if we get the slightest chance: 'And the man said, the woman whom thou gavest to be with me, she gave me of the tree, and I did eat.' (Genesis 3: 12, Authorized Version).

But if we are to know the truth of any communication, whether in daily life or from the Bible itself, it is vital to recognize that truth comes in varied packaging and by a variety of means. For instance, if I were to tell you that Samuel Taylor Coleridge had never really met an 'Ancient Mariner' who was determined to unload his guilt at having pointlessly killed a large ocean-going bird – would that have made the slightest difference to the tear-jerking message of the poem?

Similarly, we must understand that both the Old and the New Testaments use myth and story to convey truths through what we might otherwise dismiss as 'merely fiction'. We are told in the Gospel according to Matthew that Jesus Christ, Son of God, Son of Man, 'spoke all these things to the crowd in parables; he did not say anything to them without using a parable. So was fulfilled what was spoken through the prophet: "I will open my mouth in parables, I will utter things hidden since the creation of the world"' (Matthew 13: 34-35, citing Psalm 78: 2).

If you were to treat Christ's parable of 'the Good Samaritan' (Luke 10: 30-37) as factual truth, as an account of what Jesus actually observed, you would need to explain how Jesus (presumably sitting in a wayside café) could have witnessed a traveller being beaten up and robbed, then sat there watching whilst a priest and a Levite 'passed by on the other side', then felt a surge of approval when a stranger and outcast gave the necessary assistance – and yet himself have looked on all the while, never lifting a finger to help.

To treat either that parable of Christ's or the Genesis story of creation simply as though they were a factual record of what actually happened, an account such as you might find in a history book or a court record, would be to go seriously 'off-message'– and people seem to have gone seriously 'off-message' ever since the Genesis myth was first committed to writing. In the myth, the woman is the first sinner, easily conned by Satan, and the man's mistake is to take her too seriously. My wife will testify how eagerly I accept that view: uneasy at seeing women in positions of power, inclined to feel a woman is by nature less capable of judging rationally as to right and wrong, more easily swayed by feelings, the 'weaker vessel' – and centuries of males would have agreed with me. Even St Paul, though knowing perfectly well that in Christ there is neither 'Jew nor Greek, slave nor free, male nor female, for you are all one in Christ Jesus' (Galatians 3: 28) – even St Paul is inclined to argue the headship of the husband in marriage. Science cannot tell us with any confidence about the relative capabilities of the first man and woman: but there is increasing evidence from the field of psychology today that any crude division of human abilities and moral qualities between men and women – more of this quality or capacity in one sex and rather less of that in the other – is almost certainly untrue.

There is another problem created by treating the Genesis myth of the Fall of Man as if it were simply factual, and it is one that is particularly serious for our discussion of the 'Challenge of Evil' in the world at large and of any responsibility we humans might have for it. St Paul in 1 Corinthians 15: 21-22 (Authorized Version) announces in ringing terms what is the central Christian message: 'For since by man came death, by man came also the resurrection of the dead. For as in Adam all die, even so in Christ shall all be made alive.' The visionary meaning of Paul's formulation I entirely believe: the whole human race, symbolized by the mythical First Man, Adam, is now made capable of eternal life by the gift of Jesus Christ. The Man-God's self-sacrifice became necessary to put right a situation that had been caused by human error, by our desire to 'go it alone'. God's intention was, is and always shall be that Man should share in God's eternal life.

The problem arises when mythic vision is taken to be a factual statement such as science might investigate. It cannot be that death came into the world as a consequence of the wrongdoing of the first truly human couple to emerge, whenever that took place. Whether those two came by gradual evolution or by some special creation (and the fossil record does not rule out that possibility, for there are instances of creatures that appear to have emerged not gradually but from some sudden evolutionary burst), it is simply not true that death came into the world as the consequence of Man's fall. Man came on the scene very late in the history of living species – and Death was in the world many eons before the first human beings emerged. Pain, suffering and death afflicted the whole of what we may for other reasons believe to be God's divinely created animal kingdom: it is said, from the damage that appears on the bones of dinosaurs, that they must have suffered from agonizing arthritis! The whole of nature was and is, in Tennyson's phrase, 'red in tooth and claw': in the food chain, creature preyed on creature, pretty well from the beginnings of life on earth.

An especially dangerous instance of the misinterpretation of myth as if it were a factual report comes late in the re-tellings of the story of the Fall of Man, in John Milton's epic poem *Paradise Lost*, first published in 1667. It is no accident that Milton wrote near the birth of modern science as we know it: the Royal Society of London, the world's first society for the promotion of science, was founded seven years earlier, and Milton treats the Genesis myth as if it were a scientific record.

Milton's poem may put Biblical myth into the format of Greek and Roman epic – but it aims chiefly to align the Hebrew story with emerging scientific knowledge so as to cope with issues that concern us today: especially, questions as to the Goodness of God and the Challenge of Evil. The purpose of the poem is theological: to 'justify the ways of God to men' (*Paradise Lost*, Book I, line 26).

In Milton's version, Eve's taking of the apple is the immediate cause of all those evils that afflict God's creation:

> Forth reaching to the fruit, she plucked, she ate.
> Earth felt the wound; and nature from her seat,
> Sighing through all her works, gave signs of woe,
> That all was lost.
> (*Paradise Lost*, Book IX, lines 781-84)

The misfortunes that affect life on earth are then presented as a direct consequence of Eve's – and after that – of Adam's wrongdoing: God instructs his angels to create bad weather, natural disasters.

> The sun
> Had first his precept so to move, so shine,
> As might affect the earth with cold and heat
> Scarce tolerable; and from the north to call
> Decrepit winter; from the south to bring
> Solstitial summer's heat. . . .
> To the winds they set
> Their corners, when with bluster to confound
> Sea, air, and shore; the thunder when to roll
> With terror through the dark aerial hall.
> Some say, he bid his angels turn askance

> The poles of earth, twice ten degrees and more,
> From the sun's axle; they with labour pushed
> Oblique the centric globe. . . . Thus began
> Outrage from lifeless things . . .

But note that it is not only the weather that goes wrong: the whole savagery of the animal kingdom is presented as a direct result of human wrongdoing:

> but Discord first,
> Daughter of Sin, among the irrational   [*the unthinking creatures*]
> Death introduced, through fierce antipathy:
> Beast now with beast 'gan war, and fowl with fowl,
> And fish with fish; to graze the herb all leaving,
> Devoured each other; nor stood much in awe
> Of man, but fled him; or, with countenance grim,
> Glared on him passing.
> (*Paradise Lost*, Book X, lines 651-714)

No wonder the beasts, fowls and fish looked on us humans somewhat grimly: we were, after all, in Milton's story, solely responsible for a whole heap of trouble!

It would be hard to overestimate the damage this reading of the Genesis myth of the Fall of Man as straightforward fact has done to acceptance of the Christian faith – especially in that Protestant tradition to which John Milton belonged. No wonder a Christian like John Bunyan records, both in his masterpiece, *Pilgrim's Progress*, and also in his biographical writings such as *Grace Abounding to the Chief of Sinners*, a tendency to be sunk under a weight of guilt that would at times, however long he had been a believer, sink him into almost insupportable despair. The reader is already a full twenty-six pages into Bunyan's great work before Christian, burdened by the great load of Original Sin on his back, is given his release:

> He ran thus till he came at a place somewhat ascending; and upon that place stood a *Cross*, and a little below in the bottom, a Sepulcher. So I saw in my Dream, that just as Christian came up with the *Cross*, his burden loosed from off his Shoulders, and fell from off his back; and began to tumble; and so continued to do, till it came to the mouth of the Sepulcher, where it fell in, and I saw it no more.[1]

---

1.   John Bunyan, *Grace Abounding to the Chief of Sinners* and *The Pilgrim's Progress*,

The problem is that Bunyan as narrator may see the burden no more and I as reader may with Christian 'give three leaps for joy' at Christian's release – but the burden comes back for Christians again and again, both in Bunyan's story and especially to those educated in a Protestant tradition. I may tell myself as I read my morning newspaper that I am not responsible for all the evils in the universe – but that becomes more difficult if you were brought up to believe that everything that seems wrong in the natural world was simply a consequence of the wrong turn your human ancestors took.

There is a further problem for honest searchers after truth: Milton's version of the myth would seem neatly to exonerate God from any responsibility for what we see and suffer in the natural world. David Attenborough, though I've called him our 'Great High Priest of Nature', gave as his reason why he had to remain an agnostic the existence of a parasitic worm *Onchocerca volvulus*.

He said:

> My response is that when Creationists talk about God creating every individual species as a separate act, they always instance hummingbirds, or orchids, sunflowers and beautiful things. But I tend to think instead of a parasitic worm that is boring through the eye of a boy sitting on the bank of a river in West Africa, [a worm] that's going to make him blind. And [I ask them], 'Are you telling me that the God you believe in, who you also say is an all-merciful God, who cares for each one of us individually, are you saying that God created this worm that can live in no other way than in an innocent child's eyeball? Because that doesn't seem to me to coincide with a God who's full of mercy.
> (*December 2005 interview with Simon Mayo on* BBC Radio)

It's a fair comment, and one that Christians have to answer. The visionary approach to understanding who and where we are, our belief that we are created by the 'Good God who loves mankind', has also, somehow, to explain our experience of evil. But on the other hand, that supposedly scientific account of our existence, neo-Darwinism, which alleges that we came to be by an enormously lengthy process of random changes, of changes without purpose and perpetuated by natural selection, has somehow to explain our experience of good – and *that* is something Darwinian evolutionary theory has spectacularly failed to do.

ed. with an Introduction by Roger Sharrock (London: Oxford University Press, 1966), p. 169.

In Coleridge's poem it was the Ancient Mariner's spontaneous outburst of love for the 'happy living things' whose beauty no tongue might declare that redeemed him from his crime of wantonly destroying the Albatross. Now I want to draw your attention to a video clip of a similar outburst of love, filmed during the fearful fires in Southern California in late 2017, which was shown on television around the world and has had thousands upon thousands of 'hits' on You Tube.[2]

The evidence as presented to a world-wide audience is that a young man heard a wild rabbit screaming as the flames approached; he became distraught and felt impelled to risk his own safety to save the terrified creature.

Rabbit Rescue.

Why did he do it? According to the video commentary, he 'holds his head in grief', 'he calls out to the frightened animal'; finally, he can bear it no longer and dives into the flames to rescue a creature already singed – and though his mother was appalled to hear of the risk he had taken, a substantial number of the human race believed he had done well and made him an international hero.

Just what, a Darwinist might ask, could have gone wrong? If all creatures have evolved by a series of chance mutations that result in 'the survival of the fittest', something here must be seriously amiss. Maybe a mutation which evolved so that humans would look after their young and thus preserve their race has somehow got disordered and this may have led the young man into rescuing something as if it were a human baby? He does

---

2. A range of discussions of the event, its implications and accompanying videos can be accessed through a search engine by entering 'Rabbit Rescue'. See among many: edition.cnn.com/2017/12/07/US/California-wildfires-rabbit-trnd/index.html

not seem to have done what he did just so as to save a good meal from the flames, and he even went so far as to take the rabbit to an animal-welfare centre for treatment of its burnt ears and paws – presumably at his own expense. A genetic trait so malfunctioning as to put the man's own life in danger and not to contribute to his self-interest or the 'survival of the fittest' ought surely to have been eliminated by 'natural selection'?

Of course, the rest of us (and that includes the Darwinists when they are not being wilfully silly) know perfectly well what happened. The young man was hit by the Ancient Mariner's 'spring of love': he could not stand by and see another living creature suffer. But what he was moved by was that other way of knowing, quite different to the investigations of the scientific method: by the power of *nous*, by some inexplicable, instinctive insight into the things of God, he knows that another of God's creatures is also wonderful, glorious like himself – yet this one is frightened, suffering, threatened by destructive evil – and he knows that he must act. He hears the call of its Creator to rescue what God had made and pronounced good, he loves both the Maker and what has been made: and moved by love, rather by than any self-interest, he chooses to act. *We* understand: and so do most of the Darwinists – but not by their scientific method.

Nevertheless, the faith that God created all things in love is open to very serious challenge from observations and deductions about the world we inhabit that are derived from an honest scientific understanding – and we owe it in any enquiry into the 'Goodness of God' to confront the evidence

as it is. David Attenborough, much as he was devoted to and fascinated by the natural world, found that the existence of a parasitic worm that is only able to live in the eyeball of an innocent African boy made it impossible for him to believe in a merciful Creator. You might try to argue along with John Milton that all the evil in our world resulted from a wrong turn by our first parents – but what, then, would you make of this? This is an artist's impression of the Megalodon, meaning 'Big Tooth.'[3]

Artist's impression of the Megalodon or 'Big-Tooth'.

3.   From Wikipedia Commons, https://en.wikipedia.org/wiki/FileVMNH_megalodon.jpg.

Our knowledge of this creature derives from scientific deductions based on remnants of it found as fossils in rock layers laid down between 2.3 and 2.6 million years ago. Because it is mainly teeth and scales that survive, it is classified as belonging to the species *Carcharodon*, part of the shark family, jawed vertebrates whose skeletons, being cartilage, usually decay before much of them can become fossilized. Sharks are widespread today, but are thought to have existed from before the time of the dinosaurs, more than 420 million years ago – and this one is estimated to have been between forty and seventy feet long.

Here is another beauty, but this time not from the ancient past but from the present, the Barbeled Dragon Fish.

The Barbeled Dragon Fish.

Like the ancient Megalodon and the more modern varieties of shark that are alive today, the Barbeled Dragon Fish is a champion predator, surviving only by killing other creatures. At sea depths where there is no plant life, it lives solely by devouring other deep sea fish and marine invertebrates, and it has been wonderfully equipped (if you choose to think of it that way) with light-producing cells on its body to attract the attention of its victims.

Now, having contemplated both images, I'd suggest that the reader consider, first, how the species of Man, *homo sapiens*, who first appeared according to the fossil record around 300,000 years ago, could possibly by his Fall have warped the nature of the Megaladon, who existed 2.3 to 2.6 million years ago but is now extinct. Next, you might ask how Man could have corrupted the nature of creatures such as the Dragon Fish, which came to be before Man himself and still has present-day descendants.

You might keep the images of these two creatures before you as I quote once again from St Paul's confident assertion in his Letter to the Romans:

> The wrath of God is being revealed from heaven against all the godlessness and wickedness of men who suppress the truth by their wickedness, since what may be known about God is plain to them, because God has made it plain to them. For since the creation of the world God's invisible qualities – his eternal power and his divine nature – have been clearly seen, being understood from what has been made, so that men are without excuse.
> (Romans 1: 18-20)

Though in one sense I fully respond to Paul's assumption that God's nature is expressed in the wonders of the natural world, I cannot but ask what image of God's 'invisible qualities' and his 'divine nature' do those two creatures, ancient and modern, seem to project?

If we could simply take the Genesis story of the Fall of Man as a visionary expression of what most of us feel, it presents no problem: not only are we less than we would like to be, we tend also to feel we are less than we ought to be.

But to go further, and treat the Genesis story as though it were a factual account of historical events, is to make of it an instance of divine injustice, for what we had accepted when it was a visionary expression of our universal experience of doing wrong has now been transformed into an unmerited penalty imposed by God on the innocent offspring of the primal pair and from them transmitted to the whole subsequent human race through the act of sexual intercourse – so making a natural joy in bonding something driven by 'concupiscence', the desire for forbidden fruit, unlicensed pleasure. From that misreading comes the so-called 'Doctrine of Original Sin', where 'sin' is presented as something supposedly passed down like a congenital infection from Eve and Adam to every subsequent member of the human race – an image of supposed truth so grotesque that it will require a full refutation in my next-to-final chapter.

Nevertheless, though I realize how enormous is the problem that these two creatures set before us, and whilst I also recognize there is a parallel difficulty which arises from any extensive contemplation of the natural world, I still believe that St Paul's visionary statement of God's nature as expressed in his creation is a truth – as firmly as I believe that the truth does not allow us to make Man responsible for what seems the hideous aspect of creatures that existed long before Man emerged and before any wrongness of ours could have influenced them for ill.

CHAPTER EIGHT

'To See Things as They Are': the Necessary Concurrence of Vision with Evidence

At the close of my previous consideration of the 'Goodness of God and the Challenge of Evil', I undertook to continue our enquiry into the nature of the world in which we find ourselves as it is revealed by the investigations of modern science – and then to compare that knowledge with those insights which derive from vision, intuition, prayer and *nous*, the divinely-given power to tune into the mind of God, whose conclusions Christians believe are most fully expressed by the prophecies and fulfilments of the Old and New Testaments of the Christian Church.

Since the late seventeenth century and its development of scientific enquiry, leading to a supposed 'Enlightenment' from what some contemporaries held to be the shackles and fantasies of religious belief, there has been an understandable bias against the whole visionary, intuitive mode of understanding. To demonstrate quite how understandable that bias is, let me give you an illustration.

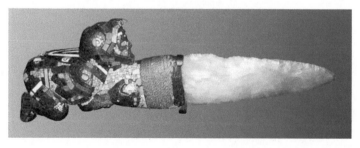

Aztec dagger for human sacrifice.

This is an Aztec sacrificial dagger, the handle carved to represent a kneeling Eagle-warrior, one of whose roles was to supply human victims for sacrifice whose hearts would be cut out whilst they were still alive, so that the God of the Sun might be 'fed' with fresh blood.

Aztec human sacrifice.

And here is an Aztec illustration of that sacrifice, from the Codex Laud, Bodleian Library, Oxford. [1]

By vision, by intuition and prayer, our forebears reached out to the Gods beyond – a striving toward reality probably as old as human self-consciousness itself. Aztec legend had it that the gods had poured out their own life-blood to make the world, and so, simple reciprocity required that the heart-blood of living human beings be poured out so the Gods could replenish themselves. Most if not all adherents to the religions of the world, including the Jews of the Old Testament, have believed that sacrifice was essential for a right relationship with the divine, for maintaining or restoring harmony and peace; and Christians believe that the perfect sacrifice of an innocent man accomplished the redemption of the world. The Aztecs were grossly wrong, not in believing that the sacrifice of *another* human being would repair a relationship with the divine, but in not intuiting that the necessary sacrifice would be made by God himself in the person of Jesus Christ (as the Jews had been led by prophecy to expect). But worse still was their failure to understand that the necessary gift required of us was sacrifice of *ourselves*. They misjudged the nature of God and the sacrifice required, because they thought God to be as savage and self-directed as they were themselves.

If I pause for a moment from consideration of recent scientific evidence about the natural world and of our own place in it, that is because the

1. From the Codex Laud, Bodleian Library, Oxford.

claims of the alternative way to understanding, by vision, intuition and inspiration, may seem to have been discredited by evidence like that derived from empirical study of the Aztecs. Yet, if vision is allied with and validated by empirical evidence, it can illuminate and transform our human understanding as though by a flash of lightning.

In my late teens and early twenties, I was much taken with the life-story of the late seventeenth-century courtier and notorious tearaway, John Wilmot, Earl of Rochester. Near the beginnings of a scientific and philosophic enterprise that would soon result in a so-called 'Enlightenment' from religious superstition, Rochester seems to have been half-persuaded by the materialism of an older contemporary, the philosopher Thomas Hobbes (1588-1679), and so held that the only reliable guide to understanding was sensory experience, which (to use Hobbes' own phrase) showed 'the life of man, in a state of nature', as 'solitary, poor, nasty, brutish, and short'. Rochester seems to have concluded that a man of sense would take what pleasure there was whilst he could still find it. In the late 1960s, Rochester's attitudes looked all too similar to those I thought I saw developing amongst the intelligentsia of my own day: cynical, unbelieving, pained by their own existence, lacking a sense of meaning, seeking relief in alcohol, drugs and unbridled sexual pleasure. I took to reciting lines from Rochester's 'A Satyr against Reason and Mankind':

> Were I (who to my cost already am
> One of those strange, prodigious creatures, man)
> A spirit free to choose, for my own share
> What case of flesh and blood I pleased to wear,
> I'd be a dog, a monkey, or a bear,
> Or anything but that vain animal,
> Who is so proud of being rational.
>
> The senses are too gross, and he'll contrive
> A sixth, to contradict the other five,
> And before certain instinct, will prefer
> Reason, which fifty times for one does err;
> Reason, an *ignis fatuus* of the mind,   [*a 'willow-the-wisp'*]
> Which, leaving light of nature, sense, behind,
> Pathless and dangerous wand'ring ways it takes
> Through error's fenny bogs and thorny brakes;
> Whilst the misguided follower climbs with pain
> Mountains of whimseys, heaped in his own brain;

Stumbling from thought to thought, falls headlong down
Into doubt's boundless sea where, like to drown,
Books bear him up awhile, and make him try
To swim with bladders of philosophy;   ['*water-wings*']
In hopes still to o'ertake th' escaping light;
The vapour dances in his dazzling sight
Till, spent, it leaves him to eternal night.
Then old age and experience, hand in hand,
Lead him to death, and make him understand,
After a search so painful and so long,
That all his life he has been in the wrong.
Huddled in dirt the reasoning engine lies,
Who was so proud, so witty, and so wise.

Whether I was just to my contemporaries, I doubt. I do know that the Chaplain of my Cambridge college, surveying his work at the end of that academic year, told me that, amongst the whole new student intake for 1958, I was the only one who had made a reverse journey, from scepticism to belief. An account of the dramatic deathbed conversion of John Wilmot, Earl of Rochester was a major factor in that change.

We have a first-hand record of the stages leading to Rochester's conversion written by Gilbert Burnet, later Bishop of Salisbury, who held a series of discussions with Rochester on philosophical and theological issues in the last year of Rochester's life, when he was already suffering major complications from a combination of alcoholism and venereal disease. Burnet was a master of five languages, a scholar, theologian and historian of considerable repute, highly respected as a clergyman. If he seemed to his contemporaries a shade self-satisfied and sometimes an unwitting buffoon, there is no good reason to accept the charge, made then and now, that he liked to haunt the deathbeds of notable sinners in the hope of demonstrating his converting power. In the same year that Rochester died (1680), Burnet published *Some Passages of the Life and Death of John, Earl of Rochester,* which on its title-page claims to have been 'Written by his [Rochester's] Own Direction on his Death-Bed'.

Rochester showed a need to talk and had previously held discussions with other thinkers. He thought his illness might prove lethal and he perhaps felt responsible for the death of one of his female companions from syphilis the previous year – a lady to whom Burnet had ministered as she was dying. It is perhaps significant that Rochester needed to assure Burnet that, in all his extravagant outrages, he had stopped short of intentionally doing another person any major harm.

More significant for our present enquiry is that, though Burnet did a thoroughly workmanlike job over several visits in laying out the arguments for believing in a Christian God, he got nowhere. Admittedly, Rochester, like most people then and now, unless they cling to an increasingly discredited Darwinian dogma of life emerging through blind chance, took the view that if a thing looked designed, it probably was so. But that, according to Burnet's account, was as far as Rochester could go.[2]

> **This** subject led us to discourse of God, and of the notion of religion in general. He believed, there was a Supreme Being. He could not think, the world was made by chance ; and the regular course of nature seemed to demonstrate the eternal power of its author. This, he said, he could never shake off; but when he came to explain his notion of the Deity, he said, he looked upon it as a vast power, that wrought every thing by the necessity of its nature ; and thought that God had none of those affections of love or hatred, which breed perturbation in us ; and consequently, could not see there was to be either reward or punishment. He thought our
>
> 60
>
> conceptions of God were so low, that we had better not think much of him. And to love God seemed to him a presumptuous thing, and the heat of fanciful men.

2. See *Some passages of the life and death of John Earl of Rochester: Written at his desire, on his Death-Bed, by Gilbert Burnet, D.D. Sometime Professor of Divinity in the University of Glasgow, and afterwards Bishop of Sarum. Containing more amply Their Conversations on the great Principles of Natural and Revealed Religion. To which is subjoined, a further account of his conversion, and Penitential Sentiments, by Robert Parsons, M.A. Chaplain to the Countess Dowager of Rochester* (?1787). Poor facsimiles of an earlier edition , printed for Richard Chiswell at the Rose and Crown in St Paul's Church-Yard, 1680, can be purchased through Amazon and accessed at Early English Books, reference: quod.lib.umich.edu/e/eebo/A30466.0001?view=toc

What changed Rochester's mind and spirit so dramatically, by a coming-together of vision and experiential evidence, was an intervention not from Burnet, who was away at the time, but from the family chaplain, who thought to read to the sick man the Fifty-Third chapter of the Prophet Isaiah, which we know as the prophecy of 'The Suffering Servant'. I'll repeat first the passage in the King James or Authorized Version, 53: 1-12, which is likely to be what Rochester heard, and then quote from what Burnet calls Rochester's 'strange account' of his response.

1. Who hath believed our report?
and to whom is the arm of the Lord revealed?

2. For he shall grow up before him as a tender plant,
and as a root out of a dry ground:
he hath no form nor comeliness;
and when we shall see him,
there is no beauty that we should desire him.

3. He is despised and rejected of men;
a man of sorrows, and acquainted with grief:
and we hid as it were our faces from him;
he was despised, and we esteemed him not.

4. Surely he hath borne our griefs,
and carried our sorrows:
yet we did esteem him stricken,
smitten of God, and afflicted.

5. But he was wounded for our transgressions,
he was bruised for our iniquities;
the chastisement of our peace was upon him;
and with his stripes we are healed.

6. All we like sheep have gone astray:
we have turned every one to his own way;
and the Lord hath laid on him the iniquity of us all.

7. He was oppressed and he was afflicted, yet he opened not his mouth:
he is brought as a lamb to the slaughter,
and as a sheep before her shearers is dumb,

so he openeth not his mouth.

8. He was taken from prison and from judgement:
and who shall declare his generation?
for he was cut off out of the land of the living:
for the transgression of my people was he stricken.

9. And he made his grave with the wicked,
and with the rich in his death;
because he had done no violence,
neither was any deceit in his mouth.

10. Yet it pleased the Lord to bruise him; he hath put him to grief:
when thou shalt make his soul an offering for sin,
he shall see his seed, he shall prolong his days,
and the pleasure of the Lord shall prosper in his hand.

11. He shall see of the travail of his soul, and shall be satisfied:
by his knowledge shall my righteous servant justify many;
for he shall bear their iniquities.

12. Therefore will I divide him a portion with the great,
and he shall divide the spoil with the strong;
because he hath poured out his soul unto death:
and he was numbered with the transgressors;
and he bare the sin of many,
and made intercession for the transgressors.
(Isaiah 53: 1-12)

Here now in Burnet's account is Rochester's response.

He said, Mr. Parsons, in order to his conviction, read to him the 53d chapter of the prophecy of Isaiah, and compared that with the history of our Saviour's passion, that he might there see a prophecy concerning it, written many ages before it was done; which the Jews that blasphemed Christ still kept in their hands, as a book divinely inspired. He said to me, that as he heard it read, he felt an inward force upon him, which did so enlighten his mind and convince him, that he could resist it no longer: for the words had an authority, which did shoot like rays or beams in his mind; so that he was not only convinced by the

reasonings he had about it, which satisfied his understanding, but by a power which did so effectually constrain him, that he did ever after as firmly believe in his Saviour, as if he had seen him in the clouds.

He had it read so often to him, that he had got it by heart: and went through a great part of it in discourse with me, with a sort of heavenly pleasure, giving me his reflections on it. – Some few I remember: *Who hath believed our report?* **Verse 1. Here, he said, was foretold the opposition the gospel has to meet from such wretches as he was.** *He hath no form nor comeliness; and when we shall see him, there is no beauty that we should desire him,* **verse 2. On this he said, the meanness of his appearance and person has made vain and foolish people disparage him, because he came not in such a fool's coat as they delight in.**

What he said on the other parts I do not well remember; and indeed I was so affected with what he then said to me, that the general transport I was under during the whole discourse, made me less capable to remember these particulars, as I wish I had done.

We might say that Rochester was hit by what I'll call 'a double whammy': the power of visionary prophecy, written down some 740 years before the birth of Jesus Christ, but confirmed and validated by observational evidence derived according to the requirements of historical science. This particular ancient vision, offering a finer understanding of propitiatory sacrifice than that of the pagan Aztecs, is a more perfect image of what true sacrifice to God should be; and the historical facts of the life, death and resurrection of Jesus Christ as the Messiah who was to come, both as foretold by Christ before his death and in the precise terms as set down by Isaiah, are validated by a mass of circumstantial evidence from a host of first-hand witnesses and secondary reporters, each confirming the others' testimony. When vision and scientific fact come together, their authority can be irresistible.

Not only did Rochester find the fulfilled prophecy undeniable: what it promised met his deepest need. The life, teachings, betrayal, trial and execution of Jesus Christ on trumped up charges, but followed immediately by his quite unexpected resurrection, offered to anyone, however corrupt they might feel themselves, a reconciliation with God and one's fellow human beings, forgiveness of all one's sins and wrongdoing, and a future of life in the enjoyment of the Kingdom of God, if only they would accept Christ's gift of himself.

Of course, Rochester was not unique in being bowled over by the coming-together of prophecy and observable fact. That was the whole message of the Christian Gospel or 'Good News' from the earliest days. From immediately after Christ's death and resurrection, it is reported that his previously demoralized followers went first to the Jews of Jerusalem, presenting themselves as personal witnesses to the fulfilment of ancient prophecy in the life, death and resurrection of Jesus Christ. There is no evidence whatever of any time-lag or recovery-period: they then went to the synagogues of Judea, then to the synagogues of the ancient East, then throughout the whole Roman world, inviting first the Jews and then the Gentiles to inspect the ancient prophecies and see how prophecy squared with the recent events that had happened in their midst. They challenged their contemporaries to face the facts of which they were the witnesses – and there is no report of any contemporary opponent managing a remotely plausible alternative explanation.

Only in the nineteenth century and onwards have sceptics made serious attempts to argue that the Christ story was a myth that grew up over a substantial period of time. Early Muslim writers might dispute whether Christ died on the Cross, preferring to maintain that, like some of the ancient Prophets, he had been carried up to heaven – but that was simply to substitute a more acceptable interpretation of events. In fact, St Paul's initial persecution of the first Christians, followed shortly afterwards by his conversion, his contact with first-hand witnesses, relatives, friends and followers of Christ, and the evidence that from the first he taught what was already the foundational Christian account of what had happened, all suggest that the facts stimulated a search of ancient prophecy, rather than prophecy generating spurious 'facts'.

Take one small example. Three gospel writers, Matthew (27: 57-60), Mark (15: 42-46) and Luke (23: 50-55) report that, after Christ died, one Joseph of Arimathea, 'a rich man' and 'a member of the Council', used his influence with Pilate to collect the body of the murdered Christ so as to give him a decent burial in a tomb he had made for himself. Are we to assume that Joseph woke up after the crucifixion and said 'God forgive me! The 53rd Chapter of Isaiah, verse 9, says "He was assigned a grave with the wicked, and with the rich in his death". I had better get up immediately and petition Pilate to let me have Jesus' body to put in my own tomb – otherwise, we won't be able to say with Isaiah that he was buried "with the rich"'?

If I have chosen to recount the story of Rochester as one victim of a modern tendency to overlook the insights of vision in favour of what is alleged to be observable scientific fact, that is because – both in my own life and in that of Rochester – the coming-together of ancient vision with historical evidence has brought intense joy in the midst of what might otherwise have been insurmountable suffering. We owe it to ourselves and to our fellow human beings to pay particular attention to those instances where vision and scientific evidence concur – and to treat with extreme suspicion those occasions where they do not.

What Rochester learned from the conjunction of vision with factual evidence was that life was a cause for rejoicing and a glorious gift – and a gift, moreover, that was potentially unending. What renders neo-Darwinist theory about the world unacceptable to responsive beings is that it is essentially joyless, unable to account for the value we humans and some at least of the creatures put on existence. Open Professor Dawkins' *River Out Of Eden: A Darwinian View of Life*[3] on a fine spring morning in England or at an autumnal fall in New England, and try reciting his summary to the scene before you:

> The universe we observe has precisely the properties we should expect if there is, at bottom, no design, no design, no purpose, no evil, and no good, nothing but, blind, pitiless indifference.

If that were really true, when we respond to the beauty or the ugliness of the natural world, when we delight in its creatures yet are repelled by the ferocity of their behaviour – or if, like the young female presenter who led the BBC's television programme *Nature Watch* the evening before I wrote this, we are enchanted by film of a nest of young birds being fed by their parents yet later moved to tears by shots of an invading weasel devouring the young and leaving the parents distraught – are we just being stupidly sentimental, caring for something that is not worth our sympathetic distress? Surely, to be as indifferent as Dawkins' theory logically requires would be to make ourselves into inhuman monsters. Yet why should this be so?

When I turn once again to exploration of the natural world, my chief interest in pursuing what are the most accurate and up-to-date observations of biological science will be to see what might be gathered from them about the likely nature of whatever power could have brought them into existence and to see how congruent those scientific observations are with the insights of that other source of human understanding – what I have designated the world of vision, insight, intuition, prayer, and the power of insight through '*nous*'.

---

3. Richard Dawkins, *River Out of Eden: A Darwinian View of Life* (Basic Books, New York, 1995), p. 133.

But before we begin such an enquiry, we had better be clear what 'vision', as expressed in the both the Old and New Testaments, implies about the actual state of the world we live in.

The same visionary prophet Isaiah, whose utterances some 2,400 years later so transformed Rochester's perception of the world in which he found himself, also presented God as testifying that the natural world had not yet attained its final state – and so had yet to fulfil God's perfect intention:

> Behold, I will create new heavens and a new earth.
> The former things will not be remembered,
> nor will they come to mind.
> But be glad and rejoice forever in what I will create,
> for I will create Jerusalem to be a delight and its people a joy.
> I will rejoice over Jerusalem and take delight in my people;
> The sound of weeping and of crying will be heard in it no more.
> Never again will there be in it an infant who lives but a few days,
> Or an old man who does not live out his years.
> (Isaiah, Chapter 65, verses 17-20)

Moreover, it seems that this new order will involve a reconciliation throughout the animal kingdom:

> The wolf and the lamb will feed together,
> And the lion will eat straw like the ox,
> But dust shall be the serpent's food.
> They will neither harm nor destroy
> on all my holy mountain, says the Lord.
> (Isaiah, Chapter 65, verse 25)

This prophecy repeats what is said earlier in the same book, about a messianic figure who will be a descendent of David the King and will put the nations under a righteous discipline that will also correct what is (to use Tennyson's phrase) a Nature 'red in tooth and claw':

> Righteousness will be his belt
> and faithfulness the sash around his waist.
> The wolf will live with the lamb,
> the leopard will lie down with the goat,
> The calf and the lion and the yearling together;
> and a little child will lead them.

The cow will feed with the bear,
their young will lie down together,
And the lion will eat straw like the ox.
The infant will play near the hole of the cobra,
and the young child put his hand into the viper's nest.
They will neither harm nor destroy on all my holy mountain,
For the earth will be full of the knowledge of the Lord
as the waters cover the sea.
(Isaiah, Chapter 11: 5-9)

In passing, I am forced to observe that Isaiah's prophecy of universal peace does not encourage meat-eaters like myself to look forward in that perfect Kingdom to roast lamb or a sizzling pork chop – we will need to explain how what will not be tolerated there could somehow be acceptable in life as we know it. If you think I may be creating an unnecessary difficulty, look at how the resurrected Christ at the end of the Gospel according to John is reported as directing the disciples where to find fish, and then as inviting them to breakfast with him by adding their catch to the fish he is already cooking over 'a fire of burning coals' (John 21: 4-13). A modern vegetarian might well ask 'How could the one whom you believe to be fully God and perfect Man permit, even encourage, such a thing?' Perhaps the best answer might be that human beings are, at present, under interim arrangements: given that things are not yet as they should be, some things are tolerated that in a perfect world will be unnecessary.

What is of particular significance in Isaiah's prophecy is the way he relates the disorder of the natural world not only to a rebellion by human beings against God's rule but to some disobedience of 'the powers in the heavens', who with their earthly followers will eventually be overthrown in a final catastrophe:

Terror and pit and snare await you, O people of the earth.
Whoever flees at the sound of terror will fall into a pit;
whoever climbs out of the pit will be caught in a snare.
The floodgates of the heavens are opened, the foundations of the earth shake.
The earth is broken up, the earth is split asunder, the earth is thoroughly shaken.
The earth reels like a drunkard, it sways like a hut in the wind;
so heavy upon it is the guilt of its rebellion that it falls – never to rise again.

In that day the Lord will punish the powers in the heavens above
and the kings on the earth below.
They will be herded together like prisoners bound in a dungeon;
they will be shut up in prison and be punished after many days.
The moon will be abashed, the sun ashamed,
for the Lord Almighty will reign on Mount Zion and in Jerusalem,
and before its elders, gloriously.
(Isaiah, Chapter 24: 17-23)

It appears that Isaiah attributes what has gone wrong in the natural
world not just to human evil agency (to the 'kings of the earth') – but
(equally and probably in their origin) to 'the powers in the heavens above'.

In the New Testament, these same 'powers' are similarly presented as
the cause of what is contrary to God's will, both in the human sphere
and in the natural world. The classic formulation of the situation of Man
and his world can be found in St Paul's Epistle to the Romans, Chapter 8,
where Paul reflects on present realities:

I consider that our present sufferings are not worth comparing with
the glory that will be revealed in us. The creation waits in eager
expectation for the sons of God to be revealed. For the creation was
subjected to frustration, not by its own choice, but by the will of the
one who subjected it, in hope that the creation itself will be liberated
from its bondage to decay and brought into the glorious freedom
of the children of God. We know that the whole creation has been
groaning as in the pains of childbirth right up to the present time.
(Romans 8: 18-22)

Paul in the conclusion of Chapter 8 of his Letter to the Romans
concedes that all creation has been 'subjected' to 'powers' that presently
frustrate the divine intention – but that disruption will not continue
forever:

For I am convinced that neither death nor life, neither angels nor
demons [NIV note: or heavenly rulers], neither the present nor the
future, nor any powers, neither height nor depths, nor anything
else in all creation, will be able to separate us from the love of God
that is in Christ Jesus our Lord. (Romans 8: 38-39)

When Paul is writing later to the Ephesians about 'powers', whether
political or spiritual, it is evident that he is referring back to the

prophecies of Isaiah: these 'powers' are not to be regarded as divinely inspired potentates or as angelic agents of God's will, but as malign wreckers. Paul's Letter to the Ephesians makes that abundantly clear:

> Finally, be strong in the Lord and in his mighty power. Put on the whole armour of God, so that you can take your ground against the devil's schemes. For our struggle is not against flesh and blood, but against the rulers, against the authorities, against the powers of this dark world and against the spiritual forces of evil in the heavenly realms.
> (Ephesians 6: 10-12)

In St Paul's letter to the Colossians (written at much the same time as he wrote to the Ephesians, and when he was already in prison), he again takes up Isaiah's theme by attributing the malfunctioning of God's creation to the twin evils of corrupt human authorities and divinely created spiritual powers who have gone wrong. Christ is 'the image of the invisible God, the firstborn over all creation':

> For by him all things were created: things in heaven and on earth, visible and invisible, whether thrones or powers or rulers or authorities; all things were created by him and for him. He is before all things, and in him all things hold together. And he is the head of the body, the church; he is the beginning and the firstborn from among the dead, so that in everything he might have the supremacy. For God was pleased to have all his fullness dwell in him, and through him to reconcile to himself all things, whether things on earth or things in heaven, by making peace through his blood, shed on the cross.
> (Colossians 1: 16-20)

CHAPTER NINE

The Witness of the Natural Sciences

The differing pieces of evidence I left you with at the end of Chapter Seven suggest two conflicting views of the world in which we find ourselves. Does the young man risking his own life to save a suffering creature from a forest fire attest to a value inherent in the animal kingdom as the creation of an inventive, infinitely ingenious, but also a loving God? Or do we, when contemplating along with David Attenborough the horror of a parasitic worm that survives only by burrowing into the eye of an African boy, or viewing the ancient and modern sea-monsters of the deep, take those particular pieces of evidence as excluding any possibility of there being a benign Creator?

I am convinced that Jesus Christ, whom I have argued on the historical evidence to be the God-Man, the *homo theos*, who in himself was reconciling the human and the divine, would have applauded that young Californian who rescued a frightened rabbit from the fire. But I am equally convinced that Jesus Christ would have sympathized entirely with David Attenborough's difficulty in squaring the existence of a parasitic worm, or of any creature that lives by preying upon others, with the notion of a loving God. Christ was a realist, with little patience for any pious, moralizing religious fantasy that ignored the facts. To the question about the man born blind and whether he had sinned or his parents, Christ answered shortly: 'Neither' (John 9: 3). He asked of a local disaster where a tower in Siloam had collapsed and killed eighteen people, 'Do you think they were more guilty than all the others living in Jerusalem?' (Luke 13: 4). If he, as a man living in the first century of the Christian era, had known what we now know from science about the late emergence of Man in the animal kingdom, he would surely have been equally dismissive of the charge that we humans were somehow responsible for everything that went wrong from the beginning of the world.

And yet Christ as a supreme realist is happy to draw on examples from the natural world so as to illustrate not only what are God's demands for humankind but also what are his benevolent concerns. We must learn to trust and to cease worrying about what we shall eat, what we shall drink, what we shall put on, how we should look to others, and instead we must: 'See how the lilies of the field grow. They do not labour or spin. Yet I tell you that not even Solomon in all his splendour was dressed like one of these. If that is how God clothes the grass of the field, which is here today and tomorrow is thrown into the fire, will he not much more clothe you, O you of little faith?' (Matthew 6: 28-30, cf. Luke 12: 27-28). The natural world is to be understood as filled with evidences of God's care: 'Look at the birds of the air; they do not sow or reap or store away in barns, and yet your heavenly Father feeds them. Are you not much more valuable than they?' (Matthew 6: 26). Then there is Christ's assurance, on the evidence of what we see happening in nature, that God is both concerned for every creature in it and for every single person in our suffering human race: 'Are not two sparrows sold for a penny? Yet not one of them will fall to the ground apart from the will of your Father. And even the very hairs of your head are all numbered. So don't be afraid; you are worth more than many sparrows' (Matthew 10: 29-31).

I will report more fully in my final chapters on the visionary approach of scripture, both in the Old and New Testaments, and on the indications there that the world of nature is not entirely as God intended it to be. At this point, it will be enough just to cite Paul's perception that there is a sickness throughout the natural world that will only be remedied by the redemption of Man himself.

St Paul writes, in his essay to the Romans setting out the fundamentals of the Christian faith, that

The creation waits in eager expectation for the sons of God to be revealed. For the creation was subjected to frustration, not by its own choice, but by the will of the one who subjected it, in hope that the creation itself will be liberated from its bondage to decay and be brought into the glorious freedom of the children of God.

We know that the whole creation has been groaning as in the pains of child-birth right up to the present time. Not only so, but we ourselves, who have the first-fruits of the Spirit, groan inwardly as we wait eagerly for our adoption as sons, the redemption of our bodies.
(Romans 8: 19-23)

If I turn shortly to recent studies by biologists of the creatures of the natural world which seem to support some of our intuitive insights, this is in part because we are conditioned by the spectacular successes of the sciences over the last one hundred and fifty years to believe that what the sciences report has some absolute authority, and so we tend to devalue the witness of those other ways of knowing, by vision, intuition and insight. If science has offered no explanation of how a phenomenon might occur, we are wary even of talking about it. A much-valued colleague of mine at the University of Newcastle, NSW, Professor Bill Walters, who was Professor of Obstetrics in our Medical School, once confided to my wife and myself, as fellow-parishioners of the Cathedral who could be trusted not to blab, that he had whilst at work been struck by an agonizing pain in the chest, and had subsequently learned by a phone call late that evening from seven hundred and sixty eight miles away in Adelaide that his father had died that very afternoon from a massive heart attack. But such evidence of intuitive contact was not something Bill found easy to confide to medical colleagues.

So before I appeal to new evidence as to the nature and experiences of the animal world, I want to draw on some personal experience of animals that a scientist would be obliged to dismiss as anecdotal, but which might explain why, when attempting to alleviate the suffering of a fellow human being, we sometimes resort to giving them a pet. When our family was in Australia, we built a substantial aviary at the rear of an inside courtyard to the house, where we kept Australian parrots. One day my daughter's cat, Pinkerton, was seen to launch himself at the aviary, climbing vertically up its front wire. As we rushed out to defend the parrots from attack, we realized Pinkerton was at the same task, scaring off a neighbour's Manx cat who had settled himself on the roof of the aviary and was terrifying the birds.

As a further sign that our cat had somehow identified with the concerns of his owners rather than followed any predatory instinct, Pinkerton gave further indication of fellow-feeling when our sulphur-crested cockatoo, Rajah, who had a stand in the courtyard to which he was tethered by a lengthy chain, was panicked by a sudden car-noise, flew off, struck his beak on a garden-wall, and then bled to death. Pinkerton, whom we had always thought to be jealous at the attention we gave the cockatoo, lay outstretched across the base of Rajah's stand for a whole day, with every appearance of joining us in mourning our unexpected loss.

Because of an animal's ability not just to call out our love for it as being an instance of God's wonderful creation, but also because it seems to return that affection and even to identify with our concerns and to sympathize with our troubles, it is a common practice in human culture to offer a suffering human being the comfort of one of nature's creatures as a pet. When we were planning to return to England after twenty-one years in Australia, it was a problem what to do with my daughter's second cat, Myshkin. Our clergyman friend, Lance Johnston, had a friend whose wife had just been diagnosed with multiple sclerosis, and her husband wanted to give her some consolation. So Myshkin was put into a wicker carrier, driven to an unfamiliar house in the Blue Mountains and released into a strange living-room – where he leapt immediately into the lap of the unknown lady and settled down: it seemed that he had understood his mission.

I notice that whenever I risk telling such anecdotes to friends, I trigger a flood of parallel experiences. We tend to dismiss such accounts as 'not scientifically validated' or as 'anthropomorphic' – that is, as transferring our human perceptions to animals as if they were like ourselves. However, the evidence accumulating from recent biological studies of animal behaviour is that the creatures of the animal kingdom may in many ways be much more like us human beings than we ever imagined.

Increased knowledge may markedly change our attitude to our own treatment of the natural world. A recent study of the nervous system of fish (who are mainly cold-blooded creatures that I had always been taught had no feelings analogous to ours) suggests that they have much the same pain receptors as human beings – so it seems that I might have been right as a boy to feel uneasy at hooking a fish from the river and then leaving it to thresh on the bank in apparent agony till it died. New knowledge may prove to be a challenge to long-held but comforting untruths.

Of the three ways I have talked about by which human beings determine the nature of their world and their position in it – through personal experience, by the reported experience of others, and finally by means of 'vision', intuition, prayer, what the Orthodox call 'nous', tuning-in to the mind of God – it is that second path to understanding, through information and opinions derived from others, which has vastly increased in quantity, quality and range over the last hundred or so years.

Photography, audio recordings, the circulation of information on film, video and CD, its distribution worldwide by radio and television, have all ensured that we have access to a far greater and potentially more accurate experience of the world than was ever available to our forebears.

Yet whether we are believers in a benign Creator or are atheistic neo-Darwinists insisting that the evolution of species is without design, purpose or direction – or even if (like the BioLogos people) we try to hold both positions at once, what has now been observed by scientific study of the natural world presents a major challenge to all theories and beliefs.

For Christians, the evidence offered contradicts the Genesis myth if interpreted as factual truth. Human beings cannot be responsible for all the pain, suffering and death that occurred before humankind arrived. The killing of other creatures for food, the brutal aggression within a species, the widespread violence, suffering, pain, illness and death, and even those parasitic life-forms that survive only by living off another creature, seem all of them to have been a part of existence on planet Earth pretty well from the first beginnings of life. That must inevitably raise doubts about the goodness of a creator-God – unless we are prepared to argue that what appears to us the suffering of the creatures is simply not real.

And yet: for the New Atheist and the neo-Darwinist, the evidence is even more threatening. The enormous expansion of knowledge of and interest in the natural world as something of amazing variety, complexity, beauty and life raises the awkward question of inherent *value*. How can something born from a process of blind chance have intrinsic worth? Is this 'value' merely imposed by human choice, human whim, even human boredom – or is the creature we observe something of value *in itself*?

Could it be some supreme value in nature that leads a David Attenborough to devote his lifetime to exploring and popularizing knowledge of the natural world – and with such passion and obvious affection? Are we really prepared to dismiss his devotion as no more than a private hobby, akin to taking an interest in whist-drives or in afternoon golf? When we applauded the courage of a young man rescuing a rabbit from death by fire, would we have given the same approval if he had burnt himself recovering a pack of cards that had fallen into the grate? Surely we should ask the Darwinians how a mindless process, directionless and undesigned, could have produced a natural world that we value so highly?

What is even more difficult for the Darwinian position is emerging evidence that animals as well as ourselves appear to value the life of other creatures, not just mourning the deaths of relatives and friends from their own species but – far worse for any neo-atheist stance – showing what looks to be an altruistic interest in other species of life, even saving another creature from injury or death. Surely the alarm-bells at any Darwinian Institute should ring?

Of course, the alarm bells do ring – and we must expect that any apparent evidence of animals grieving at death or of saving another creature for no obvious advantage will be greeted with scepticism, by charges of 'anthropomorphism', or of inappropriate sentimentality. There are bound to be complaints that we have imported a discredited belief-system into our analysis, so that we attribute the phenomena we observe to some God who designs and creates and has sown some sense of the value of what he has created among his creatures. Yet true science, to apply the standard of the philosopher Antony Flew, is to follow the evidence where it leads. To deny the significance of evidence, as some Darwinian evolutionists do, or – far worse – to actively suppress interpretations we find unpalatable, is inexcusable.

First, let me give you a comparatively simple illustration. [1]

Tanzanian lioness nurses leopard cub.

A lioness has been photographed in the wild, nurturing a leopard cub that had lost its mother – wholly contrary to the biologists' expectations from previously observed behaviour that male lions will

1. 'Tanzanian lion nurses leopard cub', *The Guardian*, 14 July 2017, and www. livescience.com.

not only kill leopards and cheetahs and their young, but will, when taking over a pride of lions, go so far as to crack the heads of any lion cubs that a female may have borne to his predecessor. So in what way could this apparent act of kindness by a lioness be a demonstration of that single and purposeless Darwinian mechanism that is said to govern the development of species, 'the survival of the fittest'? Those who witnessed such an apparent anomaly tied themselves in knots attempting to explain how what was held to be an involuntary instinct, to protect the young of her own kind, could have led the lioness mistakenly to transfer her maternal concern to another species of cat: whereas any child would react by saying what seems obvious: not that it was some aberration from biologically-conditioned lion-behaviour but just that 'she felt sorry for the baby'. Maybe in understanding the animal world we should take more notice of Christ's warning to respect the perceptions of children: 'I tell you the truth, anyone who will not receive the Kingdom of God like a little child will never enter it' (Mark 10: 15).

A similar child-like perception might best explain what has been observed in a number of the higher mammals whose brains are reported to have a size, proportion or structure nearer to our own. Reports abound of various creatures engaging in what appear to be elaborate mourning-rituals after the death of one of their kind. Whales, on the death of a young calf, have been seen to hold what looks like a funeral wake. Wild elephants are widely reported as gathering to mourn and bury their dead.

Elephant encountering a dead relative's bones.

The two video sequences of which I shall now give an account both show elephants responding to the death of a member of their species and apparently disturbed by the remains. But almost as interesting as the evidence that animals may grieve is the differing stance of the two commentators to what they are describing. I'll first direct you to a video-clip of 'Elephants Mourning', put out by National Geographic,[2] where the commentator is in no doubt as to what is going on.

The narrator insists:

2. See: youtube.com/watch?v=TjtrdpSwEUY

If there is anyone who thinks that only human beings can feel emotions like sorrow and grief, this footage will change their mind. An elephant family in Kenya's Amboseli National Park comes across the bones of their own dead matriarch. As they tend to do whenever they encounter any elephant bones, the elephants first gather round the bones in a concentric circle. Then they turn the bones over, picking them up, feeling every surface. [*The soundtrack records an elephant's anguished trumpeting.*] After this, they touch the bones with their hind feet. Scientists who have studied elephant-behaviour are certain that elephants experience deep emotions, and they don't understand about death. Everything about the way these elephants are grieving here proves that point.

Elephants coming across remains.

An elephant leaving with a discharge from its eyes.

Now, let me put against that commentary some evidence from a second video, also put out by National Geographic[3], and showing similar behaviour in elephants, but where the reporter, Shifra Goldenberg, was a doctoral student of biology at Colorado State University, and clearly nervous of overstating her case, lest she offend any prevailing scepticism among those who would examine her thesis and determine her future. Such care for precise accuracy is commendable – but the pressure is clearly there to avoid interpretations that might be professionally

3. 'Rare Footage: Wild Elephants "Mourn" Their Dead', www.nationalgeographic. com, 31 August 2016.

unacceptable. Another version put out of the same video had the title 'Rare Footage: Wild Elephants "Mourn" their Dead' – with "Mourn" in inverted commas.

A troop of elephants in the Samburu National Park, Kenya, were filmed as they happened upon the carcase of an elderly female elephant who had died some two to three weeks previously.

Though the troop is not directly related to the dead animal, they interrupt what is normally their continual search for food, and stand for a considerable time around the body, smelling it and then (so it would seem) fondling the remains. A young male elephant stretches out the ear of the dead matriarch, lets it drop, and then explores with his trunk the interior of her skull.

Elephants are noted for having strong emotional bonds, so it may be significant that, as each elephant leaves the scene, they seem to have mucus streaming from the gland behind their eyes, a sign that generally indicates they are in a heightened state of emotion. 'Whether it's mourning, I cannot say', Shifra observes, pointing out that you can ask a human being why they are crying: 'But you can't get answers from an elephant'. Having guarded herself against any easy charge of sentimentality or anthropomorphism, Shifra makes it pretty clear that she believes that elephants give every appearance of grieving at death.

Giraffes also (who are not credited with a brain capacity equal to the larger mammals and who are normally solitary) have also been filmed gathering from long distances to view the corpse of a giraffe that has died of old age, summoned (so it would seem) by some unknown mode of communication to pay their group respects.[4]

Giraffes making a rare assembly to observe a dead giraffe.

That it should matter to human beings that certain animals appear to join us in grieving at death is hardly surprising, given that (unless we are sunk in despair) death presents itself as the final enemy, as a complete negation of value, and a parting from all that we have held dear.

A central tenet of the Christian understanding

---

4.   See *Spy in the Wild*, DVD Disc 1, 'Love' (London: BBC Earth and Dazzler Media, 2017).

of 'how things are' is that death may indeed be 'the final enemy', but a loving Creator has intervened in his suffering creation in the person of Jesus Christ, who took upon himself all the consequences of our wrongdoing, was cruelly and unjustly put to death but rose 'on the third day', and now offers new life, here and in the hereafter, to each and everyone who will accept his gift of himself.

But what is also clear is that any talk of animals grieving over a death must be anathema to the committed atheistic neo-Darwinist, for there is no plausible explanation of how fruitless mourning could have evolved in the higher mammals, because in no sense could such a response have aided that central mechanism for explaining all things, 'the survival of the fittest' – the elephants in the videos seem to have skipped breakfast so as to grieve! My erstwhile mentor, C.S. Lewis, himself a dog-lover, toyed with the idea that a human being's love for a pet might raise it to a higher plane of existence in the afterlife – though he was insistent that

'Is it dead?' – 'How awful!'

Communal mourning of 'Spy Monkey' by a langur troop.

this was a hope, not a doctrine. But were he to have been an unbelieving neo-Darwinist, he would, if he had seen a dog refusing food after the death of its master, have told it in no uncertain terms that it was time to 'snap out of it – and pretty smartly!'

It would appear also, that with the animals, as with us, death is not only a cause of grief but an event where the sympathy of one's own kind may help to ease the pain. An amusing and quite extraordinary confirmation of this came during filming for the BBC *'Spy in the Wild'* series, which records the behaviour of creatures in the wild and tries to avoid any suggestion that animal behaviour might have been skewed by the presence of human observers: they introduce to the animals animated models of each species – but these conceal hidden cameras. The models look, smell, move and sound like the real thing – so much so that 'Spy Monkey' was accepted by a troop of langur monkeys, and then taken over by a young female for mothering. By accident, she dropped the model monkey and it lay as though dead. The reaction of the whole troop was astonishing and quite uninfluenced by any human presence.[5]

The whole troop of langur monkeys gather round the distressed 'mother', sharing her grief, comforting each other by gestures of affection, putting arms round each other's shoulders and treating the death of 'Spy Monkey' as a communal loss.

But Christians should note that the more it may appear that creatures of the natural world suffer and grieve much as we do, the more we will need somehow to reconcile their suffering as well as ours with faith in a good Creator. The howling in grief of a young sea lion over her dead pup, born prematurely, is so painful that the video bears a warning that some viewers may find it distressing.[6]

A sea lion grieving over her offspring born dead.

But if Christians have difficulties in squaring their faith in a good God with the evidences of suffering from observation of the natural world, the position of the New Atheists and the neo-Darwinists is even more precarious. It seems now that not only do creatures grieve to some degree as we do, but that some may even show a capacity for altruism: a quite unexpected care for others that has led to reports (and some of them now caught on camera) of higher mammals, elephants, whales and

5.   See *Spy in the Wild*, DVD Disc 1, 'Love' (London: BBC Earth and Dazzler Media, 2017).
6.   https://thedodo.com/sea-lion-mother-crying-1819338298.html

dolphins, protecting human beings from danger. The neo-Darwinists – who cannot easily admit any concern of one species for another into their system of mindless evolution, unless it can be argued to be some kind of deal that benefits both parties – they dismiss such accounts as just one more of those self-deceptions that result from human self-importance, anthropomorphism, superstition or wishful thinking.

Fortunately, thanks to modern photography and the dedication of biologists to research in the field, we now have a wealth of evidence to show that animals not only grieve at death but will intervene to protect other creatures from destruction.[7]

Orcas (or killer whales) on the hunt.

Orcas (or killer whales) drowning a grey whale calf.

Some of the most startling footage on record is from a BBC camera crew filming off the coast of California in May 2012, with Victoria Bromley as narrator. The crew had news of what appeared to be an attack by a group of orcas, or killer whales, on a female grey whale and her calf. By the time their boat could get to the scene, the orcas were well advanced in their attempt to separate the young calf from its mother and were taking turns to hold it under water till it drowned.

What happened next had never before been caught on camera. A group of humpback whales were seen to intervene and attempt to prevent the calf being separated from its mother. But despite their best efforts, the grey whale calf was successfully drowned – whereupon the humpbacks remained in the area so as to harass the killers and prevent them feeding on the corpse. They kept this up for a full six hours, themselves going hungry, despite seeing their own preferred food, krill, float by in large quantities. After six hours the killers gave up, leaving the corpse as meat for the albatrosses and other carrion-eating creatures. What is especially noteworthy is that the humpback whales seemed determined that the orcas should not benefit from their 'evil' action – their sensitivity was not to the eating of dead animal flesh in itself.

This filmed episode of humpback whales intervening to protect a grey whale calf from attack by orcas was a model of scientific procedure: from precise, extended (and now often repeated) observations, the observers

---

7. 'Humpback whales' attempt to stop killer whale attack' from BBC 1, 'Planet Earth Live', 11 May 2012, available via You Tube.

deduced what were the underlying principles at work. Nevertheless, the conclusions to be drawn from these particular observations are remarkable. Not only must the humpback whales be of high intelligence sufficient to comprehend the orcas' intentions and devise a strategy, if possible, to frustrate them: the humpbacks have also what looks to be a moral objection to murderers who try to benefit from what the humpbacks feel to have been a repellent action.

The more developed a creature is, the more it seems that higher considerations requiring unselfish, altruistic action may influence its behaviour. As in the case of the humpback whales attempting to rescue a grey-whale pup from orcas, the action is likely to be at a cost to the individual: troublesome intervention, possible injury – or simply going without a meal for six hours. Yet altruism has no place in that neo-Darwinist mechanism which is supposed to determine the development of everything: the 'survival of the fittest'. We will see this same problem arising again and again in discussion as to whether animals are conditioned to do solely what makes for survival of the race, whether 'survival of the race' is the dominant objective, or whether animals, like human beings, may in fact make choices.

As reports of humpback whales intervening to protect other creatures multiply, so does the absurdity of explanations offered by evolutionary biologists. CTV News.ca on 8 August 2016 reported another incident where a humpback in Antarctica had been observed interfering with an orca attack on a crab-eater seal, and noted that there had been 115 such interactions between whales and killer whales documented 'in the last 62 years'. In the same news item, Robert Pitman, a California-based researcher with the U.S. National Marine Fisheries Service, reported watching on a trip to Antarctica in 2009 'a humpback whale lift a seal out of the water using its chest, creating a platform to hide atop from

An orca threatening a seal and a humpback whale ready to intervene.

nearby orcas. When the seal started to slip into the water, the humpback used one its pectoral fins to nudge the animal back into the middle of its belly. It had clearly done this deliberately', Pitman told CTV News. I haven't a video record of this incident but there is a still picture on the internet of a parallel episode. [8]

A seal has secured itself from orca attack by scrambling on to a

8.   Picture from Bing, IFL Science, jpeg.

flimsy ice-flow: approaching it is an orca; breaking from the water in the foreground is the head of a humpback whale, apparently ready to intervene.

When it comes to neo-Darwinist explanations of apparent contradictions of their doctrine, it has been suggested that humpbacks are programmed to protect their young, so they respond to the cries made by orcas as they attack their prey. But that does not explain, when the humpbacks reach the scene of the crime too late and realize that the victim is *not* one of their own, why they continue for many hours to protect what they now know to be the young of another species. What is even more inexplicable in neo-Darwinian terms is that the humpback whales have been observed to go hungry for many hours and to continue to protect the dead body from being eaten by the orcas, even when rich supplies of their own food, krill, have floated into sight. Are they fasting in sympathy? – And if that is a daft explanation, is it much dafter than suggesting that the humpbacks do not distinguish their dead young from those of another species, because (though they are among the brainiest of the higher mammals) they are still *not very bright*? That was Pitman's professional explanation. Another suggestion is that, though 89% of orca attacks are made on other species – seals, sea lions, porpoises and other marine animals – and only 11% on young humpbacks, the humpback elders nevertheless see some survival-benefit for their own kind from acting as over-zealous policemen of the deep, stamping out anti-social behaviour wherever it raises its ugly head. But if that were true, we would have to see it as altruism, labouring for the good of others, whether it be just for their own family and race or inspired by a more general concern for the whole community of creatures.

Observation of the humpback whales suggests not only that they have an aversion to suffering and death but also that they have a capacity for altruism, that they feel for others. This might suggest that certain of the higher mammals have, like us, developed to the point where they are capable of valuing another creature for itself and of reverencing life. I will direct you shortly to evidence collected by the *Spy in the Wild* team of a chimpanzee cherishing a pet much as we would – but, meanwhile, I'd like to revert to that personal experience to which all religious or irreligious perceptions must appeal if they are to gain acceptance as truth.

As a young boy I was sickly and learned very early not only the fascination of pets but also how we are moved to protest at their death. Because I was so often confined to bed, my parents bought a pair of mice to amuse me, the male white, the female brown, and placed them in a bedside cage where I could watch. Of course, they did what mice do, and very soon there was a litter of baby mice, who soon became white, brown or piebald, and who, when I was well enough to walk, I persuaded the local pet shop to take and sell off to entertain other children. However, my original pair continued to breed, and the pet shop would take no more. My father was always the most tender-minded of men, releasing house-mice caught in the family mousetraps if he thought they could survive elsewhere, and delaying our Christmas dinner every year because of his reluctance to strangle the festal chicken. Nevertheless, it seems that incest between brother and sister was his sticking-point, and when the second generation of my pet mice produced offspring, he took action and drowned the lot in a water-butt. I cannot claim to have developed any affection for the pink and apparently blind creatures, but I reacted with horror. What Father did made sense – but how could he bring himself so to violate the sanctity of living things?

Had I known it, I could in my protest have cited the visionary perception of the Jains of India whose adherents are largely vegetarian, and who so venerate all living creatures that they can be seen sweeping a path before themselves as they walk, lest they should accidentally tread upon a fly. Yet such sensitivities seem to have extraordinary parallels not only in the world of men but also in the animal kingdom.

I want now to report on an extraordinary sequence, captured by the 'Spy in the Wild' team, of a chimpanzee filmed in his natural habitat, and therefore unlikely to be imitating any human behaviour that he might have observed. The team's use of extraordinarily life-like animatrons which are accepted by the animals as one of their own species, and yet conceal hidden cameras, has permitted a precise study of animal behaviour in their natural state as never before. According to the original narrator, David Tennant, this ape had adopted a tiny orphaned genet cat as a companion and can be seen on camera playing with it, even putting up with a mild nip from it, angrily protecting it from rough handling by other chimps, and in general, keeping the creature beside him as if he had for it much the same interest, amusement, empathy and affection as a human being might have for a pet.[9]

First, let us review the sequence as put out by the BBC and sold in CD form for the British market by Dazzler Media in early 2017, with its commentary by David Tennant.

Tennant's narration is explicit, emphasizing in an introduction repeated before each of the sequences, (LOVE – INTELLIGENCE – FRIENDSHIP – MISCHIEF – MEET THE SPIES), the claim that astonishing fresh insights into animal behaviour have been gained through the new

---

9. Still from *Spy in the Wild*, 2 DVDs (London: BBC Earth and Dazzler Media, 2017), Disc One, 'Love'.

Chimpanzee keeping a genet cat as a pet.

technique. The '*Spy in the Wild*' team will 'span the globe' 'to understand the true nature of animals', asking 'Is it possible they can truly love one another?', and suggesting that 'perhaps they are more like us than we ever believed possible'. That Tennant's approach is that of the team as a whole is evidenced by the cover of the U.K. issued boxed set, which claims that the team has filmed 'over thirty fascinating animals across the world . . . revealing behaviour that is remarkably like our own.'

Now let us consider exactly the same sequence, but from American sources, with a different commentator following what seems an almost identical script. But is it?[10]

This version was put out by PBS in the States, but marketed as a DVD with another narrator replacing David Tennant. The new commentary now has major omissions. Cut is the remark that the way the chimp responds to the genet cat 'shows a real emotion in animals – empathy'. Gone is the suggestion that '*Perhaps this is how human pet-keeping began*'. Gone too is the observation that (I quote) '*This is a glimpse of something quite remarkable: the first stirrings of empathy for another species*'.

I was sufficiently troubled by the discrepancies between the commentary for the original British broadcast and that for the derivative American version to ask John Downer, the producer and director of '*Spy in the Wild*', by letter, whether the alterations that his company must have authorized reflected a change of mind on the part of the makers

---

10. The version with an altered commentary was put out on the web by *Nature*, but now seems to be withdrawn, perhaps in response to my criticisms, though the American edition of the CD with altered commentary is still available.

or whether the revisions were accepted so that those in schools and universities of the United States who are teaching evolutionary biology in the official Darwinian mode should not be offended or feel contradicted. In his reply John Downer complimented me on my 'perspicacity' – but made no reply to my question as to whether the scientific conclusions of those who had gathered the evidence through their unique technique had been adjusted so as not to alienate a different market. Subsequently, on 8 February 2018 the series producer Matthew Gordon kindly reported to me by letter on an enquiry made to PBS, who had replied to the makers of *'Spy in the Wild'* to say that the narration was indeed changed 'but only slightly, so as to arrive at the conclusion of empathy instead of stating it at the top of the scene'. They had not thought it necessary to ask permission for their changes. Suffice it to say that, when I viewed the version put out on the internet by *Nature*, what was now the key and final sentence about empathy had been deleted altogether – and so it remains. The video can still be viewed in the doctored version. Hence, I reluctantly conclude that it was unwillingness to upset sensitivities in a potentially very large commercial market that led to censorship of what the researchers first believed they had observed.

(Viewing the first episode of a new series of *Spy in the Wild*, shown on 22 January 2020, it seemed, regrettably, that the makers have accepted commercial realities and we shall hear no more of animals being 'more like human beings than we ever imagined': which is probably a gain to profit, at the cost of truth.) The situation in the States is that proponents of neo-Darwinism in the schools have taken legal action to exclude any criticism of evolutionary theory by proponents of Intelligent Design – and it appears that *Spy in the Wild* did not fit the party-line.

You can see why: if evolutionary biologists were to allow the importation of concepts like 'empathy' – feeling along with another creature – into the equation, where would it end? You might start to believe there was some inherent quality or value in life-forms to which creatures other than ourselves might be responding – pure poison to those determined to believe that the development of life was from its beginning purposeless and undesigned, and that all value is only what some sentimental humans have chosen to impose on the brute facts. Already, the many reports of apes keeping pets have had to be countered by an apparently 'more scientific' observation that those apes get bored with, neglect and even eat their so-called 'pets' – to which we can only reply 'In what way is such behaviour different to what human beings do? Tell us news!' But once you start accepting that a monkey might have affection (and still worse, *unselfish* affection) for its pet, then you will have to consider seriously whether a whale that protects another creature from danger is genuinely concerned for its well-being, whether elephants and giraffes do mourn a death in the family much as we do, and whether langur monkeys really comfort one another when grieved at the loss of one of their number – and where might such thinking lead?

I don't myself intend to leave the discussion at a stalemate. In the next chapters, I shall begin by examining further the evidence accumulating from observations of the natural world. I will look at animal relationships, at the extent to which co-operation is the key to success rather than the supposed ruthless competition that is the Darwinian explanation of how all life developed. I shall consider if not only the animals we have tamed but also the fiercest of carnivores can learn to forsake what we thought to be their biologically conditioned savagery and so can relate affectionately to human beings. Most of all, I hope to explore the question of animal intelligence, whether some animals choose between imagined outcomes – which must surely mean they can envisage something that is not yet in front of them. And if they have an ability to imagine two possible outcomes and so can exercise choice, what does that mean? Can it be that, like ourselves, they make decisions whether to prefer the benefit of others to their own self-interest? I will look also at those rules that seem to govern behaviour in animal societies, at instances where rules are broken and punishments imposed, but where there seems also to be a possibility for apology and reconciliation. I will draw on recent research which appears to show that higher animals have a sense of fairness, of what is due to them as well as to their fellows. Are there criminals among the animal species? And is there, in any sense, right and wrong?

That may suggest that the God we think we see at work in the world about us is not quite so 'far unlike our books' as the priests in Fulke Greville's *Mustapha* may have feared. So in my remaining chapters I will look at Christendom's sacred books, the Old and the New Testaments, to see how their revelations – through vision, prophecy, intuition and insight, by *nous*, by contact in prayer with the mind of God – may square with what can be derived from that other rightly-valued source of understanding, the scientific method.

CHAPTER TEN

'To See Things as They Are': When Evidence Confirms Vision

In the previous chapter, I suggested that you might try reading Professor Richard Dawkins' neo-Darwinist description of the world we live in to, say, a fine spring morning in England, or before an orchard of cherry trees in Japan at blossom-time, or perhaps at those magnificent changes in leaf colour that occur during a New England fall. You might even test it in the height of a Sydney heat-wave, just at that point when the cool southerly-buster brings its welcome relief! My purpose is to expose the absurdities of Dawkins' doctrine when seen against the realities of human experience. How true then does it feel to say with the neo-Darwinists (and I quote Professor Dawkins verbatim) that our universe has 'at bottom, no design, no purpose, no evil and no good, nothing but blind, pitiless indifference'?[1] Surely, if that were believed to be scientific fact, we human beings (as well as the animals if they had any sense of their predicament) might well conclude that we would all be better off dead!

What has sustained the human race – and probably from before records began – has been what I have termed our visionary insight into truth: the perception derived from inspiration and through prayer, confirmed by experience and undeterred by suffering, that the world is good, that existence is worth having, that beauty and our joy at beauty are a reality – and that there is a designing power to whom we may

---

1. Richard Dawkins, *River out of Eden: A Darwinian View of Life* (Basic Books, New York, NY, 1995), p. 133.

respond with gratitude and love. This sensitivity is caught most perfectly by the insights throughout Judaeo/Christian scripture, and especially as expressed in the Book of Psalms:

O Lord our Governor:
 how glorious is your name in all the earth!
When I consider your heavens, the work of your fingers,
the moon and the stars which you have set in order,
What is man, that you should be mindful of him:
or the son of man, that you should care for him?
Yet you have made him little less than a god:
and have crowned him with glory and honour.
You have made him the master of your handiwork:
and have put all things in subjection beneath his feet,
All sheep and oxen:
and all the creatures of the field,
The birds of the air and the fish of the sea,
and everything that moves
in the pathways of the great waters.
O Lord our Governor:
how glorious is your name in all the earth!
(*The Cambridge Liturgical Psalter*, Psalm 81, vv 1, 4 -10)

The very first book of the Hebrew Bible, in Greek 'Genesis', the Book of Beginnings, proclaims that 'In the beginning God created the heavens and the earth' (Genesis 1: 1) and then goes on to detail that process: first, the creation of light and darkness, then of night and day, then the sky, the sea and the land, next, the creatures of the waters, of the air and of the earth: and, finally, Man, male and female, made in God's image, endowed with a capacity to rule the created world and given also the God-like privilege of inventing and creating from the material God has provided, as if they were God himself.

Against that vision, for over a hundred and fifty years, has been the atheistic, neo-Darwinian account of how all things came to be. What has brought that theory into increasing disrepute, and now to the point of collapse, has not been its presentation of a world without meaning, without value, neither good nor evil, with everything in it the product of blind chance. That has seemed to many a price worth paying, a creed to endorse, if it gave us freedom from any notion of a designing and controlling Power that might impose on us duties and obligations. Neo-Darwinism appeared to offer human beings authority to decide good and evil according to our individual taste or whim.

The validity of a scientific theory, however, is not judged by popular vote, but by the adequacy of its explanatory mechanisms to account for, and even to predict and replicate observations made according to scientific method. The problem with the Darwinian theory of 'natural selection', whereby a chance mutation gives to a creature an immediate advantage in the battle of life, and so it survives to pass that mutation to its offspring, is that from its earliest beginnings the theory of accidental evolution has proved inadequate to account for what actually takes place.

A leaf insect in best disguise.

St. George Jackson Mivart FRS in his *On the Genesis of Species* (1871), twelve years after Darwin first published *On the Origin of Species*, drew attention to the leaf insect that disguises itself from predators by looking like decaying foliage, and pointed out that, until the deception was relatively complete, presumably after a whole range of changes, it would be of little benefit to survival.

Turning now to another observable scientific phenomenon, one that also takes place, and has occurred ever since human records began, it is undeniable that a number of human beings in every year decide that their life is not worth living, and so end it by suicide. It is a tendency well established and widespread: the medical journal *The Lancet*, on 24 April 2009, estimated from records that over a million people worldwide each year destroyed themselves. The Samaritans in their 2017 Report announced that in 2015 there had been 6,639 suicides in the United Kingdom and the Republic of Ireland. *The Times* on 12 April 2018 reported that suicide rates among students in the United Kingdom had increased by 56 per cent over the past ten years.

It may well be that the teaching in our schools and universities – and now increasingly in the developing world – of atheistic neo-Darwinian theory as to the world's origins has been a factor in a growing inclination to self-slaughter.

But the truth of any scientific theory is not affected by whether we like it or if it has unpleasant consequences. Even the current failure to replicate an essential process in evolution – say the supposedly chance progress from chemicals to a living cell – does not invalidate the theory of origins: it may be that, despite our best efforts, we are not yet sufficiently skilled. And even if 'evolution' seems too often in bio-evolutionary circles to be invoked as an explanation where no real explanation has been offered, that would not invalidate the theory if it were properly evidenced. It may well be that the practice of educators is all too much like that of the magician, presenting a mouse in a cage, concealing it under an academic cloak, asking the class to cry 'evolution!' in place of 'abracadabra!', and then snatching the cloak aside to show that a mouse has been transformed into a plump rabbit. But even if a fraudulent result can be achieved by sleight of mind or hand, that does not mean that an adequate demonstration of the theory in practice could be not offered.

What does destroy a scientific theory entirely is when its central explanatory mechanism proves incapable of accounting for the facts as derived from scientific observation. The evidence for suicide in the human species from earliest times and its perpetuation in all societies up to the present day contradicts the core tenet of the neo-Darwinian theory of evolution. If accidental and undirected genetic changes are perpetuated only if they immediately benefit a creature in the battle for life, so that it survives to pass on that characteristic to its offspring, how come that a mutation that drives a creature to kill itself could survive and spread throughout the human species? Surely, the evolutionary doctrine of 'the survival of the fittest' requires that a tendency to suicide be eliminated at its first appearance?

Even worse for neo-Darwinian theory, which holds that all varieties of life are germinated solely by chance mutations over many eons of time, is that suicide is unique to the human species and has no parallel or precursor in the animal kingdom from which we are alleged to have developed by a series of undesigned changes. If you ask 'What about the lemmings?', you need to know that the story of these Arctic rodents breeding excessively and then limiting their numbers by throwing themselves *en masse* off a cliff is a modern myth, shamelessly given credence by a Walt Disney Academy Award winning production in 1958: the producers of the nature film *Wild Wilderness* bought trapped lemmings in Hudson Bay, Alaska, released them at a cliff-top in Calgary, Alberta, in Canada, then drove them over the edge and photographed them falling.

If not from the animals, from where then could the human tendency to suicide have developed? Certain animals have been observed to cease eating after the death of a mate and anecdotal evidence abounds of pets refusing food after the death of their owners. However, to treat that as

conscious suicide it would be necessary to show that an animal knew
that starvation would lead to its death. It would seem that the neo-
Darwinist theory of everything emerging through accidental change that
happened to be beneficial is contradicted by the development in humans
of a tendency to consciously self-destruct.

But when a theoretical explanation such as neo-Darwinist atheistic
evolution yields such high dividends as to free a believer from any
obligation or responsibility either to a supposed creator or to any creature
outside oneself, it is inevitable (even in the declining years of a theory)
that there will be those who will go to any extreme of incoherence or
internal self-contradiction so as to preserve what are felt to be its essential
features.

In December 2013, three intrepid European savants, two from
university-linked hospitals in Paris and another from a laboratory for
Medical Psychology in the Free University of Brussels, Belgium, in a
paper for the *International Journal of Environmental Research and Public
Health*, attempted the heroic feat of reconciling what they termed 'The
Evolutionary Puzzle of Suicide' with traditional neo-Darwinist doctrine.[2]
That doctrine, you will recall, insists that only genetic changes that
immediately enhance a creature's chances of survival will be perpetuated
in a subsequent generation. Despite the authors' citation of 82 relevant
papers, the quality of their argumentation may be judged by their
introductory concession that 'Suicide and homosexuality are the two
phenomena that have been most difficult to reconcile with evolutionary
theory'. Homosexual behaviour may offer a pleasurable reward similar
to heterosexual congress, but, as many instances illustrate, that does not
prevent a homosexual passing on characteristics by heterosexual means.
In contrast, suicide kills any potential transmission of characteristics
stone dead.

The 'rabbit from the hat' by which our savants sought to solve the
evolutionary puzzle of suicide was to introduce a new concept to the
system: a concept of *'altruistic* suicide', whereby an individual may
kill him- or herself to enhance the survival chances of the race. Such
behaviour is well-evidenced in nomadic societies, where a sick or elderly
person who slows the necessary movement of the group may consent to
be left behind to die. However, the cost of introducing such a concept
into evolutionary doctrine is to resort to notions that evolutionary
biologists of a Darwinian persuasion and especially those who document

2. Henri-Jean Aubin, Ivan Berlin and Charles Kornreich, 'The Evolutionary Puzzle
    of Suicide', *International Journal of Environmental Research and Public Health*,
    Vol. 10, no. 12 (December 2013), pp. 6873-86.

the behaviour of animals have (as we have seen) been at pains to avoid: it introduces concepts of comparative value and meaning, of possible choice, of responsibility to others outside oneself, and maybe even to a creator to whom one might have to answer, and whose demands it has been the central attraction of neo-Darwinism to deny. You save the theory by introducing internal contradiction and so to deny any true unbeliever that apparent benefit for which ancestral vision and ordinary common-sense have both been sacrificed.

Long before this desperate attempt to rescue a declining theory by introducing a concept of altruism quite foreign to its central explanatory mechanism, observation of the behaviour of animals in the wild had required revision of the Darwinian concept of ruthless competition, so as to accommodate that high degree of cooperation observed both within a species and even between species. Rather than pontificating from afar, therefore, I shall seek to draw on actual observation to indicate the nature of our world and the character of whatever power might be presumed to direct it. The seventeenth-century sceptic Rochester was prepared to admit the probability of a divine power of which we could otherwise know nothing; but to spare the sensitivities of the neo-Darwinists, I will for the moment call my imaginary constructing force 'Mr Chance'.

Of course, to label such a power as 'Mr Chance', who by a series of small, accidental changes over eons of time has brought forth from a single original a variety of creatures that have features in common such as four limbs and two eyes, is no more than a concession to Darwinian weakness. Given the paucity of evidence from the fossil-record for such gradual, step-like changes, it would make as good if not better sense to imagine a designer or designers who have based their multiple inventions on one or more basic blueprints.

So let us, just for a moment, turn aside from Darwinian theory to the life-history of the dragonfly, whose ancestors appear in the fossil-record as much as 325 million years ago, whose existence spans three habitats, water, earth and air, whose reproductive processes are extraordinarily complex, which begins first as an egg in water, where it develops through a succession of stages as a larva called a 'nymph', then climbs out on to dry land to shed its larva-skin, dries itself off till its new body can burst from its old carcase, drawing its new abdomen from the old shell, and finally inflates its wings and takes to air. So complicated a process would seem to cry out for a designing hand – though of course it may be that Mr Chance was blessed with extraordinary beginner's luck so long ago – or perhaps, he just wanted to show off![3]

3. Photo by L.B. Tettenborn, licensed by Wikipedia Creative Commons. https:/

*A dragonfly leaves
its larval state,
passing from water
to earth, to air.*

'Mr Chance', if he exists at all and is rightly named, does also seem to have been almost obsessively inventive. He appears to delight in an immense variety of creatures, in strange beauty and bizarre ugliness, and has brought about a world where (as we have seen earlier) life is valued and its loss regretted not only by human beings but (so it would seem) by some at least of the higher mammals. Nevertheless, if affection within a species of animal is evident, and grief also when relationships are broken, so also is brutal savagery, both within and between species. Yet, despite the natural world's apparently mixed quality, we have in our day seen our fellow human beings put such value on the world of nature as to make its preservation into something like a religious crusade.

'Mr Chance' does also seem – presumably more by luck than judgement – to have engineered an environment where not only human beings but also some of the higher mammals, and even the larger sea-creatures,

commons:Wikimedia.org/wiki/File_Anax_Imperator(loz).JPG.

the so-called 'Leviathan', can 'sport in the deep' (to steal a phrase from the Old Testament *Book of Psalms*[4]). Certain of the higher mammals observed today seem to enjoy just larking about. How Professor Dawkins squares such enjoyment with his Darwinian assertion that 'The universe we observe has precisely the properties we should expect if there is, at bottom, no design, no purpose, no evil and no good, nothing but blind pitiless indifference', I cannot imagine.

In contrast, the wealth of photographic evidence of animal behaviour gathered in recent decades reveals – to take a phrase from the BBC series *Spy in the Wild* – 'that they are more like us than we ever imagined'. Observe for a moment this sequence of a group of macaque monkeys in India, amusing themselves at an abandoned water-trough, diving from a great height, to the alarm of those monkeys who are swimming in the trough, or disporting themselves around it, or teaching their youngsters to swim.[5,6]

Macaque monkeys high diving.

A macaque high diver arrives!

Following the theme of the initial *Spy in the Wild* series, that animals 'are more like us than we ever imagined', it is clear that these macaque monkeys are having fun, like us finding it pleasurable to exercise their skills in a challenging environment, in company with their fellows, giving any hesitant jumper a helpful shove, then landing amidst bystanders who receive a mild but unexpected shock. But note also that this society, like ours, has rules and bounds: to offend the dignity of an elder, or to frighten the young who are being trained by a parent to swim, is to invite correction – even if that correction is within limits and looks more threatening than it really is.

This capacity of creatures large and small to parallel the behaviour of human beings, whether they live largely solitary lives or exist in communities that have social hierarchies and strict codes of conduct, together with their ability to

---

4. Psalm 104:28b, *The Cambridge Liturgical Psalter*, p. 160.
5. Still from *Spy in the Wild*, DVD Disc 2, 'Mischief' (London: BBC Earth and Dazzler Media, 2017).
6. Still from *Spy in the Wild*, DVD Disc 2, 'Mischief' (London: BBC Earth and Dazzler Media, 2017).

devise (so it would seem) ingenious solutions to the common problems of existence, has largely determined the direction of biological research in recent years. Recordings on film of animal behaviour, un-influenced as far as possible by any human presence, have become a mode of mass entertainment and instruction. The account I shall now give, of a pair of Red-billed Hornbills, part of a sequence in *Spy in the Wild* on 'Love', presents a model of relationship between the sexes that might well serve as a video for marriage counselling! Scientific research is not dispassionate but driven by our human need to understand what is, what was, and what shall be, for reasons that are at once practical, intellectual, philosophical, and even religious. So, as a married man approaching a fiftieth wedding anniversary, I cannot but see in the Hornbills a reminder of what was and is, of what could and what should be.

The Red-Billed Hornbill.

The male Red-Billed Hornbill[7] is a magnificent creature – just as well, since the convinced neo-Darwinist must see the bird as a prime example

7. Photo by Sumeet Moghe, from Wikipedia Creative Commons.

of what behaviour might be required for a species to be perpetuated by 'natural selection' – whereas for a Christian believer the matrimonial conduct of both male and female is so exemplary as to stir a faint wish that, just once in a way, they might be tempted to be that little bit naughty![8]

The hidden cameras of the *Spy in the Wild* team reveal the complex interactions of a courting couple of Red-Billed Hornbills in southern Kenya. The male Red-Billed Hornbill seeks out a hole in the trunk of a tree to see if it can be made secure against predators. Once satisfied he has found something suitable, the male makes a little dance-display to attract the female Hornbill to his find, who also explores its suitability for laying eggs and bringing up a brood of chicks, and appears to signify her approval by starting to clear out any rubbish inside – or so we must presume. But it is when they work together to narrow the entrance-hole with mud that they seem to manifest knowledge and understanding as well as intelligence that is hard to account for simply by a succession of fortuitous evolutionary accidents: they add to the mud poisonous millipedes that will keep any nest-raiding pests at bay.

Once the female has settled herself, the two set about narrowing the entrance still further with plastered droppings, so that the female is protected, but effectively locked in – whereupon the male embarks on what seems the ceaseless task of carrying food to his mate and also, as soon as eggs are laid and the young hatched, of finding food for a large family with ever-increasing appetites.

Being, as we might say, 'only human', the female eventually finds being locked in with ever-growing, demanding and constantly bickering offspring too much to endure, and she chips her way out of the nest – though she and her mate are careful to seal the entrance yet more securely after she has left, leaving only sufficient room to drop titbits into ever-open mouths. The parents are seen to act as 'meals on wings' until all the young have scrambled out of the nest, flexed their own wings, and are able to forage for themselves.

And as if that were not enough, the paired birds return year after year to breed in the same place, and they remain a pair till divided by death.

If, however, I were to find this product of evolutionary development just a little mawkish, there is plenty of behaviour along the same supposed 'evolutionary chain' that might better suit my inclinations. If I were a rapist or a wife-beater, I might derive some sense of 'only being natural' from animals that are nearer to us on the supposed evolutionary chain,

---

8. See *Spy in the Wild*, DVD Disc1, 'Love' (London: BBC Earth and Dazzler Media, 2017).

from (for instance) the higher carnivores, the lion or the tiger, where the male pursues a female on heat (in the case of the lion, fighting with her till she submits to his advances), and where the males of both species largely abandon any resulting offspring to the care of the female – and also on occasion crack the heads of any young that have been born to a previous male. How that benefits the 'survival of the fittest' is for a Darwinian to explain. At some point in the development of the various species there were changes in behaviour, apparent choices between alternative modes of being – but whether by a designer or designers, by the dictates of survival, by accident or even by choice of the creature, is anyone's guess.

The meerkat, a small South African carnivore belonging to the mongoose family, is of only moderate rank in the hierarchy of being that we think of as culminating in ourselves. That meerkats have attracted so much scientific attention is because of their similarity to human beings in their social organization and behaviour. The Kalahari Meerkat Project, jointly funded by Cambridge University and the Kalahari Research Trust, is 'a long-term project studying evolutionary causes and ecological consequences of cooperative behaviour in meerkats'. One spin-off from that research has been the 'animal soap opera', *Meerkat Manor*, produced by Oxford Scientific Films, which in a series of episodes invited its audience to follow the lives and loves of a number of named meerkats, to the extent that, where there was no film of a particular event, 'stand-in' meerkats with a resemblance to members of the original cast were brought in as actors to supply the footage that was missing.

Meerkats might be seen as paralleling and even improving on human behaviour. They live in communities where cooperation is the norm, but like us they compete, sometimes violently, with other meerkat communities for territory and resources. But within a community there appear to be strict rules, with only the dominant male and female permitted to mate, and their offspring (even when biologically mature) denied sexual relations. Instead, the young busy themselves with nurturing their parents' subsequent offspring – which they do with evident enjoyment and a degree of cooperation that extends even to an unmated female lactating and nourishing the more recent arrivals. A subordinate female who breaks the rule against mating will be driven out of the community, together with the fruit of her wrongdoing – though human sympathizers may be comforted to hear that there seems to be an opening for forgiveness and reconciliation. A meerkat mother with her illegitimate offspring, who found it impossible to survive as an outcast, has been filmed achieving re-admission to her original clan, after what seems very much like an act of contrition.

The difficulty – and perhaps the impossibility – of achieving so-called 'scientific detachment', especially where animal behaviour appears to parallel the human, can be judged by audience-response to an episode of *Meerkat Manor*, where a dominant male was filmed killing the offspring of a subordinate female who had given birth to unlicensed young. Viewers objected that the film crew should have intervened to stop such behaviour. The crew responded as if they were war-correspondents: the truth might be unpalatable, but their duty was to record it as it was.

Once the distorting lens of neo-Darwinist theory is removed from our view-finder, we find ourselves confronted by a natural world filled with inexplicable wonders that nevertheless cry out for explanation. Foremost among them is that apparent capacity for altruism which attracts us to studies of the meerkat – an altruism that I have argued to be quite contrary to any purely Darwinian account of evolutionary change and development. Let us for a moment consider an episode of meerkat life as presented by the makers of *Spy in the Wild* and ask if the commentary fairly describes what is going on.

A solitary meerkat sentry, on the highest tree-branch, exposed to predators.

Meerkat sentry continues to challenge 'Spy Cobra'.

To witness a group of meerkats undertaking different tasks and then coping with what appears a potential threat to survival rouses questions that science is ill-equipped to answer. One meerkat will serve for about an hour as sentry[9], accepting to go hungry whilst others eat and drink. Presumably, it is conditioned to or has agreed to repress its natural appetites because the safety of the community is paramount. But who appoints that sentry, what dictates the length of its service, and who nominates its successor? And if the sentry's behaviour is conditioned, and therefore a characteristic inherited by the whole race, why do not several meerkats respond at once to the same emergency?

9. Stills and the original commentary cited from *Spy in the Wild*, DVD Disc 2, 'Friendship' (London: BBC Earth and Dazzler Media, 2017).

The Sentry is not only exposed to birds of prey: in the video he is seen actually falling from his perch, thanks to a temporary loss of concentration! But on sighting what seems a dangerous snake (in fact, *Spy in the Wild*'s 'Spy Cobra'), the Sentry rushes to confront it.

You may see just why the University of Cambridge has undertaken a long-term study of the social organisation and group interactions of meerkats. Put bluntly, they seem, though early in the supposed progressive developmental order of creatures, to have arrangements, responsibilities, actions and interactions that are disturbingly similar to our own.

We may not as yet have persuaded the younger females in our human families to forego breeding so as to devote all their time and energy to their younger siblings, even to the point of lactating so as to take a share in nourishing them – but I suspect there might be more than a few human voices to say 'More's the pity!' – and there may be some even now who would think that the meerkats might have found a humane solution to the problem of excessive population-growth world-wide that threatens our ability both to sustain our own species and also to ensure the survival of all the other species on our planet.

Already, we humans, like the meerkats, have imposed in some countries a limitation on the number of children that can be born to a parental pair. We also appoint members of our communities to do guard-duty, to watch for enemies, even if at risk to themselves: we expect them to be diligent and courageous, to forego food and entertainment whilst they are on watch – and we take care not to over-extend the period of their service.

Like the meerkat, when we are ourselves in a position of guardianship, our first impulse also is to confront the enemy rather than disturb the peace of the community – and only when the danger proves too much to handle do we call for help from our neighbours.

But what perturbs me most is to accept that even a humble meerkat may have its pride. And what astonishes me most is to think that a meerkat may have an ability, perhaps even a responsibility, to choose between good, bad, not so bad and indifferent – just as I do. Furthermore, if both we and they have a capacity to choose our action and inactions, does that apply to other so-called 'rational' creatures – and if so, where would that lead?

As for the 'sense of pride': why, when a threat is detected, does the sentry meerkat take immediate responsibility, apparently risking its life for the good of the community, and only calling to the rest of the group for help when its own efforts have proved inadequate? If you were to say the meerkat is programmed, as if it were a man-made android, or a computer or some other machine, who then devised its programme? And if, like my Cambridge philosopher friend, you would prefer to attribute all apparent choice, whether in animals or in humans, to changes in the chemical balance of the brain, will your theoretical explanation survive the test of experience? If my dog bites your ankle or if I punch you in the face without you having offered any provocation, will you be prepared to put everything down to random changes in the level of hormones? The same problems in interpreting what is happening in neo-Darwinian terms arise in the case of a animal higher on the supposed developmental chain, the wild dog.

As with meerkat society, so with the family of wild dogs: it is clear that aspects of those habits of behaviour which the narrator dubs 'Love' and 'Friendship' could be accommodated in neo-Darwinian doctrine: such characteristics enhance a creature's chances of survival and so are likely to be passed on to future generations. What is not conformable to neo-Darwinism with all its talk of 'selfish genes' is the capacity for altruism that has been observed in both species: an extreme of love that, in the case of the meerkat, leads it to forego eating so as to undertake sentry-duty and then brings it, on behalf of the meerkat family as a whole, to confront a snake when that threat appears.

In another episode of *Spy in the Wild*[10], which filmed the behaviour of wild dogs in the African savanna, we learn once again just how far survival of a species may depend on social cooperation – but we also observe what appears to be altruism in a mother who is prepared to sacrifice herself so that her pups may survive.[11] Lions seem to regard wild dogs as rivals, so when a lioness picks up the scent of wild-dog pups in their underground den, she begins to dig them out so as to kill them.

Finally, as the lioness continues to paw at the entrance to the den, it is the distraught mother who decides to risk her all, by offering herself as the closest attraction. She teases and tempts the lioness again and again, until, after a full forty minutes, the weary lioness accepts defeat and takes herself off elsewhere – whereupon the liberated cubs are joyfully reunited with their mother.

In the case of the wild dog mother, altruism – potential self-sacrifice – manifests itself in an impulse that drives her to protect her cubs, even though it may be at the cost of her own life. Such impulses are inexplicable in terms of neo-Darwinist theory, given that a breeding mother, were she to continue to live, would give birth to a succession of replacement litters. The doctrine of 'survival of the fittest' should have ensured that selfishness won out over altruism. Any tendency towards self-sacrifice should (according to the doctrine) have been bred out after

---

10. *Spy in the Wild*, DVD Disc 1, 'Love' (London: BBC Earth and Dazzler Media, 2017).
11. Stills from *Spy in the Wild*, DVD Disc 1, 'Love' (London: BBC Earth and Dazzler Media, 2017).

A lioness scenting wild dog pups, while pack members seek to distract her.

The mother wild dog offers herself as the major lure.

its first appearance, since the bearer of so odd a mutation would not easily survive to pass on that characteristic to any descendants. Nevertheless, if we were to attempt to answer that hard question posed by the narrator of *Spy in the Wild* as to 'whether animals can truly love one another', we might apply a test proposed by Jesus Christ in the Gospel according to John: 'Greater love has no one than this: that he lay down his life for his friends' (15: 13). If altruism, unselfishness, is the true measure of love, would we be prepared to say 'Greater love has no wild dog than this: that a mother is willing to risk her life for her pups'? To talk in such a fashion, we would have first to resolve an even greater mystery, and again one that cannot be decided simply by scientific observation: the question whether animals – or even just some animals – can be said to choose.

But before we begin to approach the question whether animals and even human beings do make choices, we need to recognize that 'choice' is a slippery concept. What seems to be choice may be no more than behaviour imitated from an elder and perhaps even compelled. Footage exists of a leopard attempting with difficulty to wean her cubs off mother's milk and on to freshly killed meat. The cubs show no eagerness to make such a change, for the milk has satisfied their need for nourishment till it is withdrawn. As for the greater question of whether a choice to be carnivorous, living off the flesh of other animals, was made many eons ago, either by some ancestral creature or even by an as yet unrecognized designer or designers, that is something that cannot be answered from the evidence to hand.

There may also be an appearance of choice simply because the actual determining factors are not understood. I may seem to choose to have my morning toast covered with thick marmalade, rather than with just a thin spread of butter. In fact, I have always had a very sweet tooth, and that conditions my behaviour. The evidence that there is, at breakfast, most of the time, not much choice involved is that I almost never vary my practice.

However, I was aware from my earliest days that choice existed and that my sweet tooth could land me in trouble. I had a passion for condensed milk, so the occasional tin that fell to the family's ration-share in the war years was placed in a cupboard out of reach but not hidden from intelligence. You might stand on a chair to get at what was forbidden: but not being smart enough to notice that my dips from tin to mouth left a cobweb of condensed milk from cupboard to chair-back, I learned from very early on both that some choices might be unwise and that there was danger in leaving evidence of criminality behind!

To be an animal or a human capable of making a genuine choice between two or more possible courses of action, you would seem to need certain intellectual skills. You would need a memory to recall what had happened in the past, either to yourself or to others, as a consequence of a particular way of proceeding. You would seem also to need a capacity to imagine the likely consequences of an action not so far taken. If you were, for example, a tree-dweller threatened by an advancing predator, you might need to estimate the likely strength of nearby branches before choosing an aereal get-away, as against committing yourself to the density or otherwise of available ground-cover in which to hide. An unwise choice would not ensure your 'survival among the fittest'! (Take Darwinian theory to its logical conclusion, and it would seem that, over time, the 'bird-brains' ought, all of them, to have been eliminated!)

However, a series of enquiries over recent years into the intelligence of crows does seem to suggest that they at least are not 'bird-brains' but have the intelligence to choose between alternative courses of action, working out which will be the most rewarding. Witness my brief summary below of studies of intelligence by biologists at the Universities of Auckland and of Cambridge, entitled 'Experiments with a Crow' and viewable on You Tube.[12]

A crow raising a titbit to the surface by dropping stones into water.

In **'Experiment 1: Sand and Water'**, the crow faces two glass tubes, one filled with water and one with sand, each with a treat near the surface, and works out that you can drop stones into water so as to raise the water-level and get at the floating titbit – but the same process won't work for sand.

In **'Experiment 2: Light versus Heavy'**, the crow shows it knows that heavy weights dropped into water will raise the water-level more quickly than light ones – and you see it chucking a light weight aside with what looks like irritation!

12. Search 'Causal understanding of water displacement by a crow' at youtube.com/watch?v=Zer4bHmuY04 .

In *'Experiment 3: 'Solid versus Hollow'*, the crow registers that a solid, heavy weight will displace more water than a light, hollow one, so the treat will rise more quickly.

In *'Experiment 4: Narrow versus Wide'*, the crow works out that a tidbit floating in a narrow tube of water will rise quicker if blocks are added to it than if the same blocks were dropped into a broader tube.

In *'Experiment 5: High and Low Water-Levels'*, the crow understands that a treat already high in a tube half-filled with water will be obtained more quickly by dropping weights into that tube than if they had been dropped into a tube where the treat was floating at a lower level.

In *'Experiment 6: the U-Tube'*, the crow, when facing what looks like an interconnected three-tube apparatus, learns by trial and error that dropping a weight into the right-hand tube will raise the water-level in the central tube where the treat is located, whereas a weight in the left-hand tube will do nothing.

Experiments like these indicate that crows have an ability to comprehend the physical properties of inanimate materials and can apply that knowledge toward achieving a desired goal – in this case, the tasty titbit. But anecdotal evidence (and some of it captured on film) suggests much more: that a crow may have some understanding of those cooperative arrangements between different species that exist for mutual benefit, right up the chain of being from fish to ourselves. Crows given food by an engineer who spread it out on a path leading to his workshop have been observed depositing nuts and bolts at the same place – presumably as an act of reciprocity, bringing to a benefactor presents that he has been seen to have some taste for, however odd!

When it is a case of the relation of human beings to domesticated animals such as cows or sheep, you might argue that we humans, like the mafia, have imposed a deal impossible to refuse: 'Give us your milk or your wool, and we'll protect you from predators and ensure you get a square meal and a roof over your heads'. However, a deal between two quite different animal species, each independent and hostile to strangers, is harder to explain.

Here is a still from a video that presents the extraordinary pact whereby Banded Mongooses, at the signal from a Warthog indicating its willingness to be groomed by rolling over on to its side, begin a lengthy and intensive search for ticks, parasites and bits of dead skin, no doubt with the occasional reward of a juicy morsel, but not sparing their patient, whatever discomfort the warthog may endure in the process. [13]

---

13. *Spy in the Wild*, DVD Disc 2 'Friendship' See also 'Mongooses Give Warthog Spa Treatment': https://www.youtube.com/watch?v=VHHDi-XC1Ro and https://www.youtube.com/watch?v=43dbH_JLiCk.

The grooming of warthogs by banded mongooses.

You might, I suppose, by a stretch of neo-Darwinist imagination, envisage an incident eons ago when a group of mongooses came across a warthog willing to be de-bugged, and the experience so enhanced the mood of both sides and increased their chances of survival that knowledge of the deal was passed to their progeny and spread amongst all their successors. But moving to our next example, can you explain in any way how the complex deal between a pair of dikkop birds and a female crocodile could ever have come to pass?

This extraordinary evidence as to some pact for mutual benefit being understood and observed by what are vastly different creatures has been made possible by a novel technique for recording behaviour of animals in the wild by constructing models that look, feel, move and even smell like the subjects to be observed, yet have hidden cameras that record animal behaviour without the distortions that might result from any detectable human presence.

In what I'll call 'The Crocodile and Dikkop Deal',[14] we first observe a vast female crocodile emerging from the water and then making for its island nest, shepherded on land by a pair of tiny dikkop birds, who with outstretched wings but still walking along the ground, guide the crocodile away from the birds' own nestlings and toward a cache of semi-hatched crocodile eggs (among which are some cameras disguised as semi-hatched young). Only when the croc is clearly settled amidst her crocklings do the dikkops relax and return to their own young. It seems fairly clear that the crocodile female – originating, of course, far earlier in the lengthy chain of evolution – is easily forgetful of any recent deal and needs to be reminded – though, it seems with no offence given or taken on either side!

---

14. Stills from *Spy in the Wild*, DVD Disc 2, 'Love' (London: BBC Worldwide and John Downer Productions Ltd, 2016). The episode can be viewed at: https://youtube.com/TFAOnPvNyQI

*A pair of dikkops
guiding their crocodile.*

Very soon after, we realize just why the dikkop birds feel safer sharing the nesting-ground of a crocodile, for another crocodile comes out of the water to invade the territory of the first. Female crocodiles when nesting are fiercely territorial, so the second crocodile is driven off after a fierce battle, with much clashing of open jaws and baring of teeth. From the dikkop-birds' viewpoint, it is clearly a case of 'Better the crocodile you know!'

All is calm – till the heat of the day inclines the nursing croc to take a cooling dip. A monitor lizard rises out of its burrow – and monitor lizards will eat the eggs of both dikkops and crocodiles. This lizard gets its teeth into some crocodile hatchlings and in the process bites on the camera metal of a Spy-Egg. But then the female dikkop remembers her obligations under the deal and leaves her nest to harrass the monitor lizard, trying to frighten it off with her outstretched wings. The male dikkop bird joins his mate and both harrass the lizard, wings outstretched, threatening it and even nipping its tail, but at the cost of exposing their own nest.

The hen-bird retreats to protect her own young, whilst the male bird chirps insistently for help. Within seconds, the crocodile responds to the alarm-call, heaving herself out of the water - and the monitor lizard runs for cover. Both crocodile and the dikkop birds rest together, their pact honoured and security for both sets of young restored.

*The dikkop pair facing
the monitor lizard.*

To set up a similar protection-deal between members of the most intelligent species on earth – ourselves – we would need all parties to have some initial appreciation of the advantages of cooperation and then to understand the details of any agreement: what were the duties and responsibilities incumbent on both sides, what actions might be required, either in predictable or unpredictable circumstances, what infringement of the rules would cause our partnership to break down – and what would be the cost of failure to either party and to both.

If I were Mr Dikkop, I'd look for an honest broker to ensure that I, my female partner, and the third party each fully understood the rules. And given that the crocodile seems aggressive and is perhaps unreliable, and has already had to be reminded to keep off my nestlings, I think I would require that the whole agreement be set down in black-and-white. How on earth such conditions could be agreed and observed between bird and beast, I cannot begin to imagine. Maybe we have no alternative but to call-in the Intelligent Designer!

Perhaps both crocodile and dikkops and all members of their species are conditioned by some external or internal conditioning power to behave as they do? It has been suggested to me by my philosopher son Kim Frost that an experiment which brought a crocodile of the same species from a region where there were no dikkop birds might help establish whether the contract was 'in the genes', so to speak, so that the newcomer instinctively knew that dikkop birds could be partners in a scheme for mutual protection of the young. If the croc immediately preyed on the dikkops or devoured their eggs, we would have good evidence that there was no such inherited, involuntary cooperation. And if, after a period of association with the local crocodiles, the newcomer learned to behave herself, we would still know nothing about how the original deal was set up, but we would at least know that her behaviour was learned, and not instinctive.

The obvious problem with any scientific understanding of animal behaviour is that, unlike human beings, the animals can give us no account of the whys and wherefores of their actions: they seem to have limited self-awareness, and any language they may have is so primitive as to render them unable to communicate anything more than the simplest information. One starting-point for studies in human psychology is asking people to describe how they experience their minds working: such accounts may be true, partially true or false, but animals cannot give any such information.

The question of whether animals have a sense of fairness is of deep interest both to traditional believers in some divinely ordained order of right and wrong and to those who insist, like the makers of *Spy in the Wild*, that 'the animals are much more like us than we ever imagined'. But it also concerns those neo-Darwinists who are troubled by what seems the ruthless code of 'survival of the fittest' and are eager to believe that undirected evolution favours corporate cooperation and so selects those individuals who have a sense of what is due both to themselves and to others. I'll refer now to an experiment, often repeated with dogs, birds, chimpanzees and other animals, that purports to show that a capuchin monkey will object to unfair treatment. An excerpt from Frans de Waal's TED Talk had had over sixteen million viewings when I last checked.[15] It reports on an experiment first carried out ten years before; and on this filmed occasion it presents two monkeys who have never before undergone the test, so that their responses are fresh, spontaneous – and passionate! Two capuchins from the same group are placed in neighbouring compartments of a cage, divided only by a wire partition, so that each can see exactly how the other is treated. They have been trained to take a stone from their cell, hand it to a keeper through a hole in the outer wall of the cage – whereupon each of them receives in return a reward. On the first run of the experiment, both monkeys get a slice of cucumber. But on the second run, however, one capuchin, overlooking the other, sees his fellow this time being rewarded with a much more appealing titbit – a grape. So he fetches a stone, to once again make an exchange – but is again given a piece of cucumber, which he throws at the keeper in evident anger and disgust – and once again looks across at his neighbour to confirm that such an outrageous injustice has taken place.

This experiment certainly appears to demonstrate that a monkey will demand equality of treatment with a neighbour; and similar experiments are reported to have produced parallel results with chimpanzees, crows and other intelligent creatures. But I am not convinced that we have been shown that these animals genuinely understand that a principle of 'equality and equal rights' requires that the other creature must always have the same treatment. If the second monkey had been given two grapes instead of a bit of cucumber and had then offered one of its grapes to the monkey that clearly felt hard done by, that might be better evidence of it understanding a more abstract principle of 'fairness'. An experiment that gave to one monkey nothing and to the other two grapes when a similar stone token was traded would surely test the limits of simian generosity. In a situation where even a very young human child might give away a grape to a disappointed sibling, if only for the sake of peace, I suspect that, with apes as with grown men, it will be more common to discover an attitude of 'What's yours is mine – and what's mine is my own!'

15. See 'Capuchin monkey fairness experiment', https://www.youtube.com/watch?v=-KSryJXDpZo.

We may suspect, even if we cannot prove it, that certain creatures – the meerkat sentry defending its colony, or the wild dog mother protecting her young – are each making a moral choice, choosing the good of others, even if at risk to their own lives. We may also feel that the African drongo bird[16], caught on film exploiting its intelligence to cheat a group of meerkats out of their breakfast, is only one more parallel to those loveable con-men that human society has, somewhat reluctantly, agreed to condemn, even though they choose to engage in a mild degree of mischief that does no one any serious harm.

The drongo bird ready for mischief.

The drongo bird not only displays almost as sharp an intelligence as the crow: it also raises the same question as we might ask in the case of the capuchin monkey: whether there are unwritten codes of behaviour, generally understood, that cannot be transgressed without consequences. The drongo bird inhabits the same neighbourhood as the meerkat on the South African savannah. It is perfectly capable of surviving on a diet of flying insects that it catches whilst on the wing. However, the canny bird has observed that the meerkats feed at the surface and in the open air – and it has also learned to imitate the alarm call of the meerkat sentry. So at a time when the meerkats are feeding in the open, after a preliminary trial where the drongo gives an alert for what was a genuine threat (a passing bird of prey) the same drongo now gives a false alarm-call. The meerkats again scatter for cover, and this time the drongo dives down to pick up any tasty morsel they might have left behind in their haste.

Eventually, the meerkats realize that their meerkat sentry remains unperturbed even when what seems to be the alarm has been sounded, so when the drongo again fakes an alarm-call, they angrily intercept the drongo as it dives for plunder – leaving the human observer to wonder,

---

16. 'Drongo bird tricks meerkats', BBC Earth (Africa), excerpt available at: https://www.youtube.com/watch?v=tEYCjJqr21A. See also *Spy in the Wild*, DVD Disc 2, 'Intelligence', the Drongo.

not just at the intelligence shown by both sides, but whether there is some code that gives an individual creature rights to what he or she has worked for – rights that the drongo is testing to the limit.

Another thought occurs. It would certainly be within the intellectual capacity observed in meerkats for them to devise a trap for the drongo by laying out food, giving the alarm – and then pouncing on the drongo as it dives down to take the bait. They have not been reported so doing –which raises the question as to whether animals observe what human beings would recognize to be a 'proportionate response'. The drongo is not, by its 'naughtiness', threatening the life of any meerkat – so it would not be 'proper' to exterminate it, even if that were easy and led to a good dinner. At this point, I yield to the injunction of the author of Ecclesiasticus: 'Seek not the things that are too hard for thee, neither the things that are above thy strength!' (verse 3: 21, AV).

Such exploitation by the bright of the not-so-bright has been shown to occur not just between species but within a family of animals. To 'squirrel something away' for hard times is standard squirrel practice. However, individuals from the North American grey squirrel population have been observed to watch where a more provident squirrel has buried some nuts, to wait till its back is turned – and then dig up its winter-supply to make a ready meal. It is estimated that American squirrels lose as much as 25 per cent of their hidden nuts to theft, whilst some in the same squirrel family (though not all) may get as much as a quarter of their nourishment by such thieving. Not surprisingly, to be caught stealing provokes an angry protest from the victim.

The last animal to which I want to direct your attention is one that has caused immense problems, both for those among us who accept the Old Testament picture of a God who 'saw all that he had made, and it was very

THE TIMES | Wednesday July 12 2017

Recognise me? A huge cuckoo chick does its best impression of a reed warbler. Cuckoos lay eggs in other birds' nests and chicks pretend to be part of the brood

good' (Genesis 1: 31) and for the atheistic neo-Darwinists who see blind chance as the origin of everything, and 'survival of the fittest' as the evolutionary mechanism by which all things came to be. The creature has given its name to a phrase in the English language that characterizes a monster of ingratitude: 'A right cuckoo in the nest!'

The central facts about the North European Cuckoo are well-known and undisputed. It, or its Maker, or some Evil Seducer (if we are to believe in either power or both), or maybe that supposed Darwinian force, blind Chance, has somehow found a way for the cuckoo to evade all those chores of normal life that attend on producing offspring and finding a place in which to shelter and nourish one's young. The cuckoo has turned parasitic, laying its egg in the nest of a much smaller bird, such as a reed warbler or the common redstart. Though the cuckoo's egg and any subsequent hatchling may be of significantly greater size than those of its tiny host, and though the cuckoo egg hatches faster and a young cuckoo soon becomes strong enough to throw out of the nest any competing young that have sprung from its foster-parents, the warblers seem not to mind and continue to feed the voracious appetite of the interloper as if it were their own, even when it is a fully fledged adult – since they are, it would seem, too dumb to understand that the cuckoo cannot be their progeny but is in fact a murderer who has done away with their natural heirs.

Obviously, such warbler dumbness would appear to frustrate that fundamental Darwinian mechanism for the continuance and evolutionary development of life, the 'survival of the fittest': these smaller birds look singularly ill-equipped to identify and combat a major threat to the continuance of their species. Consequently, the cuckoo and its victims have attracted from evolutionary biologists a disproportionate amount of observation and have occasioned what looks from the outside to be some rather desperate and even anthropomorphic interpretations of how the birds behave. We have been assured that warblers have been seen joining with other creatures to warn off any big bird in the vicinity of their nests. No one to my knowledge has suggested that there might be some deal that benefits both cuckoo and reed warbler, like that between the dikkop birds and their crocodile. However, Professor Nick Davies FRS, Professor of Behavioural Ecology in the University of Cambridge Department of Biology, after more than thirty years of observing cuckoos and reed warblers interacting at the neighbouring Wicken Fen, writes in the trailer to his 2016 Darwin Lecture about 'an endless game of trickery and defence, [where] the cuckoo and its hosts engage in an "arms race" involving mimicry of many kinds – from the patterning of eggs to the demanding twittering of chicks – as the two species weigh up the risks of being duped and discovered'.[17]

Professor Davies is confirmed in his image of a continuing and now international conflict between cuckoos and their victims by (I quote

---

17. See Professor Nick Davies, 'The Reed Warbler and the Cuckoo: An Escalating Game of Trickery and Defence', available at https://www.cam.ac.uk/research/features, 22 February 2016.

again): 'exciting discoveries . . . now being made in Africa by Claire Spottiswoode and in Australia by Naomi Langmore. In both places, the arms race between cuckoos and hosts has been going on much longer and has escalated to new levels . . . in Australia some hosts reject chicks unlike their own and their cuckoo has combated this by evolving a mimetic chick. And in Africa, cuckoo hosts have the most remarkable egg signatures in the form of individual spots and squiggles which make it easier for them to detect a foreign egg.'

'The Reed Warblers' Revolt!'

This might inspire a cartoon for that story book by which the evolutionary propagandist, Professor Dawkins, proposes to save young children from religious indoctrination: a group of reed warblers in their nest in full military uniform, with a large propaganda poster of the enemy cuckoo hanging over its side, ready with black markers in hand, and at the cry of 'Evolution!' to label each of their emerging eggs with an identifying squiggle!

Unless Professor Davies is a proponent of 'Intelligent Design' as well as being what he calls himself, 'an evolutionary biologist', it should be obvious that his description of creatures competing for survival as though at war is full of anthropomorphic metaphors that contradict the supposedly fundamental role in evolution of blind chance. He credits animals with a human ability to understand the nature and causes of a conflict, to rightly identify a current threat, as having foresight to anticipate where an assault might come from next, with power to estimate the strength of an attack, and skill to analyse the weaknesses of any proposed defence. The creatures would need some gift of invention to support any such escalating conflict, so as to counter a new challenge with an appropriate counter-ploy. Yet if you were to wait for evolution to devise a method of marking your own eggs, given that the theory demands that such a means of identification has to arise accidentally and by a chance mutation, you and your fellow-warblers would probably have died out long before it could occur. And if anyone wants to survive in any such inter-species war, never make a reed warbler or a common redstart your general!

But before we score an easy 'victory-on-points' for supporters of Intelligent Design in what looks like an ever-escalating war with proponents of blind and meaningless Evolution, we should recognize that the North European cuckoo is bad news for either side. It shows an aspect of animal behaviour that would be counted as criminal if we saw it in a human being, and thus makes it hard to explain how the creator God of the Book of Genesis could have seen 'all that he had made, and it was very good' (Genesis 1: 31).

One solution to our conflicting and conflicted responses to the natural world has been the doctrine of a so-called 'Law of Kind': it is alleged that God indeed 'created all things good', but he has given to each of the living creatures a rule for their own particular nature. It is 'natural', therefore, for the lion, the tiger, the leopard or the tiger shark to be predatory and ruthless killers. But for human beings to behave like them, or to be a cheat and murderer like the cuckoo, would be 'bestial', 'brutish', 'unnatural' and 'un-kind'. Claudius in Shakespeare's play, Hamlet, in murdering his elder brother, usurping his throne and then cuckolding him by taking over his wife, has been in Hamlet's words 'a little more than kin, and less than kind' (Hamlet, I. ii. 65) – his conduct has violated the code set down for humankind.

The advantage of the doctrine of kind for a believer is that it seems to absolve God from creating what we would otherwise call 'evil'. However, even if we were willing to take the Genesis vision literally as a factual account of creation, the charge would still lie: for though we might accept with Milton and others that the Fall of Man did in fact corrupt all creatures and a large portion of them retrospectively, there still remains the Serpent who seduced the Primal Pair, presumably also made by God but supremely competent in evil suggestion and already 'fallen'.

There is a quality-test for any person, thought or action, and one recommended by Christ: 'By their fruits ye shall know them' (Matthew 7: 20, Authorized Version). One fruit of the doctrine of differing laws for different creatures has been an insensitivity in human beings, if not outright cruelty, when making use of animals from the world we share. As a trophy-hunter might say when slaughtering big game, or as my mother certainly did say to my father when asking him to strangle the Christmas chicken: 'They're not like us, dear!'

Maybe not. But when I wince at film of a lion cracking the heads of cubs of which he was not the father, when I see and hear the wail of a female seal over its still-born young, or when as a boy I grieved with my father at wringing the neck of the festal chicken that had just looked us in the eye, I am put in the position of feeling myself more sorrowing, more sympathetic, more loving than the creator God himself – which is nonsense, contrary to all I experience and believe.

St Paul wrote of the whole creation groaning as it waits for the glorious liberty of the sons of God; and long before, Isaiah prophesied 'a new heaven and a new earth' more compatible with the will of God, where 'the lion shall eat straw like the ass', 'the child shall put its hand on the cockatrice's den' and where 'a little child shall lead them'.

The oddity is that there has been in the world for two thousand years since the birth of Jesus Christ a 'full, perfect and sufficient' explanation of the Goodness of God and the Challenge of Evil, one foreseen, described by scientific method, revealed in a new species, *Homo Theos*, the 'God/Man' to which our human race is invited to join itself – and yet somehow key aspects of that solution have dropped out of our consciousness. I will try in my concluding chapters to recover what has been lost.

Richard Dawkins on the modern 'Ship of Fools'.

CHAPTER ELEVEN

'To See Things as They Are':
Mr Toad on 'The Ship of Fools'

The clever men at Oxford
Know all there is to be knowed.
But they none of them know one half as much
as intelligent Mr Toad!

The animals sat in the Ark and cried,
Their tears in torrents flowed.
Who was it said, 'There's land ahead'?
Encouraging Mr Toad!
('Toad's Song', Kenneth Grahame,
The Wind in the Willows, 1908)

Save for one crucial intervention, there has been little in human thought over the past two-and-a-half thousand years to alter the Greek philosopher Plato's perception of our human existence as being unwitting passengers on a 'Ship of Fools', whose initial construction and purpose can only be guessed at and whose final port is unknown.

Plato's ship has a captain (we are to presume, the Philosopher himself) who, though only partially sighted and a shade deaf, had some knowledge of the seasons, tides, winds, waves and tempests that might assault his vessel, and who directs it by reference to certain fixed stars in the heavens that allow him to plot a course – but whatever he may privately believe, he certainly does not declare openly any ultimate destination, either for the ship, its cargo, or its passengers.

On board the Ship of Fools are a rabble of sailors, each quarrelling over the steering, begging the captain to let them take over, killing or throwing overboard anyone who has been given even temporary control, and finally incapacitating the captain with drugs or strong drink. The crew then mutiny and take command, boosting each another with a reputation for seafaring know-how that not one of them possesses, yet presuming that their new authority allows them to make free with the ship's stores and cargo.

'How', in such a situation, Plato asks, 'will the true pilot be regarded? Will he not be called by them a prater, a star-gazer, a good-for-nothing?'[1]

What little has been recorded of the history of human self-knowledge since *homo sapiens* first began its journey of discovery suggests that, amidst constant squabbles, there have been two main modes of understanding our situation: on the one hand, what I have termed the path of Vision, intuition, insight, inspiration, prophecy and prayer, the capacity for *nous*, for tuning-in to the mind of God – and, on the other, knowledge by way of Scientific Method, through precise observation of the world as it presents itself to our five senses, and by deduction of underlying causes and principles from what can be observed.

Admittedly, the voyagers on our Ship of Fools have on occasion been inflamed by some incendiary mystic or dispirited by an equally persuasive sceptical materialist. Yet by and large, our two ways of knowing, through divine inspiration or by scientific enquiry, have existed side by side, with a degree of tolerance and even some mutual appreciation, well into modern times. In the sixteenth century of the Christian era, Francis Bacon, one of the forerunners of scientific method, liked to speak of the twin volumes of knowledge, the Book of God's Word and the Book of Nature. A century later, Isaac Newton, founder of modern physics, was both an inspired scientist and mathematician and a highly competent theologian.

But now it would seem as though a gang of half-crazed evolutionaries, thinking of themselves as no more than a chance derivative from some higher ape, have sought to disown any past alliances and to assume sole intellectual sway over our 'Ship of Fools'. They counsel fellow-travellers to stop their ears against any chatter about design or purpose, either as regards the ship itself or any of its passengers or contents: it is all no more than an accidental assembly of flotsam, born out of nothing when time

---

1. Plato, *The Republic*, VI, translated by Benjamin Jowett, The Internet Classics Archive, classics.mit.edu/Plato/republic.7.vi.html.

began and destined to a slow but inevitable disintegration as the universe first over-stretches itself, and then collapses back into the nothingness from which it came.

The problem for any intellectual enquiry, whether it be in historical studies or in the field of biological science, is that once you start from a non-negotiable premise – that the Holocaust never happened or that God does not exist – you lose hold on that basic principle of enquiry as Antony Flew defined it: of 'following the evidence wherever it leads'. You are tempted to pass over any observation that might seem to contradict your premise, you ignore alternative explanations, and press on in the hope that some eventual progress in human understanding will resolve what now seems puzzling or contradictory. Such a process lures the researcher toward absurdity: to following that Cambridge Professor of Behavioural Ecology who posits a conscious and escalating international conflict between simple-minded reed-warblers and cuckoo-kind, or to our 'clever man from Oxford', Richard Dawkins, who with Toad-like self-confidence offers his bestselling diatribe, *The God Delusion*, free of charge to any Muslim who will accept it, in the expectation that it will prove mightily effective against the world's evils, especially what may derive from *jihad* (witness the report in *The Times*, 19 March 2018, p. 3).

Those twin means of knowledge that I have identified, the modes of Vision and of Scientific Method, are both driven by our uniquely human need to understand, to comprehend. We do not seek to know simply in order to use that knowledge for some practical advantage.

Rather, we appear often to search out wonders that indulge our passion for experience, without any obvious material need. Alone among living creatures, only a human being would walk a tightrope across Niagara Falls or ascend to the highest peak of Mount Everest, primarily to know what that was like. We are beings lured from one experience, from one puzzle, to another, and we tend to be somewhat sharp with any theory, whether it be religious or philosophical or even evolutionary, if it seems to fall short of what it purports to explain. And not surprisingly, given we are compulsive problem-solvers, we seem most to enjoy those answers to an immediate enquiry that look almost to be designed to lead on to some further puzzle.

As for this present study, it began as an attempt to find something helpful to say to a fellow human being suffering the unavoidable stresses and pains of being human. That enterprise was not entirely altruistic, for we are searching for something to say to ourselves as much as to others. Our motive was not merely palliative, either for those with whom we sympathized or for ourselves: comforting lies will not suffice. Only what we believe to be true could resolve the problem of how the Goodness of an omnipotent God might co-exist with the reality of Evil. And yet it is somehow enticing as well as daunting to realize that any adequate consideration must explain not only those sufferings that result from human malfunction, whether originating from ourselves or from others, or from the ravages of disease, or from that 'last enemy' to all existence, death itself, but also that we must take into account those so-called 'natural' evils – earthquakes, volcanic eruptions, avalanches, tsunamis, storms and tempests, mudslides and forest fires, extremes of cold or heat that induce crop failure, famine or the excesses of plague – where it would seem there must be some fault in the system itself, some error in any supposedly benevolent plan. Yet what strange creatures we are, that it is in some way exhilarating to be persuaded that the intellectual Everest we sought to conquer is in fact several thousand feet higher than we at first supposed!

This realization of the full scope of what my topic required drove me to take a Sunday respite from what the twentieth-century poet T.S. Eliot has described as 'the intolerable wrestle with words and meanings'. I made a short journey with my wife into the East Anglian countryside – where we were waylaid and pleasurably captivated by a spectacular fenland sunset, an experience that a seventeenth-century religious poet, George Herbert, characterized as like encountering 'traps laid open, millions of surprises', and which C.S. Lewis, an admirer of both writers, alluded to in the title of his spiritual autobiography, *Surprised by Joy.*

Herbert, as an Anglican parish priest early in the seventeenth century, gave such experiences, whether of anguish or delight, a moral effect, recording them in a poem he entitled 'Sin' and including among his 'millions of surprises' 'Bibles laid open'. Lewis saw the experience of unexpected joy as a series of tasters, designed to lead him on to an ever-deepening encounter with the Divine. The poet Wordsworth (from whom Lewis took the title of his autobiography *Surprised by Joy*), writing at a time midway between the other two writers, when the development of our technological society and its commercial concerns seemed increasingly to divide human beings from their natural environment, was concerned not to promote or dismiss any moral or religious interpretation but to recover a more primary, childlike experience of the world about us:

My heart leaps up when I behold
A rainbow in the sky:
So was it when my life began;
So is it now I am a man;
So be it when I shall grow old,
Or let me die!

> The Child is father of the Man;
> And I could wish my days to be
> Bound each to each by natural piety.

Even if Wordsworth had had a modern understanding of how light breaks into glorious colour when passed through a refracting medium, that knowledge was not a pre-condition for his child-like experience. Such immediate spontaneous delight is just one further marker of that enormous gulf which separates humanity from all other living creatures. Evolutionary biologists may become excited by apparent parallels or pre-echoes when apes or crows make use of primitive tools, they may speak of 'language' developing among animals at first hearing of a creature signalling to its fellows a warning of approaching danger – but how often do we hear accounts of our supposedly nearest relative on Darwin's Tree of Life, the chimpanzee, taking time off to contemplate a rainbow or a sunset? And if, as Darwinian doctrine dictates, such activity could be perpetuated in a species only if some accidental genetic variation was of immediate benefit, how might such time-wasting in man or monkey be held to contribute toward 'the survival of the fittest'?

For a more persuasive account of what it is to be human we would do well to turn not to the experimental psychologists or to their well-intentioned colleagues, the clinical psychiatrists, but to the world's poets, dramatists and story-tellers. Few on either side of the arts/sciences divide would deny that a fundamental characteristic of humankind is the need for relationship, the requirement to be valued, to be loved. A human being condemned to strict solitary confinement quickly deteriorates, both mentally and physically. By domestication of our pets we may make animals to a degree dependant on our affection and so get something in return. However, in the world of nature, with the one exception of a general maternal care for the young, there would appear to be little or no parallel or fundamental need for our necessary relationships of love – except, of course, in a creature such as the Red-Billed Horn-Bill, which shames us by its degree of marital devotion! Male lions may fight for the chance to copulate with a female but for much of their adult existence they seem, like tigers, bears and other predators, to survive quite healthily as solitary beings. And however much a meerkat community may relish its communal life, there seems nowhere in the animal world to be a craving analogous to that of Shakespeare's King Lear, to be loved at whatever the cost. Whether we have developed by evolution or by design, we are beings desperate to relate.

King Lear's mistake, in the tragedy of that name, was to attempt to compel an expression of affection that can only truly satisfy if it is spontaneous and freely given. It was an error from someone who 'hath ever but slenderly known himself' (I.i.292-3) – and from one who, for that matter, has had so little understanding of those about him as to imagine that affection could be bought by gifts of power and property or compelled by threats to withhold it if certain conditions were not met. When Lear's aggressive demands lose him whatever shreds of feeling his elder daughters may have had for him, so that they conspire to drive him out homeless and friendless (as they think) into 'the pitiless storm', his primary concern is for his sanity: 'O Fool, I shall go mad!' (II.iv. 285). His instinct is to latch on to whatever human company there is, whether it be his professional Fool or the apparently mad 'Poor Tom'.

Lear's sense of identity depends not so much on his position as king as on loving and reciprocal relationships, and it is significant for his and our perception of what it is to be human that, in his rage against those that have denied him love, he is driven to see his 'un-kind daughters' (III.iv.70) as inhuman, as 'unnatural hags' (II.iv.76), as having a 'wolvish visage' (I.iv.306), as a 'detested kite' (I.i.260), 'like a vulture' (II.iv.132) or 'most serpent-like' (II.iv.158), as being, in the more precise and evocative phrase of Kent, Lear's most loyal supporter, 'his dog-hearted daughters' (IV.iii.45). In incipient lunacy, Lear's failing grip on reality causes him to hallucinate a trial of his offending daughters, re-classifying them as 'you she-foxes' (III.vi.22).

As for Lear's desperate need to recover a sense of identity – 'Who is it that can tell me who I am?' (I.iv.227) – it is noteworthy that it is at the furthest point of his disintegration as a human being that he is drawn to an error to which exponents of the scientific mode of enquiry seem especially prone: to assume that the reality of anything is adequately summed up by observation and enumeration of its constituent parts and the effects of their interaction. Sliding toward mental disintegration, Lear first seems to countenance such reductionism chiefly as a rhetorical device: 'Let them anatomize Regan, see what breeds about her heart' (III. vi.74-75), as if there might be some physical disorder of a vital organ that has caused emotional malfunction. But Lear at his most disturbed and unreasonable, bordering on delusive hallucinations, accepts the naked, apparently deranged beggar 'Poor Tom' as essential man: 'thou art the thing itself; unaccommodated man is no more but such a poor, bare, forked animal as thou art' – and he seeks to join him by tearing off his own clothes: 'Off, off, you lendings: Come, unbutton here' (III.vi.74-5).

When I suggested that the capacity for joy might be one defining characteristic of what it is to be human, I passed over the countervailing experience of its absence or loss. The death of a loved one, the destruction of what has been appreciated as beautiful, the traumatic realization that one's failing sight or hearing must eventually result in an inability to experience a sunset save in recollection or to respond to a favourite song or appreciate a Beethoven symphony except in memory are all equally capable of provoking Lear's cry of existential anguish: 'Who is it that can tell me who I am?' That cry must have had its pre-echo down the ages, ever since *homo sapiens* first emerged into painful self-consciousness. 'Life will pop a question on your plate', as the saying goes – and whether it is now or is to come – as another Shakespearean protagonist, Hamlet, says as he approaches the catastrophe of his story – 'the readiness is all'.

In February 2016, Richard Dawkins, a leading exponent of the neo-Darwinist atheistic theory of evolution suffered what was described as 'a minor haemorrhagic stroke' – though later in the same year he reported that he had 'almost completely recovered'. Understandably, the media were keen to know if the experience had in any way modified his scientific opinions: predictably, he answered 'Not at all!'

Professor Dawkins, like me, has been a lifelong academic, and held the Oxford Chair for Public Understanding of Science from 1995 till 2008. If that sounds more like a post for the dissemination of opinion than for basic research, it surely requires a belief that science ought to be recognized, on balance, as of benefit to humanity. Certainly, Dawkins was willing to commit profits from the sale of his 2006 book promoting atheistic neo-Darwinism, *The God Delusion*, to fund an altruistic message on the side of buses that announced 'THERE'S PROBABLY NO GOD. NOW STOP WORRYING AND ENJOY YOUR LIFE.' His humanitarian concerns have led him of late to offer to donate *The God Delusion* free of charge to any Muslim who will accept it.

Anyone who teaches is certain at one time or another to meet a request for advice that is beyond the limits of their competence. I have served in two hemispheres, in three universities in three different countries: as a junior Lecturer in the University of Wales, Cardiff, as a Fellow of St John's College, Cambridge, Director of Studies in English and a University Teaching Officer, then as Professor of English Literature and Chairman of Religious Studies in the University of Newcastle, New South Wales, and finally, in retirement, as honorary Principal and Administrator of the Institute for Orthodox Christian Studies, Cambridge. On at least five occasions, I have been responsible for people who advised me they were inclined to take their own life. Two we saved, three we lost - and it is little consolation to know that the three who were lost were at the time of their suicide technically out of my care.

Since an increasing number of our students in the developed world are drawn to self-slaughter, I cannot but wonder how Professor Dawkins copes. My guess is that he does not, in a crisis, think it opportune to rehearse his supposedly scientific conclusion that all life is a chance product, without direction or meaning, but that he (like the rest of us) will take the sufferer home to meet the family, will settle him or her beside a crackling fire, or in summer will draw back the living-room curtains to reveal a moonscape over the garden – and then over a cup of tea or a glass of wine, he will seek to establish what are the most pressing problems, and will then suggest that, as with his own recent stroke, even major troubles can sometimes, somehow, be averted or contained.

Whether he will realize later that evening that he has applied the classic remedies of faith, hope and love, and so might consider binning his writings about a world with no meaning, is another matter; it is not easy to accept that you might, in your primary activity, have been always something of an ass.

To start from a non-negotiable premise – that life has no design and no direction except chance –may well blind us to other schematic solutions that would better accommodate all the evidence – as I hope to demonstrate in my final discussion. At present, it will be sufficient to observe a preference amongst neo-Darwinists for evidence that anticipates the darker side of human nature: the competition between creatures for dominance, their battles for control of food and territory, their fights over sexual partners, the murder of unwanted offspring of their own species. Evidence that might seem to foreshadow what is undeniably a caring side to the human race tend to appear, save in the reporting of how animals nurture their young, to be much less acceptable. We have seen previously how the significance of a chimpanzee that seems to keep another creature as a pet and then to guard it from harm is hotly contested, even to the point of editing out any talk of 'altruism', whilst a lioness that nurses an abandoned leopard cub is treated as a puzzling anomaly. Reports of marine animals such as whales or dolphins aiding other creatures who are in danger of being injured or killed are commonly dismissed as poor observation or a sentimental human fantasy. Darwinists seem willing enough to accept as persuasive any analogies in the animal world to the darker side of human nature: but they prefer to ignore or understate what are the vast differences.

To return again to the poets, they report an unbridgeable distance between our own species and any other creature, such that it is impossible to envisage a process by which an unplanned development of life-forms might turn by stages, but in a remarkably short period of aeonic time, into a human being. Shakespeare's Hamlet, though he is in the depths of self-loathing and dislocation from his human relationships, remembers enough to rehearse what was a renaissance commonplace:

> What a piece of work is a man, how noble in reason, how infinite in faculties, in form and moving how express and admirable, in action how like an angel, in apprehension how like a god: the beauty of the world, the paragon of animals!
> (*Hamlet*, II.ii.303-307)

As the 'paragon' of animals, humankind exceeds the capacity of any other creature by the difference between a cuckoo's nest or rabbit's burrow and the Taj Mahal; or if it be just a question of the ability to relocate oneself, by the complexity and scale of the flight of an eagle or an osprey over earth or water as against a manned journey into outer space. The disproportion in skills, abilities, comprehension and achievement between human beings and the most advanced of other species is so immense as once again to provoke my question: 'What possible payoff could be so great as to blind evolutionary biologists to the scale of the problem before them, in presuming that the one simply morphed into the other?'

The extent of human curiosity, of our longing to comprehend other creatures, of our need to understand and if possible to relate to and nurture them, is so great that it is hard to think of an example of any living creature that has not been captured for a zoo or an aquarium, been stuffed for some natural history museum, examined in a laboratory, protected in a nature reserve or preserved in its natural environment. It is also equally true that there are few creatures in the wild, however unappealing, that have not been kept by some human being, somewhere, as a specimen or even as a pet. Such unbridled curiosity, such passionate desire to relate, whatever the cost in effort, discomfort or danger, has no parallel in any other species and cannot be explained by any Darwinian doctrine of 'the survival of the fittest'.

A further large distinction between a human being and our nearest putative relative in the natural world is that animals submit to a leader, whereas men and women look for a hero. It may well be that a meerkat shows altruism in defending its colony or a prairie dog in protecting its young – but only human beings select a role-model. The ideal of the hero arose early in the short history of our race and has remained largely unchanged right up until the present day.

A modern aspirant to that role is the entrepreneur Elon Musk, billionaire and director of companies (and also a skilled self-publicist), who has

acquired extensive power and influence, yet presents himself as using his
authority for the benefit of his fellow human beings and for the fulfilment
not just of their more pressing needs but also of their wilder aspirations.

On 11 July 2018 Elon Musk, as Chief Executive of *Tesla Incorporated*,
announced the establishment of a 'giga-factory' in Shanghai, China, that
would manufacture half-a-million electric cars per year, thus significantly
reducing those levels of atmospheric pollution caused by vehicles using
carbon-based fuels.[2]

Another of Musk's companies, *Space X*, has for many years
manufactured and launched the rockets that put communication
satellites into space, thus vastly increasing the capacity of human beings
to fulfil their passion for relating to one another as far, as widely and
as immediately as possible. To further indulge our insatiable curiosity,
our yearning for contact and our likely need, Musk has committed
Space X to building a rocket capable of carrying an exploration team
the 300 million miles from Earth to the planet Mars so as to establish
safe lodging for the human species, in the event that pollution of the
environment, warfare and a possible nuclear disaster will have rendered
our Earth uninhabitable.[3]

But what has elevated Elon Musk to assured heroic status has been his
announcement of an intention to travel in the first manned exploratory
rocket himself, setting aside the possibility that space radiation on the
journey might kill him, despite the likelihood that, if he survived the
impact of landing on Mars, he would be unable to return, and disregarding
the probability – even if a settlement on Mars could be established – that
he would eventually die in an environment as hostile to life-forms as
could be imagined. Mars appears, from previous unmanned probes, to
have no magnetic field, no ozone layer to protect life from lethal cosmic
radiation, an atmosphere about one hundred times thinner than that of
Earth and 96% comprised of carbon dioxide. Worst of all, Mars appears
not to have – and may never have had – the liquid water essential if life-
forms as we know them are to exist.[4]

What confirms Musk's aspiration to be seen as a modern hero is his
citation of an advertisement supposedly placed in the *London Times* in
1914 by Sir Ernest Shackleton when seeking companions for a further
journey to the South Polar region – an expedition which Musk presents
as requiring similar qualities to his own:

---

2. See: http://www.bbc.co.uk/news/business-44789823.
3. See: https://www.independent.co.uk/life-style/gadgets-and-tech/news/elon-musk-
    mars-launch-2019-bfr-spacex-next-year-sxsw-falcon-heavy-a8251081.html.
4. See: https://www.youtube.com/watch?v=Dfg1n7Lh62Q.

'MEN WANTED for hazardous journey, small wages, bitter cold, long months of complete darkness, constant danger, safe return doubtful, honor and recognition in case of success. Ernest Shackleton'.

My point is not to mock heroic endeavour, which only carries a human passion to explore and comprehend to its further extreme. What is remarkable about heroism is our willingness to endure hardship, cold, darkness, danger and possible loss of life, all for the sake of honour and recognition from our fellow men. It is the ancient alternative of 'Death or Glory!' – but it raises for the evolutionary biologist what seems an insurmountable question: how could a universal genetic conditioning to survive turn by some unhappy chance mutation into a willingness to suffer and die for the sake of a name or a cherished cause, and thus be perpetuated?

Elon Musk seeks to align himself with modern explorers and the ancient heroes of Greece and Rome rather than with that yet more mythical figure, Darwinian Man, conditioned by his genes to be above all a survivor. What it means to be a hero is captured in a poem by Alfred Lord Tennyson, where he imagines a veteran of the Trojan Wars, 'the wily Ulysses', embarking in old age on one final journey:

It little profits that an idle king,
By this still hearth, among these barren crags,
Match'd with an aged wife, I mete and dole
Unequal laws unto a savage race,
That hoard, and sleep, and feed, and know not me.

I cannot rest from travel: I will drink
Life to the lees: All times I have enjoy'd
Greatly, have suffer'd greatly, both with those

That loved me, and alone, on shore, and when
Thro' scudding drifts the rainy Hyades
Vext the dim sea: I am become a name;
For always roaming with a hungry heart
Much have I seen and known; cities of men
And manners, climates, councils, governments,
Myself not least, but honour'd of them all;
And drunk delight of battle with my peers,
Far on the ringing plains of windy Troy.

I am a part of all that I have met;
Yet all experience is an arch wherethro'
Gleams that untravell'd world whose margin fades
For ever and forever when I move.
How dull it is to pause, to make an end,
To rust unburnish'd, not to shine in use!
As tho' to breathe were life! . . .

Come, my friends, 'Tis not too late to seek a newer world.
Push off, and sitting well in order smite
The sounding furrows; for my purpose holds
To sail beyond the sunset, and the baths
Of all the western stars, until I die.
It may be that the gulfs will wash us down:
It may be we shall touch the Happy Isles,
And see the great Achilles, whom we knew.
Tho' much is taken, much abides; and tho'
We are not now that strength which in old days
Moved earth and heaven, that which we are, we are;
One equal temper of heroic hearts,
Made weak by time and fate, but strong in will
To strive, to seek, to find, and not to yield.[5]

Earlier in this discussion, I drew attention not only to our human
inclination to insistently interrogate the world we live in, but also
to what seems a built-in tendency of that world to provide us, as
compulsive problem-solvers, with answers that lead on to further
questions. It hardly looks as though students of the natural sciences are
in any immediate danger of running out of topics for research! How did
the Japanese puffer-fish acquire and store in its tiny brain the skill to

5. See: https://www.poetryfoundation.org/poems/45392/Ulysses.

create a large, complex and beautiful design in the sands of the sea-bed, sufficient to attract the attentions of a mate? Or how do the inhabitants of the ant-factory comprehend that, if they do not open air vents in its mud-walls, the gases that arise from their feeding of inedible reeds to a fungus which they are able to digest will lead eventually to their death? And if they do not individually know, who or what *does*? Though human intelligence has observed in great detail how a spider constructs its web, we are still no nearer than St John Chrysostom was, sixteen centuries ago, in understanding how, without human intelligence, it could manage to do so.

Exploring further this capacity of questions about the world we live in to lead on to yet further questions, it seems all too often that the doctrine of Evolution now serves as a new 'God of the gaps', on constant standby to account for whatever we are otherwise unable to explain.

At various points in what might be termed the 'Late Plasticine Era' (a period of indeterminate extent where the laws of cause and effect seem to have been somewhat less rigid than they are today), a phenomenon occurred and recurred at intervals in a variety of creatures that is so complex and puzzling that the easiest way to get our heads round it is to say simply that 'it evolved'. Various creatures, at various stages in the development of species, learned somehow to avoid danger by pretending to be dead. This practice or trick, known to the trade as '*thanatosis*' or 'tonic immobility', can be seen in this picture of the Virginian Opossum, who gave to the English language the phrase 'playing possum'.[6]

A Virginian opossum, 'playing possum'.

'Playing possum', pretending to be dead as an effective way of coping with a threat, has been observed in a whole range of creatures, from fish, insects and reptiles, through to birds and animals, in mice, rats, gerbils, guinea pigs, rabbits and pigs.

Here is another instance of *thanatosis*,

---

6. See:WikimediaCommons:https://en.wiipedia.org/Apparent_death=media/ File:Opossom2.jpg.Johnrible own work, unconditional use.

again from North America, in the tiny Western Hognose Snake[7], species
Heterodon of the genus Colubridae, which is thought to have emerged in
the Oligocene Epoch, roughly 23 to 34 million years ago.

A hognose snake playing dead

The hognose snake, when threatened, goes into what appears to be
its death-throes, rolling over on its back with mouth open and tongue
lolling. It may vomit up any undigested food, but it also emits a foul
smell that resembles rotting flesh. Yet all the while it stays conscious and
will seize any opportunity to escape.

A ploy that biologists have categorized somewhat ponderously as
'adaptive behaviour', which has been observed in a variety of creatures
including modern man, relies on a characteristic of most predators that
they will avoid eating stale meat. Possibly, Darwin's doctrine of 'the
survival of the fittest' has meant that it is mainly fussy eaters who avoid
infection and so get to pass on their genes and their instinctive habits.

However, the biologist's jargon about 'thanatosis', 'tonic immobility',
or 'playing possum', disguises the fact that what seems similar 'adaptive
behaviour' has a very different causation in man and beast. Humans

7.   Still from youtube.com/watch?v=ICPVGstdNjU.

faced by an aggressive brown bear are advised to play dead: they are to lie face down, covering their face with their hands, arms and elbows, in the hope that the bear will lose interest and wander off.[8]

Human beings act on information, animals, it would appear, by instinct – which is a discreet way of admitting that we have only a limited comprehension of how their behaviour is motivated. As with our puffer-fish and the ants in their ant factory, we do not know how they do what they do.

It is here that the modern 'God of the gaps', the fall-back explanation that is Evolutionary Theory, fails us entirely. The theory as propagated by neo-Darwinists would see the capacity for *thanatosis*, for shamming dead when threatened, as appearing first in fish, some thirty or so million years ago, then spreading along the branches of the Tree of Life into a variety of creatures as they develop at many times and in many places – creatures that include the modern hognose snake and ourselves.

For such a transmission no intelligent designer seems to be required, and, except for ourselves, no special knowledge or understanding on the part of the creature: only a chance happening upon a mode of behaviour that aids survival. But once the ploy has been discovered, it can not only be taught to the young but will be perpetuated in a wide range of descendants, according to the principle of 'the survival of the fittest'.

So far so good – but the problem with this mechanical theory of transmission is that the theory doesn't square with the facts. Given that evolution is supposedly driven by the passing-on of accidental changes in the genes that prove beneficial, how come that 'thanatosis' does not manifest itself in many of those other creatures supposedly related to the death-shammer on the same branch of the Tree of Life? And if an accidentally-arrived-at survival strategy is not activated in future generations, surely it follows that it can no longer be perpetuated or transmitted by the principle of 'survival of the fittest'? Can a behavioural strategy lie dormant, asleep in the genes over eons of time, and yet be re-activated in another species, in special circumstances, at a later date? And if that is possible, why are we able only to teach dogs to 'lie doggo', whereas a pig (so we are told) can do it naturally and unbidden?

If practitioners of the Scientific Method have difficulty squaring their theories with observable fact, believers in inspiration, Vision, as a mode of enquiry are even more likely to have their insights dismissed on the available evidence, as being mere fantasy, wishful thinking.

The prophecies of Isaiah and of the Book of Revelation as to 'a new heaven and a new earth' (Isaiah 11: 6-9, 65: 17-23; Revelation 21: 1ff.),

---

8. See https://www.mnn.com/earth-matters/animals/stories/how-to-survive-a-bear-attack.

where 'the wolf will live with the lamb, the leopard will lie down with the goat', where 'a little child shall lead them' and a young child can safely 'put his hand into the viper's nest' – all such visions, despite St Paul's perception that creation currently groans as though in the pains of childbirth (Romans 8: 18-23), tend now to be relegated to that ever-growing category of science fiction, where harsh realities can be recognized, challenged and find relief – but only in the land of 'Never-Never'.

Enter now, stage-left, a hero of the internet, one 'Christian the Lion', by nature amongst the most savage of predators, yet here seen embracing two human beings with such evident delight as to give hope to the sixty-one

'Christian the lion' embracing two humans.

million, six hundred and eighty-six thousand, three hundred and twenty nine viewers who by 24 December 2018 had accessed You Tube clips about him: – the hope that the dream of some rapprochement between man and beast might one day be fulfilled. The video of 'Christian Lion'[9] introduces a couple of young men who once bought a lion-cub from Harrods department store in London but, as it grew towards maturity and became more difficult to manage, arranged for it be released into a wild-life reserve

9.   See: https://www.youtube/watch?v=hLHDp_dL5Uk

in Kenya. Hearing some three years later that Christian had settled into the wild and had established a pride for himself, his former owners travelled nine thousand miles to seek a possible reunion. Christian and another lion are seen sussing out the apparent intruders, till Christian recognizes who it is, runs towards them, leaps playfully onto the two men in turn, wrapping his front legs around their shoulders and nuzzling their faces. Subsequently, the two lionesses who are with Christian, together with a cub, all establish a similarly affectionate relationship with their human 'relatives'. What followed made plain that the reconciliation between man and beast looked forward to by the prophet Isaiah more than two and a half thousand years ago remains a world-wide yearning: by June 2009, several versions of the video had been viewed millions of times on You Tube, and one is reported to have had over eighty million hits.

Another popular internet hero, the South African Kevin Richardson, known as 'The Lion Whisperer', has throughout his management of a succession of wildlife sanctuaries and game-reserves been able to bond with the creatures in his care, preferring 'from birth if possible' to 'establish a relationship based on love and respect'.[10]

When considering the implications of Richardson's achievement (which has been criticised as not being in the best interest of creatures who ought to be prepared for survival in their 'natural' habitat), it is important to recognize also that most, if not all, of the predators filmed embracing human beings are creatures just re-united with people who had reared them when they were young and who later felt compelled to send them to a zoo or to release them back into the wild.

Nevertheless, it would seem that creatures who evolved as predators by nature have somehow acquired an ability to modify what is alleged to be their genetically determined behaviour – in much the same way as our family cat Pinkerton could identify with his owners' concerns enough to defend our collection of Australian parrots against an intruder and also to grieve at the death of our sulphur-crested cockatoo – and yet still retain enough instinctual capacity to plaster the left-over entrails of an invading rat all over an outside-wall.

What is crystal-clear from observable evidence is that creatures who supposedly evolved through blind chance over eons of time have, nevertheless, a capacity either to follow or to deviate from their inherited patterns of behaviour. This is a death blow to any supposedly undirected or meaningless process of evolution. 'Tell it not in Gath', nor publish it in the pages of *National Geographic* – but it looks as though living creatures

10. Simon Crear, 12 April 2013, *The Courier Mail (Australia)*, p. 23. See: www. couriermail.com.au>national>news-story.

other than ourselves not only act on information they have no obvious way of knowing and perform feats that require an ability well above what they appear to possess: they seem also to exercise choice. And freedom of choice and conscious purpose cannot be accommodated within a Darwinian system of accidental Evolution.

One last point, as an introduction to our final discussion. Whether we are assiduous believers, dedicated scientific researchers, or both, we have sooner or later to accept that there will remain at the end of all our exploration 'a Cloud of Unknowing'. On 1 October 2018, the London *Times* reported what was then a media sensation – but so disturbing in its implications that by 26 December 2018, when I reviewed all available media material, one whole aspect of the story had been quietly edited out, preserved only in a record of *The Times'* initial report.[11]

One Karen Tunmore, aged 36, a respected sports instructor, on a Tuesday night in July of that year, had walked into Middle Engine Lane police station, Wallsend, supported by a friend, and there confessed to having, some fourteen years earlier, used a baseball bat to savagely club a teenager, who later died from his injuries.

What caused the initial media furore was the reason Karen gave for handing herself in. She had sat quietly by and allowed the boy's father to be accused of the murder – though he was subsequently acquitted on grounds of insufficient evidence. But after staying silent for fourteen years, she began to hear 'voices' that persistently urged her to kill again. She attempted to silence the 'voices' by taking an overdose of drugs and, when that failed, she confided in a workmate – who advised Karen that the only way out might be to make a clean breast of what she had done.

If Karen's workmate served as the proverbial 'good angel', what in heaven or earth was the origin of Karen's 'voices'? The local newspaper, *The Chronicle Live*, brought in Laura Farrugia, a lecturer in Forensic Psychology at the University of Sunderland, to explain that it was possible that Tunmore's good deeds and community-spirited actions were her way of feeling better: 'If they can make it up to the persons they have hurt, they will, but if they can't, they do stuff for others to make them feel better. It's a way of managing their guilt and overcoming the negative feelings.' Dr Farrugia did not comment on the 'voices' – but presumably we were meant to conclude that Karen's mind was 'doing stuff' to make her admit her guilt and so feel better.[12]

---

11. See: https://www.thetimes.co.uk/edition/news/football-coach-hands-herself-in-to-police-14-years-after-killing-teen-6kcf6qlvt.

12. See 'A killer with a conscience? Why murderer Karen Tunmore was devoted to good causes, *The Chronicle*, 4 October 2018, https://www.chroniclelive.co.uk/

The difficulty with any simplistic diagnosis of Karen's 'voices' as some internally generated mental disturbance is that sufferers from schizophrenia do not, in general, recognize such voices to be illusory or as hearable only by themselves. Moreover, schizophrenics commonly fear their 'voices' as controlling, whereas Karen was able effectively to devise a means by which to defy their suggestion that she kill again. Nor is it universally accepted that all such 'voices' must be a product of sickness or malfunction: the worldwide 'Hearing Voices Movement' is only one of several organizations that exist for those who hear 'voices' but find them a positive, even a spiritual experience: it held its Tenth Anniversary International Conference in the Netherlands in 2018.

Yet it was simpler for editors simply to airbrush out material incompatible with the dominant zeitgeist – and hence *Chronicle Live*'s 'Full story behind Karen Tunmore's dark secret and confession', where Detective Chief Inspector John Bent of Northumbria Police sanitized the whole story for modern taste:

> It's so unusual. I don't remember in my 24 years somebody walking into a police-station and confessing to a murder. There was no real trigger. She just said she couldn't live with it any longer.
>
> She said it had been replaying in her mind and she couldn't deal with it anymore.[13]

The insistent scientific effort expended on understanding schizophrenia and on the 'hearing of voices' as an identifiable symptom has arrived at one observable fact: that the same portion of the brain as scans show to be activated by hearing actual speech will respond similarly when a schizophrenic reports the onset of an illusory 'voice'. As for how that might be, we are already at the edge of that 'Cloud of Unknowing': we have no persuasive explanation of how the various parts of the brain might organize themselves so as to simulate and convey a fraudulent message.[14]

---

news/north-east-news/killer-conscience-murderer-karen-tunmore-15226714.

13. See 'Scott Pritchard murder: The full story behind Karen Tunmore's dark secret and dramatic confession', *The Chronicle*, 1 October 2018, https://www. chroniclelive.co.uk/news/north-east-news/scott-pritchard-murder-full-story-15220542.

14. See: https://wikipedia.org/wiki/Schizophrenia, 32 citing 223 learned papers; Kenneth Hugdahl, 'Auditory Hallucinations: A review of the ERC "Voice" Project, *World Journal of Psychiatry*, Vol. 5, no. 2 (June 2015), pp. 193-209, surveying 117 learned papers, available online at: https://www.ncbi.nlm.nih.gov/pmc/articles/PMC4473491/.

On the other hand, that alternative path to human understanding, the way of Vision, has a well-documented record of true and of lying 'voices', together with a theory both of their origins and their transmission.

To conclude this part of the discussion, I have selected two of the best-known reports, one from the Old Testament and one from the New, one certainly and the other probably from first-hand accounts and both corroborated by supporting testimony, with the sanity of either experiencer evidenced by a subsequent lifetime of effective activity and successful human relations.

The first, of course, is St Paul around 33-36 A.D., on the road to Damascus on official business, in savage pursuit of a dissident Jewish sect, but hearing a voice asking 'Saul, Saul, why do you persecute me?', which then re-directed his journey toward becoming a prime expositor of the new Christian faith. The record is from Luke, Paul's regular companion, writing in the Acts of the Apostles (9: 1-19), and Luke also reports as an eye-witness how Paul gave the same account when he was arrested in Jerusalem but was allowed by the commander of the Roman troops to address a hostile crowd 'in Hebrew', probably Aramaic (Acts 21: 27 – 22: 21). Later, when Paul makes his defence before King Agrippa (Acts 26: 12-18), Luke again has him testifying to having heard a 'voice' and this time reporting also that Christ had observed: 'It is hard for you to kick against the goads' (Acts 26: 14).

Paul's own letters refer to the experience more circumspectly; but when writing to the Galatians he claims to have received directly 'the revelation of Jesus Christ' (Galatians 1: 12-16), and when presenting his credentials to the Corinthians he asserts an apostolic status on the ground that he also had experienced with eyes and ears a resurrection appearance of Christ: 'last of all, he appeared to me also, as to one abnormally born' (1Corinthians 15: 8). To question that status moved Paul to exasperation: 'Have I not seen Jesus our Lord?' (1 Corinthians 9 : 1).

An even more dramatic record of hearing 'voices', on this occasion accompanied also by visual 'hallucinations', is the Old Testament Prophet Isaiah's written account of his calling, which he dates to the last year of King Uzziah of Judah, who is usually held to have died in 740 B.C.E. Isaiah being amongst the greatest poets of the world, influential in his own day and throughout the subsequent course of human history, his 'voices' and their content are an obvious case for scientific study – but not, surely, for medication or hospitalization. They also speak to anyone like myself, embarking on the theme of this current study.

In the year that King Uzziah died, I saw the Lord seated on a throne, high and exalted, and the train of his robe filled the temple. Above him were seraphs, each with six wings: With two wings they covered their faces, with two they covered their feet, and with two they were flying. And they were calling to one another:

Holy, holy, holy is the Lord Almighty;
the whole earth is full of his glory.'

At the sound of their voices the doorposts and thresholds shook and the temple was filled with smoke.
'Woe to me!' I cried. 'I am ruined! For I am a man of unclean lips, and I live among a people of unclean lips, and my eyes have seen the King, the Lord Almighty.'
Then one of the seraphs flew to me with a live coal in his hand, which he had taken with tongs from the altar. With it he touched my mouth and said,
'See, this has touched your lips; your guilt is taken away and your sin atoned for.'
Then I heard the voice of the Lord saying, 'Whom shall I send? And who will go for us?'
And I said, 'Here am I. Send me.'
(Isaiah 6: 1-8)

CHAPTER TWELVE

What is Truth?

'For this reason I was born, and for this I came
into the world, to testify to the truth.
Everyone on the side of truth listens to me.'
'What is truth?' Pilate asked.
(John 19: 37-38)

Throughout the previous chapters, which began as an attempt to help our fellow human beings to cope with the vicissitudes and disasters of daily life, I have been preoccupied with the question of what can be said to be true. Did the universe and everything in it, including ourselves, have any creator or creators? Or are we, and all that we experience and struggle to comprehend, simply – as the atheistic neo-Darwinists would put it – the products of a blind and meaningless chance?

The intuitive comprehension that I have termed 'Vision' or *nous* enables us to react both to the glory and the repulsiveness of the natural world in all its multitudinous varieties of life. It brings us to thrill at the beauty of a sunset or to be overawed by a majestic landscape, responding to what we appreciate as wonderful, without any formulae, precise criteria or calculations that might aid us in identifying and explaining what we see. Above all, 'Vision' instructs us that each human being has a unique and irreplaceable value. It ensures that certain behaviour towards our fellows 'feels right', whereas other alternative ways of acting and reacting towards them 'stink to high heaven'. All such 'gut reactions' are matters of central importance about which science and the scientific method, by its self-imposed but necessary restrictions and limitations, is ill-equipped to pronounce.

One supreme mystery in human experience, the power of music, is incomprehensible in scientific terms – though I have encountered one 'dare-devil' explainer, who described our widespread delight in rhythm as being something learned by the human foetus through hearing its mother's regular heart-beat when in the nine-months' comfort and security of the womb. (Whether this possibility has been followed through by studies as to the effects a mother's arrhythmic or otherwise unusual heart-beat might have on the musical tastes and emotional development of her offspring, I have yet to hear.) However, all such 'explanations' of music seem absurd if put beside this response to its wonders by the Sufi master Jalāl ad-Dīn Muhammad Rūmī, though he speaks entirely in the language of 'Vision':

> We, who are parts of Adam, heard with him
> The song of angels and of seraphim.
> Our memory, though dull and sad, retains
> Some echo still of those unearthly strains.
> Oh, music is the meat of all who love,
> Music uplifts the soul to realms above.
> The ashes glow, the latent fires increase:
> We listen and are fed with joy and peace.[1]

When it comes to assisting a fellow human being in distress, our ability to help depends on how accurately we can understand their problem. If it be the four-year-old child of a family friend who has come out in a red, maculopapular skin-rash accompanied by high fever, a cough, a running nose and inflamed eyes, we may suspect measles. Experience has shown that measles is best treated by supportive care whilst the body's natural immune system copes with the threat. But the dramatic decline in deaths from measles, mainly in the under-fives, from 2.6 million in 1980 to seventy-three thousand in 2014, can plausibly be attributed to a worldwide vaccination programme, a triumph of science that has, by administering a single vaccine, boosted the capacity of the human body to resist three such invaders: measles, mumps and rubella.[2].

---

1. From R.A. Nicholson, quoting the poet, in *Rūmī, Poet and Mystic* (London: Allen & Unwin, 1950), p. 32.
2. *Wikipedia*, accessed 17 May 2019.

The relief that resulted from scientific identification of the illness and observation of the most effective means to treat it was in part made possible by the development of an electron microscope in 1940 that allowed researchers to see and identify the cause of the problem: 'a single-stranded, negative-sense, enveloped RNA virus of the genus *Morbillivirus*, within the family *Paramyxoviridae*.'[3]

Even if Professor Richard Dawkins and his ilk assure us that the evolutionary process is blind and without meaning, medical science has responded to the measles-virus as if it were the product of a malign agency whose activities must be curtailed by the best available means. The terms we use and the decisions we take are based on a quite contrary belief-system and are heavy with value-judgements: the measles virus is 'parasitic', unable to survive outside a living host, animal or human, and it prefers to prey on other life-forms as an uninvited and exploitative guest.

Historical evidence suggests that measles initially infected animals, but in the eleventh to twelfth century of the Christian era it ventured to invade human beings – an unwise move, in that human beings, alone amongst earth's life-forms, have developed the expertise to mount a conscious counter-attack. Unlike one group in the grand variety of our species, the Jains – who are said to hold all life in such esteem as to sweep a path before themselves lest they tread inadvertently even on an insect – we Westerners have subscribed, even if unconsciously, to a hierarchy of value: the measles virus is a lowlife predator, who has forfeited any right to existence by its temerity in attacking young children before they had the opportunity to fully experience life. The supreme value we place on human life sentences the measles virus to summary execution, with no right of appeal. And were I even to hint that the measles virus might be a means by which a provident Nature sought to cope with a growth in human population that threatens the survival of our planet and every life-form on it, I would be condemned – and I think rightly – as being knowingly and mischievously perverse.

It should be noted that, whereas refinements in the scientific mode of investigation by repeated observations, varied tests and the elimination of false conclusions have resulted in an enormous leap in human understanding and a consequent benefit to what human beings take to be their well-being, what we understand to be our 'well-being' is not something decided on the narrow criteria of what has now arrogated to itself the name of 'science'. In living memory, subjects for study such as mathematics, anatomy, astronomy, physics, history, philosophy,

3. See entry entitled 'Measles Morbillivirus' on Wikipedia, accessed 2 March 2020.

psychology and even poetry were listed as '*scientiae*', means of knowing, alongside what was respectfully known as the 'life sciences' – as also was theology, once 'the queen of the sciences', at their head. For an erstwhile propagandist of scientific knowledge such as Professor Richard Dawkins to insist that evolution was known to be undirected, blind and value-free was a betrayal of science, elevating a mere personal preference to the level of universal truth.

The prime concern of the natural sciences with 'observable' truth – a truth category which is inevitably limited – should not allow us to condemn as mere fantasy an illness quite as destructive as measles and widely reported from different parts of the world, from various cultures and diverse societies: the well-attested experience of being 'over-shadowed', 'over-looked' by the 'evil eye', of being oppressed by some malign influence, human or otherwise – an influence so powerful, in the estimate of an Australian aboriginal, as to make it possible to 'sing a man to death'.

Both I and my Indian wife were educated in a western university tradition, and though she comes from a long line of Brahmin scholars, savants and administrators who can trace themselves back to a sixteenth-century Hindu saint, Apayya Dikshitar (1520-1593 CE), we both felt equally awkward when my mother-in-law in India, at the close of a joyful family reunion, performed the traditional ritual for averting the 'evil-eye'.

My own embarrassment was compounded by the irony that I had, not so long before, sought help for just such an apparent 'oppression' – real enough, whatever its origins, to drive me to take counselling from persons in the staid and rational Church of England, for fear that what I was experiencing might make my judgements erratic whilst I was serving as an examiner for the Cambridge English Tripos, Part 1. I was passed along a line of specialists, who, as any doctor might, enquired as to my precise symptoms, sought my recollection of when such unpleasant phenomena first appeared and asked me what I thought to be their likely cause. A diagnosis was made, I was prescribed a strict regimen of do's and don'ts, assured that the problem was not unique and that action would be taken on my behalf that was known to be effective. So it proved: my assessment of exam papers was not questioned, I recovered my emotional balance, my sense of oppression was significantly reduced – and I returned to my default position of hovering between scepticism and belief about the causes of such phenomena.

But here it is necessary to insist on a simple philosophical distinction: to say that we know no precise means whereby an influence hostile or benign might be communicated unobserved is not the same as declaring such communications to be impossible. Human beings certainly affect the well-being of their fellows by aggressive words, dark looks, foul gestures and violent actions, in the rational if unlovely expectation that their victim will feel diminished and depressed. All that is needed for a victim to be afflicted from a distance is some means of communication: a letter through the post, a phone-call made, or nowadays a connection by video-link or Skype, often between continents and even from outer space.

To say, as does the sceptical brand of science that has tended to commandeer Wikipedia, that telepathy is 'pseudo-science' is to assert that something cannot happen, simply because we have not yet discovered how it might. A large portion of the world's population lives in fear of oppression by means of an 'evil eye', whilst an even greater number have varying degrees of faith in the efficacy of prayer. When a highly regarded medic such as my sane and otherwise reliable friend Professor Bill Walters of the Medical Faculty of the University of Newcastle, New South Wales, is convinced that he was hit by an excruciating pain in the chest at the precise moment his father was killed by a sudden heart-attack in Adelaide some 768 miles away, or whilst countless mothers report an intimation that their child is in danger, only to find by a long-distance phone call that their intuition was more than justified, I prefer to avoid premature assertions as what may or may not be possible by way of communication. No doubt, after the discovery of radio-waves and their characteristics, or subsequent to the invention of the telephone, there were some red faces amongst the savants, whether officially appointed or self-proclaimed.

In 1986 Robert Shapiro, then Professor of Chemistry at New York University 'and an expert in DNA research and the genetic effect of environmental chemicals', published a study of evolutionary theory entitled ORIGINS: A Skeptic's Guide to the Creation of Life on Earth.[4]

Shapiro was unusual, possibly unique, in prefacing his account of evolutionary theories with a Prologue that details an imaginary exchange between, on the one hand, the Skeptic of Shapiro's title, who pops up in the book at intervals to expose the limitations of any particular theory under discussion, and on the other, a Guru who rehearses traditional wisdom – which is accorded parallel respect as a path by which human beings strive to penetrate further into what has elsewhere been called the 'Great Cloud of Unknowing'.

The Guru recites over six days a series of creation myths from around the world, including as 'Wednesday's Tale' the neo-Darwinist account of how life began (now widely taught but dismissed by Shapiro later in his

---

4. Robert Shapiro, *Origins: A Skeptic's Guide to the Creation of Life on Earth* (New York: Summit Books, 1986); this citation is from the Bantam edition (1987).

discussion because, unlike accounts of how our blood circulates or how the planets move, 'It does not rest securely' (ORIGINS, p. 31). As 'Saturday's Tale' the Guru is brought to conclude his week with the Biblical account of beginnings found in the Book of Genesis, which describes how the Judaeo-Christian God, in a mere 'six days' and by his supreme power, created the universe and all that is in it, out of nothing. At this point in the dialogue the Skeptic protests, conceding that some accounts such as the Genesis myth 'may be very good religion' but 'I came all this way for a scientific answer' (ORIGINS, p. 29).

Shapiro, like the rest of us, was a child of his time, and oriental approaches to the beginnings of life were then back in fashion and by his account had made their way into scientific thinking about evolution:

> The *Rig-Veda* of India speaks similarly of a primal unknowable chaos from which the form of things arose. The Chinese philosophy of Lao-tzu tells of the *Tao*, a quiescence without form, which by spontaneous action created all things. This ancient alternative tradition of mythology has, in our times, reappeared in the heart of the scientific approach to the subject: life arises from pre-existing matter that is unorganized, but has within it the potential to create the forms we know.
> (ORIGINS, p. 37)

I take it that Shapiro was not there registering a personal belief-preference, but only pointing to the danger that any preconception derived from myth could distort conclusions of a scientific enquiry based on observation. Whether he would have concurred with the time-honoured principle, applicable as much to theories as to persons – 'By their fruits you will recognize them' (Matthew 7: 16) – I am not aware.

But for me, as an academic within a Literature Department of the 1980s, who had come to accept one possibly mythological tradition that the universe was created by a Supreme Being of immense capacity and benign intent, the impact of oriental thought seemed only to further undermine any hope that the Department might be able to agree as to what we thought was desirable to teach and what was not. If you held that every member of the genus *homo sapiens* had arisen from lifeless matter and yet had developed a unique power to determine their actions without reference to any pre-existent system of thought, you were left with no established measure by which to assess right and wrong, and no way to decide anything except by individual taste and inclination. Pride or self-opinion arrived at without the concurrence of others was no longer under suspicion. There was no generally accepted way to determine the worth of any literary creation, and so, to avoid quarrels, our decisions as to course-content were determined as much by chance alliances of interest as by customary estimates of value. More often than not, the spread of courses and their content could be arrived at only by an arbitrary fiat from the Head of Department.

The impossibility of arriving at supposedly 'scientific' conclusions about the nature and origin of life such as Shapiro's Skeptic required is a consequence of the dependence of the so-called 'natural' sciences on direct observation and confirmatory experiment. 'Science', as Shapiro defines it, 'is not a given set of answers but a system for obtaining answers' (ORIGINS, p. 33). It could be that all living things developed out of some Primal Egg, or that life on earth originated from a chance lightning-strike on a suitable blend of chemicals in some primaeval soup (as Darwin himself seems to have half-believed). But even if, as proposed more recently by the same Francis Crick as uncovered the structure of DNA, the seeds of life on earth arrived from some distant source in the universe in the form of spores carried on a falling meteor[5], to be convinced we would need, ideally, evidence from someone who saw it happen. But as with speculation as to how in the past one species of animal life might, on the instant or by slow degrees, have morphed into another, the problem is that we had no one there to witness the actual process. Worse still, modern experiments in the breeding of animals with different characteristics suggest that there are, and may have been in the past, limits to what might be achieved by any process we have so far imagined.

The capacity of the human mind to invent possibilities is matched only by the power of rational discourse, by rules developed over several thousand years, to assess such notions and to bin the bulk of them. If, as Lao-Tsu is reported as proposing, matter has an inherent ability to generate life-forms spontaneously, we must presume, given the extent of the universe and what is judged to be its immense age, that somewhere in that vast expanse of space and time the same undirected but creative power would have generated an intelligent life-form like ourselves – and one likely to be as anxious as we seem to be to make contact, whether for good or for ill. But though we have photographed a 'black hole' at the far edge of the universe and may claim by studies of background radiation to have dated the present universe to around 13.8 billion years from the 'Big Bang', nothing like ourselves appears to have developed elsewhere in

5. Francis Crick, *Life Itself: Its Origin and Nature* (New York: Simon & Schuster, 1982).

the universe that might wish to make its presence known. Our loneliness is palpable, our need for fellowship intense: starved of substance, we resort to substances and the fantasies of science fiction.

That oppressive 'Cloud of Unknowing' which obscures both our origins as a species and our contemplation of any likely destination for ourselves and our world has led, at the beginning of the twenty-first century of the Christian Era, to a catastrophic breakdown of communication within one of those areas of human enquiry on which we all depend for our understanding of who, what and where we are: the field of biological science.

Two studies for the general reader published at the beginning of 2019, Paul Davies' *The Demon in the Machine: How Hidden Webs of Information Are Solving the Mystery of Life*[6] and Michael J. Behe's *Darwin Devolves: The New Science About DNA That Challenges Evolution*[7] both illustrate, the one from its content and the other by its reception, just how catastrophic that breakdown may prove to be.

The oddity of Paul Davies' latest study is that it appears to run counter to his previous work as a physicist and cosmologist, where he demonstrated how an improbable conjunction of factors was necessary if life were to emerge and develop on earth. *The Goldilocks Enigma: Why is the Universe Just Right for Life?*[8] considers the question why everything was 'not too hot, not too cold, but just right!' and would seem to point to the necessity for a designing and regulating power. But Davies now proposes a new 'physics' that will be a foundation for all scientific study – maybe to gratify those in more complex scientific disciplines in whom Michael Behe detects some 'Physics envy', but more obviously to be a new approach less likely to offend any friend or colleague of a neo-Darwinist persuasion.

The answer, we are now told, to the mystery of life is in 'fundamentally new concepts' (so Davies' Preface). 'I believe there are new laws and new principles that emerge in information-processing systems of sufficiently great complexity, and that a full explanation for life's origin will come from a detailed study of such systems' (*The Demon in the Machine*, p. 179).

It should be evident from Davies' sub-title, '*How Hidden Webs of Information Are Solving the Mystery of Life*', that we are already way

---

6. Paul Davies, *The Demon in the Machine: How Hidden Webs of Information Are Solving the Mystery of Life* (London: Allen Lane, 2019).

7. Michael J. Behe, *Darwin Devolves: The New Science About DNA That Challenges Evolution* (New York, NY: Harper One, 2019), accessed in the Kindle edition (Sydney, Australia: Harper Collins, 2019).

8. Paul Davies, *The Goldilocks Enigma: Why Is the Universe Just Right for Life?* (London: Allen Lane, 2006).

out in fantasy-land, if not in dangerous delusion. The 'hidden webs', so far unrevealed, are not at present solving anything, the necessary 'information theory' has not, it would seem, developed that far, the programmes and the advanced computers that would apply it have yet to be designed – and when and if they are, it will be human intelligence and skills that created them – and so we will be back with the same old problem as we shall meet if ever a human being creates life from its constituent chemicals. If we are such clever-clogs – who or what could have produced or designed *us*?

As for Davies' main title, '*The Demon in the Machine*', that might alert us to what looks to have been an attempt to warn us, more than 150 years back, of the unanticipated consequences of introducing some supposedly controlling agency into what seems a natural process. In 1867 the physicist James Clerk Maxwell devised what he termed a 'thought experiment' to explain how the second law of thermodynamics might hypothetically be violated if a 'being' could sit at a little window between two chambers of gas at differing temperatures and prevent the natural evening-out of temperature by opening and closing the window at will, admitting the swift, heat-bearing molecules and excluding the slower, cooler molecules. A friend of Maxwell, William Thomson (later Lord Kelvin), a Scottish Episcopalian, proposed that Maxwell's imaginary 'being' be called 'a demon' – well aware, I guess, that the Greek word 'daemon', meaning simply a divine power, would in English have been more neutral, but choosing to make his point – whilst at the same assuring the reader that he was not in any way implying that the 'demon' Maxwell had proposed was an evil being, since this one was 'mediating rather than malevolent'.[9]

When, late in the twentieth century, the notion finally emerged into popular consciousness of a possible problem-solving capacity latent in artificial intelligence, that introduction was more demonic than benign. A trio of immensely successful science-fiction films, *The Matrix* (1999), *The Matrix Reloaded* (2003) and *The Matrix Revolutions* (also 2003), lured their audiences into a screen-environment that would subsequently be revealed as an illusion manufactured by artificial intelligences that had taken control of the world in the late twenty-first century, exterminating almost all of its original human inhabitants, yet imprisoning a remnant in a 'virtual reality' where they could be farmed in order to provide the victorious machines with a regular supply of human 'bio-electrical' power!

9. Sir William Thomson, 'The Sorting Demon of Maxwell', *Nature*, Vol. 20, no. 501 (1879), p. 126.

Returning to science as we know it, Michael Behe's most recent account as a cell biologist of how 'in the late twentieth and early twenty-first centuries biology unexpectedly discovered astounding sophisticated machinery at the molecular foundation of life' (*Darwin Devolves*, p. 5) serves to update and elaborate on his earlier discussions of an 'irreducible complexity' to be found in the construction and functioning of even the most primitive of living cells.[10] Whether Behe now regrets his use of the term 'irreducible' in that initial formulation of the problem I do not know: but his reminder that no human being has yet engineered a process whereby chemical constituents are transformed into a living form, together with a perhaps tactless implication that no human being ever could or ever would achieve such a feat by artificial means, has led to Behe being pilloried by the atheistic neo-Darwinist establishment, with his phrase 'irreducible complexity' hung about his neck. Now, after publication of his latest contribution, and by means of a review in the pages of *The Washington Post*,[11] Behe has been despatched to summary execution without trial, as an allegedly self-confessed 'Creationist'.

My protest to the editor of *The Washington Post* five days after the appearance of that review, to the effect that Jerry Coyne's comment had 'more the intellectual level and tone of a Donald Trump than something one would expect from a responsible journal', was an intervention I have never before been moved to make, in an academic career that has spanned more than half a century. My objection was that Coyne's review, headed 'Intelligent design gets even dumber' was 'grossly abusive, and offers no substantive critique'. My motive was to point to a breakdown within an academic discipline, which, by challenging a man's beliefs rather than his scientific conclusion, and by failing to engage adequately in debate, threatens not just the field of biological science but every other intellectual enquiry. Regrettably, avoidance or suppression of argument is a ploy increasingly resorted to by neo-Darwinists whenever their shaky alliance seems under threat. For example, as I have already mentioned, in response to A.N. Wilson's *Charles Darwin: Victorian Mythmaker* (2017), a *Guardian* commentator suggested that the only way to deal with such sniping at atheistic neo-Darwinism might be simply to ignore all such criticism.

10. See Behe, *Darwin's Black Box: The Biochemical Challenge to Evolution* (New York, NY: Free Press, 1996), and *The Edge of Evolution: The Search for the Limits of Darwinism* (New York, NY: Free Press, 2006).

11. Jerry A. Coyne, 'Intelligent design gets even dumber', *The Washington Post*, 8 March 2019: 'Jerry Coyne is a professor emeritus in the Department of Ecology and Evolution at the University of Chicago. He is the author of "Why Evolution is True" and "Faith as Fact: Why Science and Religion are Incompatible"' (Editor's introduction).

Behe's actual offence, as seen from the perspective of an observer from another intellectual discipline, would seem to be that he keeps on reporting an observation which is beyond the current capacity of biological science to explain: that within the simplest of living cells, the cell being defined as 'the structural and functional unit of an organism consisting of cytoplasm and a nucleus enclosed in a membrane'[12], there is activity so various and so complex as to invite comparison with the organised and interactive operations of a small factory.

That same problem, of finding an adequate explanation for what is observed, must have confronted human beings from their earliest attempts to understand the natural world and their place in it. Relying on themselves as the only organizing and directing power of which they had inward knowledge, yet noting also that their fellow human beings and even some of the other living creatures appeared to have a similar self-directing capacity, the great majority of the human race has presumed and still does presume that everything in ourselves and in the universe at large is designed, and so is likely to have had a Designer or designers. There is nothing essentially 'dumb' about that.

But the problem for any card-carrying neo-Darwinist is that an unexplained complexity in what has been observed is seen as posing an immediate threat to an atheism that is founded more upon faith than on sight. It is neither forgotten nor forgiven that the philosopher and lifelong atheist Antony Flew, once he became acquainted with DNA, that complex yet elegant coding for life which is in each and every living cell, turned apostate and declared for God. Nevertheless, I have considerable sympathy for a committed neo-Darwinist such as Jerry Coyne. It looks sometimes as though existence itself has been designed to entrap human beings, who are by nature compulsive problem-solvers, into an obsessive consideration of the likelihood of a Designer, and from there to anxious questionings about the nature and requirements of such a Being, and finally to an absolute dread of what the terms and conditions of any relationship might be. If the Old Testament Psalmist believed that 'The fool has said in his heart "There is no God"',[13] both the ancient Hebrew Scriptures and the New Testament writers of the first century of the Christian era are clear that 'It is a fearful thing to fall into the hands of the living God'.[14]

It is entirely understandable that someone might wish to devise a theory that would keep such a bogeyman at bay. But the problem for

---

12. *The Oxford Compact English Dictionary* (Oxford: Oxford University Press, 1996), p. 152.
13. Psalms 14:1 and 53:1 in *The Cambridge Liturgical Psalter*, pp. 15 and 77.
14. Hebrews 10:31, in the King James Authorized Version.

atheistic neo-Darwinism is that it reverses the standard processes by which the natural sciences seek to establish truth. Instead of prolonged and repeated observation of phenomena, followed by deduction from what has been observed to what may be an underlying law or principle of organization, neo-Darwinism begins with a non-negotiable premise – that there can be no Designer – and so concludes that all life must have emerged through blind and meaningless chance. Only then does the neo-Darwinist go looking for confirmatory evidence – with perhaps an occasional side-swipe at anyone like Michael Behe who dares to suggest a possible contradiction. If neo-Darwinism is science, it is science upside down and back to front.

Of course, the best way for human beings to render the notion of a Creator God redundant would be to construct a simple life-form themselves. But it is now sixty-eight years since Stanley Miller and Harold Urey simulated what were thought to be the conditions on earth in its early years and showed how the chemicals then present might fuse into the twenty or so aminoacids that are the currently recognized building-blocks of life. Since then, despite the power and the glory that await, there have been only false claims and embarrassed silence.

In answer to the query 'Have Scientists Ever Created Life in a Laboratory?', **evolution: frequently asked questions**[15] replies:

> As of the time of this writing, no, scientists have never created cellular life in a laboratory from scratch. The technology simply does not yet exist to manipulate molecules with the precision required to create all of the inner workings of a cell, built one atom at a time.
>
> However, many of the important building blocks of life have indeed been created in a laboratory, including amino acids, self-replicating RNA molecules, and self-sealing and self-replicating lipid bubbles (i.e. cell membranes) which are profound steps toward the goal of one day creating fully-synthetic life.

That comes across as blithely self-confident: rather as if a workman turned up with nails, saws, drills, wood, bricks, tiles and mortar, and then assured you that your house was as good as built. Once again, I am reminded, being an academic from an arts discipline, that introduction to the laws of logic and some formal training in rational debate are no longer a prerequisite for university education, as they once were – or not

---

15. evolutionfaq.com/faq/have-scientists-ever-created-life-laboratory, accessed 27 August 2019.

necessarily, it would seem, for those in the natural sciences. As for the writer's complaint that 'the technology simply does not yet exist', I recall an adage prevalent among the artisans of South London when I was a boy: that 'A bad workman blames his tools'.

Yet, even if **evolution faq** can hold out hope for an explanation of Behe's supposedly 'irreducible complexity' as observed in the simplest living cell, it seems to do so without any sense of the coach-and-horses that would drive through neo-Darwinian evolutionary doctrine, by introducing the agency of an informed and skilled human artificer.

Not only does the possibility of an effective human facilitator run counter to the central role of blind and meaningless chance in neo-Darwinist theory, it revitalises a doctrine fundamental to the Jewish and Christian faiths: that all life derives from a divine creator, that human beings both male and female are made in the image and likeness of God,[16] that they are necessary sharers in the creation of new life, and as individuals are far superior in creative potential to any other living creature.

Michael Behe may signal neutrality in the evolution debate by reminding his readers that the Roman Catholic Church to which he belongs has never contested the theory of evolution of species, nor the scientific evidence adduced to support it. Nevertheless, when Behe reiterates his finding that there is an unexplained complexity at the level of the simplest living cell and implies that such interacting components require an organizing power, he is, willy-nilly, arguing for the probability of his own underlying belief-system. He is also at the same time exposing neo-Darwinists to the charge that their fundamental atheism is ill-evidenced or at the least unproven, and therefore has no place in a science supposedly validated by observation. A properly scientific response to Behe's challenge, contrary to what his neo-Darwinist reviewer has suggested, is not to exclude Behe from further discussion but to attempt to meet his objections.

Michael Behe has been kind enough, in response to my request as a stranger, to furnish me with a short summary of what conclusions he derives from the latest observations in his field of study:

> Modern research reveals that Darwin's mechanism suffers from a previously-hidden, fatal weakness: not only are random mutation and natural selection grossly inadequate to *build* complex structures, they strongly tend to *break* them. Darwin rightly touted natural selection as relentless, as "daily and hourly

16. Genesis 1:26-27, 5:1, 9:6, in the Jewish and Christian scriptures.

scrutinising . . . every variation, even the slightest; rejecting that which is bad, preserving and adding up all that is good." Yet, since the mechanism has no foresight, and since in many circumstances the random *damaging* of genes can be *helpful* to an organism, then selection "adds up" those degradative changes only in the sense that broken pieces of machinery might be added to a growing pile of junk.

Unfortunately, the whole atheistic neo-Darwinist account of origins has the disadvantage of being strongly counter-intuitive, whether your survey be across nations or over time – as was demonstrated by the British Museum exhibition from 2 November 2017 to 8 April 2018 that I have referred to in Chapter Three by its title: 'Living with Gods: Peoples, Places and Worlds Beyond'. Yet the experience I recall most vividly is an episode at least forty-five years earlier, when I was a junior Fellow of St John's College, Cambridge and had teamed up with a colleague from the natural sciences who was similarly unversed in music. We had agreed to practice our newly-acquired recorders in the security of his college rooms. On my way out after a joint session, I passed a small table in the lobby on which was a two-foot-high model, carved in beautifully polished wood, of what looked like a pair of large, stretched-out but loosely intermingled bed-springs. It was, of course, more significant than that: a model of the double-helix of DNA, discovered by Francis Crick and colleagues some years previously to be the coded instructions for all life. 'That, David', said my friend, with a smile but not a touch of self-consciousness, 'is how God does it' – and that from a scientist I had never once seen in chapel!

Not only did Darwin assert his atheistic version of the origin of all life-forms against what I'll dare to call the 'natural flow' of human thought: he differed on this point from his friend and colleague Alfred Russel Wallace (who had independently developed a similar theory as to the evolution of species through natural selection), by insisting that blind chance alone must be central to the whole process of species differentiation. Darwin had felt betrayed when another friend, St George Jackson Mivart, found it impossible to believe that a creature such as a leaf insect could disguise itself from its predators by a series of tiny, accidental developments in its appearance over a period of time (as I reported in Chapter Three): as Mivart saw it, for a creature to successfully present itself as only a tatty leaf, it had to look like a tatty leaf, not by stages over a period of time, but right from the start. It would seem that Mivart and Darwin parted company permanently over the key role that Darwin insisted on giving to chance.

On the other hand, Darwin remained a loyal friend, even when Alfred Russel Wallace eventually departed much further from the Darwinist stance by declaring that only an intervention from 'the unseen universe of Spirit'[17] could explain at least three key developments in the history of life on earth: the creation of life from inorganic matter; the emergence of consciousness in the higher animals; and, finally, the generation of those higher intellectual capacities in human beings that not only made possible developments such as music, mathematics, the arts and sciences, but also that surprise delight in any intellectual discussion, the opportunity for a joke! When Wallace in later life became desperately impoverished, it was Darwin who got him a small government pension.

Mounting dissatisfaction with Darwinian theory as now presented has led to a widespread demand amongst neo-Darwinists for yet another 'new synthesis' that would better enable a defence against critics.[18] But even though Darwin himself plainly had some temperamental bias against theistic explanations for life on earth, that does not absolve his successors from considering Behe's evidence for an alleged complexity of structure and function in the simplest living cell that would seem to require an organizing power. Still less is it acceptable simply to dismiss Behe's most recent contention, that new evidence as to the functioning of DNA suggests not that fresh developments may emerge from some chance accident but that they can arise from a process whereby the DNA that coded for a particular form and function is broken down and re-directed to produce a different result. Novelty, therefore, (as Behe suggests) may arise not always from evolution but from 'devolution' (to use his own formulation) – and the question then arises, by what means or by what power does such a change in instructions come about?

The same problem had already arisen from the well-supported discovery that DNA not only replicates itself but has the capacity to self-repair. Who or what discovers that an error in instructions has occurred and determines to put it right? Even observing my own body, full of aches and pains from concentration on mounting an argument, I am aware that I need to take a break – but I am aware also that bodily processes I

---

17. For an exhaustive account of Wallace's developing views, see Wikipedia, en.wikipedia.org/wiki/Alfred Russel Wallace

18. Between 7 and 9 November 2016 the Royal Society, in partnership with the British Academy, held a well-attended conference in London entitled 'New Trends in Evolutionary Biology' – but it would seem that little emerged that promised any agreed 'new synthesis'.

can only assist must do the actual work. Similar healing processes exist in all living things – but where else does a repair mechanism exist that human agency has not designed?

I have expressed earlier my alarm at what looks to an outsider to be a breakdown in communication within the field of biological science, consequent on an unwarranted intrusion from two other modes of intellectual enquiry, the disciplines of philosophy and theology, where assertions as to necessary direction and apparent meaninglessness more properly belong.

The founders of modern science, pioneers such as Francis Bacon and Isaac Newton, however adept they might have been at other intellectual pursuits, were insistent that the new mode of enquiry into what could be observed must at all times be kept independent from what one might otherwise expect or hope to see.

In contrast, Darwin knew what he was to find before he found it. From the outset, his whole theory of 'natural selection' presumed that all life, whether past, present or future would not and could not (save for those slight modifications within a species produced by human skill in breeding for a certain quality) be attributed to any design or Designer. Evolution of and within a species occurred by blind chance – full-stop – and nowhere in his writings does Darwin express much more than a token regret at the loss of any notion of an overseeing power.

The pay-off for such a negative doctrine as Darwin's would seem to be immense. In all things, in all relationships and all situations, you have (at least theoretically) absolute freedom to choose between alternative possibilities, without obligation to a design or Designer, or reference to any code of behaviour that you have not chosen for yourself.

Richard Dawkins has set out so confidently the advantages of the neo-Darwinists' libertarian creed, in lectures, discussions, broadcast talks and writings such as *The God Delusion*, that no more needs to be said – except perhaps to wonder if the widely reported increase in anxiety, depression and rising suicide rates amongst the young could in any way be related.

It would, nevertheless, be a pity if the spectacular advances of recent years in tools for investigating cell mechanisms, and the imagination and industry that has gone into their application, should be denied their proper recognition and reward, simply because of the conclusions that Michael Behe has derived from them.

But it would be far worse for the whole of scientific endeavour if the unpalatable opinions of a Behe should be cast out chiefly on doctrinal grounds, as his *Washington Post* reviewer recommends. Far better, since burning at the stake is now out of fashion, to engage with and, if possible, refute Behe's conclusions as mistaken, rather than hope that they will eventually go away of their own accord.

All a bystander can do, whose qualifications are more in literary, historical and theological studies, is to attempt to take some of the irrational passion out of debate, by adopting a ploy from J.B. Phillips, the author of *Your God is Too Small*:[19] 'Tell me what you think your God to be – and I'll tell you why I don't like Him either!'

There is an obvious error in Jerry Coyne's review for *The Washington Post* – and one that occurs so frequently in neo-Darwinist polemics that it is unlikely to be a simple blunder. Behe is dismissed as just one more 'Creationist in a cheap tuxedo' and on that ground alone is judged unworthy of a hearing. In fact, Behe declares himself to be a Roman Catholic and is a Senior Fellow at the Discovery Institute, which brings together persons of various religious persuasions or of no particular persuasion at all, but who subscribe to the 2014 Mission Statement of the Institute:

> The mission of Discovery Institute is to advance a culture of purpose, creativity and innovation.
>
> Philosophy
> Mind, not matter, is the source and crown of creation, the wellspring of human achievement. Conceived by the ancient Hebrews, Greeks and Christians, and elaborated in the American Founding, Western culture has encouraged creativity, enabled discovery and upheld the uniqueness and dignity of human beings. Linking religious, political, and economic liberty, the Judeo-Christian culture has established the rule of law, codified respect for human rights and conceived constitutional democracy. It has engendered development of science and technology, as well as economic creativity and innovation.

In contrast, 'Creationism' emerged as a late nineteenth- and early twentieth-century movement, chiefly amongst English-speaking Protestants, who sought to return to doctrinal fundamentals that they saw threatened by too generous a liberality in the established Christian Churches.

Unhappily, by their naive understanding of the metaphorical language of 'Vision' in the Old Testament as if it were a factual, eye-witness

---

19. J.B. Phillips, *Your God is Too Small* (New York, NY: The Macmillan Company, 1953).

account of the beginnings of mankind, Creationists turn what had hitherto appeared as only an occasional if at times widespread doctrinal blemish in the Christian understanding of our human situation into a major distortion that has had and will have, if allowed to go unchecked, disastrous psychological consequences for human self-esteem and well-being (as I indicated when discussing John Milton's account of the Fall of Man in Chapter Seven).

The Book of Genesis, Chapter 1, verse 1 to Chapter 9, verse 19, is a collection of statements about human origins that express in visionary terms a perception of the situation in which we human beings find ourselves. The compilers were clearly not troubled by what may now seem some of the contradictions in the resulting narrative: it was sufficient that the visions cohered around a recurrent theme – that God is the originator of all things.

It is at the opening of the Book of Genesis, Chapter 1, verse 1, that God creates light and divides it from darkness. Yet only after he has separated 'the waters above the earth' from 'the waters beneath the earth' and established both dry ground and the seas (1: 6-10) and has then populated land and water with living things (1: 11-12), does he create 'lights' in the sky 'to give light on the earth' (1: 14-19). We are then told in Genesis 1: 20-24 that God first created living things in the waters, then birds and wild animals in all their variety, including the creatures that 'move along the ground' – and, only finally, according to Genesis 1: 26, did God create Man 'in God's own image', to rule 'over all the creatures'.

Very obviously, even if the process of development of life on earth – first, creatures in the waters, then land animals and birds of the air, followed at last by humankind – is largely confirmed by scientific enquiry, the overarching concern of the authors whose accounts are collected in the Book of Genesis is to establish a truth that is visionary, and not empirically observed: that God is at the root of all things.

Aspects of the Genesis account, if taken literally, can seem a shade ridiculous. Was God really so clapped-out, after his six days' labour in creation, that he was obliged to take a Sabbath rest? Or is that just a visionary's inspirational reminder that human beings made by God need a weekly respite from worldly concerns so as to re-connect with the world of the Spirit?

It is vital to recognize that the incidental details of Vision are not observed fact and must be subjected to critical examination against the more comprehensive understandings of a coherent belief-system. The Aztecs (as I indicated at the outset of Chapter Eight) were not wrong in holding that sacrifice was necessary to establish a right relationship with the Divine, but – by what I would identify from my own belief-system to be a Satanic perversion – they believed that the accord they desired with their gods was best achieved by sacrificing the heart-blood of another human being while the victim was still alive.

Conversely, it was when the Earl of Rochester saw the harsh realities of his human existence illumined by what was presented to him as the recorded facts of Christ's life, death and resurrection, that Christian Vision, endorsed by evidential observation, gave him joyful release.

Nevertheless, a terrible danger lies in taking a visionary insight as though it were in all respects an observed fact – a danger recognized by most hearers and readers up until the late nineteenth century. Genesis 1: 27 has God creating the first of the human race together, presumably as equals, though divided into two sexes, male and female:

> So God created man in his own image;
> in the image of God he created him;
> male and female he created them.

However, from Genesis 2: 3 onwards we have a second, somewhat contradictory account of creation, where the beginnings of mankind follow a different sequence. Instead of a simultaneous origin, the male human being has priority, the woman being fashioned from his rib. Moreover, the creation of woman takes place *after* the creation of a natural environment in the Garden of Eden and after God has made 'man from the dust of the ground and breathed into his nostrils the breath of life' (Genesis 2: 7). Prior to Eve's creation in this second Genesis account is the establishment of plant and animal life in the Garden of Eden and the commission from God to Adam 'to work it and take care of it' (Genesis 2: 15).

Much more perturbing for consequent estimates of woman is that Eve in this rather different narrative is created well *after* God has established 'the tree of the knowledge of good and evil' and *after* he has warned Adam that: 'You are free to eat from any tree in the garden; but you must not eat from the tree of the knowledge of good and evil, for when you eat of it you will surely die.' (Genesis 2: 16-17).

After this warning has been given to Adam whilst he is still solitary, God, in what appears from this second account of creation to be a significant after-thought, creates woman from a rib of the first man – and for a reason well understood by philosophers and physicians from the beginnings of recorded time: that 'it is not good for man to be alone' (Genesis 2: 18).

As a happily married male, gratitude at the implications of this further visionary account of human origins can move me to tears:

The man said,
'This is now bone of my bones
and flesh of my flesh;
she shall be called "woman",
for she was taken out of man.'
For this reason a man will leave his father and mother
and be united to his wife,
and they will become one flesh.
(Genesis 2: 23-24)

But when this second account of origins moves to an explanation of how human beings came to be so alienated from a God who is presented in the Liturgy of St John Chrysostom and elsewhere in Christian devotion as 'the Lover of Mankind', the visionary author of Genesis Two introduces elements into the story that present the first woman as a gullible fool – even though she has not been warned (as was Adam) about some lurking danger, and even if (as would appear from the Genesis account) she had never heard directly from God his apparently arbitrary restriction on the eating of fruit. We may guess that Adam kept Eve up to date with the new rulings from on high – but that is something we have to add ourselves to the Genesis story. Adam is portrayed as misled, both by female charm and by the natural appeal of an apple, into a foolish action whose implications and consequences neither of the primal pair could fully understand. As for God, he comes across as an arbitrary tyrant who demands unquestioning obedience to his 'say-so' on its own, with no intelligible explanation given, and who subsequently imposes a lethal penalty for disobedience that is vastly disproportionate to any supposed crime.

As for the serpent, whom later interpreters identified as Satan, the instigator of all evil-doing (so the Book of Revelation 12: 9, 20: 2), God is shown to be the creator, before the Fall of Man, of a serpent 'more crafty than any of the wild animals the Lord God had made' (Genesis 3: 1) – so it would appear, from this second visionary narrative in Genesis, if taken literally, that God was himself both the originator of evil and its punisher.

All this comes from taking metaphoric language as if it were factual. Worse still is the doctrine of 'Original Sin' as derived from the Genesis stories, developed well after Christ's life and death, yet upheld by many of the Church Fathers, and promoted especially amongst certain of the sixteenth- and seventeenth-century Reformers. For reasons that can now only be guessed at, these enthusiasts misrepresented the God-given delights of sexual intercourse that bind a couple together in love and may result in the blessing of children, and turned sexual congress into a means of contamination whereby the curse and punishment of the primal pair for their ignorant disobedience toward God was supposedly transmitted through 'concupiscence' (or carnal desire) to generation after generation of innocent children, without exception and to the end of time. Sometimes, the supposed transmission of evil through sexuality to the unborn is treated only as emerging in a slight preference for doing wrong: at its extreme, the doctrine of 'Total Depravity' meant that no human being who had not been 'saved' could do any good – except by chance.

Why such a doctrine should ever have proved acceptable to believers in a loving God may, perhaps, be because of the difficulty pious males have had in suppressing, or even controlling, their own sexuality, especially in religious cultures that gave – and still do give – a special kudos and spiritual regard to a self-imposed celibacy, and who insist, in two at least of the larger Christian denominations, on promoting to highest office (contrary to apostolic practice) only those who are unmarried.

If you were to squawk back at me that 'This is all scripture! This is the Bible!' I would have to say that in part that may be so – but in no sense is it the Christian faith.

Nowhere in all Christ's sayings as recorded in the Four Gospels does he once mention Adam and Eve by name, and he alludes to the Genesis account of how all things began only when asked about divorce. Mark reports him as citing the visionary account of woman created from a rib of man, but only to signify a fundamental unity between man and wife that Moses had permitted to be broken only 'because your hearts were hard' (Mark 10: 2-12).

In contrast to any supposed doctrine of an initial corruption transmitted to the young by the sexual congress of their parents, Christ celebrates, in saying after saying, the fundamental innocence of young children[20].

Take Matthew 18, verses 1 to 6:

At that time the disciples came to Jesus and asked, 'Who is the greatest in the kingdom of heaven?' He called a little child and had him stand among them. And he said: 'I tell you the truth, unless

20. Matthew 11:25, 18:1-6, 18:10-11, 18:14, 19:13-15; Mark 10:13-16; Luke 9:46-48, 10:21, 17:1-2, 18:15-17.

you change and become like little children, you will never enter the kingdom of heaven. Therefore, whoever humbles himself like this child is the greatest in the kingdom of heaven.

And whoever welcomes a little child like this in my name welcomes me. But if anyone causes one of these little ones who believe in me to sin, it would be better for him to have a large millstone hung around his neck and to be drowned in the depths of the sea'.

Returning for a moment, painfully, to the evidence given by myself and others in 2016 to the *Australian Royal Commission into Institutional Responses to Child Sexual Abuse*, relating to an alleged abuse of minors by clergy of the Anglican Diocese of Newcastle, New South Wales some thirty or more years previous, it has always been a mystery to me to account for what was then reported by one of my mature students: that her son, whilst at a diocesan youth camp, had been woken at midnight to take part in a hunt through the woods by clergy, whose prize was to sexually abuse any boy who had the misfortune to be captured. Why did they not recall that warning about a consequent drowning with a millstone about one's neck, and have it ringing in their ears? These were men known to me as professed Christians, competent pastors, and some of them were friends whom I had myself consulted for advice – and yet they seemed driven, like the Aztecs, by some bizarre misunderstanding of divine requirements – and even, perhaps, by some Satanic perversion of Christian love.

It may be that a predilection for young males as sexual objects amongst the Catholic and Anglo-Catholic clergy of New South Wales was not just a consequence of antipathy to the female sex *per se*, but was encouraged by an aversion to heterosexual love as the vehicle that had transmitted the taint of Original Sin to future generations. St Paul, who knew that men and women were created equal, was nevertheless inclined to see the male as superior in certain respects and himself chose to remain celibate, though aware that his was merely a personal preference which he hoped others might follow. He tended, nevertheless, to encourage social customs that endorsed the subordination of women, and certain of his attitudes suggest that he might have been uncomfortable with sexuality – an edginess on which later theologians could and did build.

However that may be, it is almost certainly unjust to hold St Paul responsible for the doctrine of Original Sin. He mentions the story of Adam in his surviving letters only four times or so[21], and there Adam

---

21. Romans 5: 12-19; 1 Corinthians 11: 2-13, 1 Corinthians 15: 21-22, 45-49; 1 Timothy 2: 13-14.

stands as the representative of all mankind. Sexual congress is not mentioned as the mode by which sin is transmitted, and Paul's emphasis is less on our release from sin and death as on that glorious new life attested by Christ's resurrection: 'For as in Adam all die, even so in Christ shall all be made alive' (1 Corinthians 15: 22, in the King James Version).

The exception to this generalization about Paul's views is in his supposed private letter to a protégé, the First Epistle to Timothy, where a rather different attitude to women is expressed:

> A woman should learn in quietness and full submission. I do not permit a woman to teach or to have authority over a man; she must be silent. For Adam was formed first, then Eve. And Adam was not the one deceived; it was the woman who was deceived and became a sinner. But women will be saved through childbearing – if they continue in faith, love and holiness with propriety.
> (1 Timothy 2: 11-15)

As a student of literature, I am impressed by a technical argument from biblical scholars who report that some 306 Greek words used in this supposedly Pauline epistle are not found elsewhere in Paul's writings.[22] It is alleged that a majority of modern scholars now doubt, for a range of reasons, the authenticity of those Pastoral Epistles attributed to Paul. Marcion around 140 CE formed a canon of scripture that does not mention 1 and 2 Timothy and Titus. Nor is 1 Timothy included in the fourth century Codex Vaticanus, a major early collection of Christian scriptures, though it is found in that other major manuscript collection of similar date, the Codex Sinaiticus.

But it is my own re-reading of Paul's brilliant and astonishing exposition of Christian hope in his Letter to the Romans, followed immediately by a further reading of what is alleged to be Paul's First Epistle to Timothy, which leaves me wondering just what degree of tiredness, sickness, or perhaps boredom with a communication that was just a chore to instruct an underling about matters of administration, could possibly explain such a vast difference in literary and doctrinal achievement.

The stance of the First Epistle to Timothy towards females as necessarily inferior does not square with the esteem accorded by Paul to influential Christian women among his associates, such as Priscilla, the wife of Aquila. Nowhere else in Paul's writings is Adam given such priority over Eve, or woman presented as the first sinner and Adam as

---

22. Stephen L. Harris, *The New Testament: A Student's Introduction*, fourth edition (Boston, MA: McGraw-Hill, 2002), p. 366.

chiefly a victim of her crime. But what is even less likely to be a genuine opinion of Paul, whether he were feverish, careless or in his cups, is the assertion that 'women will be saved through childbearing'. Are we to believe that spinsters or the infertile are forever cast out? For the genuine Paul, the only possible salvation for the whole human race, whether male or female, was through Jesus Christ: 'As in Adam all die, even so in Christ shall all be made alive.'

It is undeniably the case that prominent figures in the Early Church such as Irenaeus (c.130 – 200 CE), Tertullian (c.155-240 CE), Cyprian (c.200-258 CE), Ambrose, who died on 4 April 397 CE, Ambrosiaster (who pre-dated Augustine) and Augustine himself after a change of heart and mind around 412 CE, as well as later church leaders such as Luther and Calvin amongst the Renaissance Reformers, were attracted to the doctrine of Original Sin, and held that the process by which children came to be was unavoidably tainted by 'concupiscence' and therefore involved all mankind in an inherited corruption. The Roman Catholic Church, by two formal decrees 'Concerning Original Sin' at the Council of Trent, 'celebrated on the seventeenth day of the month of June, in the year 1546', explicitly endorsed the doctrine[23].

Curiously, the concept of Original Sin transmitted through sexual congress to the young seems not to have been taught by the scribes and Pharisees with whom Christ contended and has not figured in Jewish rabbinic teaching. Rather, it seems to have emerged in the course of Christian conflicts with Gnostic groups who argued for an eternal opposition between two equal cosmic powers, one good, one evil, so it is possible that the doctrine of Original Sin appeared at that time to be a means of asserting the overall dominance of the One True God.

Given the number of instances in the Four Gospels where Christ bears witness to the fundamental innocence of children,[24] the emergence of a doctrine that sees all human beings as born with a hereditary taint transmitted by the sexual intercourse of their parents would seem to require more the services of a psychiatrist than those of a theologian.

Not all of the early Fathers of the Church were led astray. It is claimed that Eastern Orthodoxy has never accepted the doctrine.[25] St John Chrysostom (c.349 to 14 September 407 CE), Archbishop of

---

23. See: https://en.wikipedia.org/wiki/Original sin, accessed 10 August 2019.
24. Matthew 11:25, 18:1-6, 18:10-11, 18:14, 19:13-15; Mark 10:13-16; Luke 9:46-48, 10:21, 17:1-2, 18:15-17.
25. Archimandrite Vassilios Papavassiliou, 'Original Sin: Orthodox Doctrine or Heresy?', 25 February 2017, at: http://pemptousia.com/2017/02/original-sin-orthodox-doctrine-or-heresy, accessed 13 August 2019.

Constantinople, in his *Homily LXII on* Matthew 19: 13-15 exclaims at what is reported as a saying of Christ: 'This is the angelic life; yes, for the soul of a little child is pure from all passions.'[26] St Cyril of Alexandria (c. 376-444 CE) is also clear that 'A babe, then, as knowing very little or nothing at all, is justly acquitted of the charge of depravity and wickedness . . .'[27]

If I turn back from what the author of *Upstart Crow* might term the 'Puri-titties and Satan-shitters' of the sixteenth century to the purer air of the Gospel narratives, I am struck, not by some belief in a pervasive human wickedness, but by a natural capability in even the worst of us to do good. As Christ observes: 'If you, then, though you are evil, know how to give good gifts to your children, how much more will your Father in heaven give good gifts to those who ask him?'(Matthew 7: 11; cf. Luke 11: 13).

Both Matthew and Luke present Christ, near the outset of his ministry, as preaching what we now call the 'Beatitudes', a series of blessings and encouragement for those who are already yearning to progress toward the good:

> Blessed are those who hunger and thirst after righteousness,
> for they will be filled;
> Blessed are the merciful,
> for they will be shown mercy.
> Blessed are the pure in heart,
> for they will see God.
> Blessed are the peacemakers,
> for they will be called sons of God.
> Blessed are those who are persecuted because of righteousness,
> for theirs is the kingdom of heaven.
> (Matthew 5: 3-10. Cf. Luke 6: 11-23)

More significant still is that encounter with the 'rich young man' which all three synoptic gospel-writers place immediately after Christ's assertion as to the basic innocence of young children.[28] The 'rich young man' asks 'What must I do to inherit eternal life?' (Mark 10: 17-21). He is told that he must obey the commandments. When he responds by asserting that 'all these I have kept since I was a boy', Jesus does not denounce him either as a hypocrite or as someone self-deceived: rather,

---

26. St John Chrysostom, *Homily LXII on Matthew XIX*, 4.B#54, p. 385.
27. St Cyril of Alexandria, *Commentary on the Gospel of St Luke*, Homily 121, B#42, p. 484.
28. Mark 10:17-23, Matthew 19: 16-26, Luke 18: 23.

we are told by Mark that 'Jesus looked at him and loved him'. What the young man finds impossible is Christ's demand to 'sell everything you have and give it to the poor, and then you will have treasure in heaven. Then come, follow me', for that involves a willingness to let go of all those securities that human beings most naturally cling to. Yet the alternative is worse: 'It is easier for a camel to go through the eye of a needle than for a rich man to enter the kingdom of God' (Matthew 19: 24, Authorized Version).

To return at last to Robert Shapiro's ORIGINS: a Skeptic's Guide to the Creation of Life on Earth, Shapiro's 'Skeptic' made a very clear distinction between those insights drawn from what I have termed 'Vision', which he saw expressed in the world's creation-myths and were perhaps at their best in the Genesis account of how all things came to be (which he conceded 'might be very good religion'), as opposed to a scientific understanding derived from observation of the present and also from plausible reconstructions of how life might have evolved in the past, so far as can be surmised from archeological, geological and biological residues still remaining.

But what neither Shapiro nor his Skeptic allowed for was that unique conjunction of inspirational insight with verifiable observation that constitutes the truth-claim of the Christian religion. We have seen already the revolutionary impact on the Earl of Rochester of what he took to be visionary revelation supported by undeniable fact. The man Jesus Christ, according to what I shall argue to be well-documented evidence, claimed to be not only the One who was to come, as promised by Jewish prophecy, but also to be the incarnation of the one Creator God: 'Anyone who has seen me has seen the Father' (John 14: 9). If Christ was not deluded or a fraud, then atheistic neo-Darwinism is bunkum – and vice versa.

The opposition of two such mutually exclusive alternatives – of blind, meaningless Darwinian evolution as against a conscious, controlling and yet benevolent Creative Power – would be sufficient in themselves to fuel passionate debate, even without that further and apparently preposterous insistence from committed Christians: that the same eternal, benevolent and Creative Power has made itself accessible and intelligible to the human race in the person of Jesus Christ.

There has been an assiduously propagated assertion in the Western news media that we have now entered upon a predominantly unbelieving and atheistic era, as signified by a widespread decline in religious observance and a concomitant and perhaps consequent failure of moral standards.

In fact, it would seem, from recently reported research led by the University of Kent[29] as part of 'The Understanding Unbelief Programme', that thousands of people drawn from six different countries – Britain, the United States, Brazil, China, Denmark and Japan – who identified themselves as atheist or agnostic – have by no means rejected all belief in the 'supernatural'. The majority of those who claimed to have no faith accepted one or more aspects of common belief-systems:

> such as life after death, reincarnation or astrology. They also sometimes believed that some events were 'meant to be' and that there were forces of good and evil . . . 71% of atheists and 92% of agnostics held at least one supernatural belief, which might also include karma.

Comparisons of the beliefs of declared unbelievers with the general population were similarly revealing:

> About a third of atheists and 40% of agnostics in Britain believe that some events are 'meant to be', compared with just over 60% of the general population. Almost 20% of atheists believe in life after death, compared with 55% of the general population.
> Almost a third of atheists and around 45% of agnostics believe in underlying forces of good and evil, compared with almost 60% of the general population.

Given that atheistic neo-Darwinism is increasingly exposed as more a form of negative faith than a defensible scientific theory, and given also that its more vociferous proponents now recommend blind devotion as opposed to any attempt to engage with critics, and given, especially, that the most recent research has revealed that self-confessed atheists and agnostics in six national populations currently display a marked inclination to harbour notions of the supernatural, it is a wonder that our Christian communities, with so much evidence in their favour, should appear at present to be making so little progress against what has traditionally been taken to be their ancient enemy, the 'Father of Lies', as expressed in atheistic neo-Darwinism.

Since the strategy of this study has been to encourage the reader to confront reality as it is, rather than as we might like it to be, and since I am on the point of presenting a summary of evidence for the Christian

29. Anna Behrmann, 'Atheists have belief in the supernatural', *The Times*, 3 June 2019, p. 11.

account of that reality, it is time to admit to my experience over sixty years: that any attempt to further that Christian interpretation has invariably been, to a greater or lesser degree, accompanied by acute physical, mental and even spiritual discomfort, without any obvious physical or psychological cause. In Chapter Two of this book, I issued a health-warning to anyone about to follow my enquiry into the truth-claims of atheistic neo-Darwinism. Now, honesty requires me to admit that the same experience, of being under intense attack, internally and externally, has occurred at four points in what has been a lengthy academic career: first, in my twenties, when, as a member of the Church of England Liturgical Commission, I composed prayers for services in modern English; second, in my early thirties, when I undertook preparation of a poetic version of the Book of Psalms in modern English; third, in my seventies, when acting as my wife's editor for her study of Hinduism and Christianity; and now, at the end of my career, when challenging the truth-claims of atheistic neo-Darwinism. I have thought hard about the wisdom of committing such an admission to print, because the obvious retort will be that such phenomena are occasioned by the psychological stress of defending the discarded truths of an outworn creed. There is certainly a cost to be met – but there are also further questions to be asked. Why should such a cost be exacted? And do any proponents of the atheistic account of human origins suffer a parallel disturbance? – And if not, why not?

The answer that I would give – and one that might empower the Western-based Christian Churches to challenge more effectively the pervasive influence of atheistic neo-Darwinism – is one learned from a close personal friend, Archbishop Gibran Ramlaoui, Antiochian Orthodox Archbishop of Australia, New Zealand and Dependencies, on whom my wife and I relied for spiritual counsel during our twenty-one year sojourn 'down-under'.

Gibran would say, when confronted by what seemed a doctrinal conundrum: 'It's all part of the package'. The problem that faces Christian Churches in the West, and increasingly the rest of the world when influenced by Western ideas, is that we have all benefited enormously from what was a true 'Enlightenment' over the last three centuries or so, which by taking a scientific approach progressively exposed a morass of pervasive and destructive superstition. But now, as the saying goes, the danger is that we will 'throw out the baby with the bathwater' – the baby in this instance being Jesus Christ. In the Western Churches at large and within my own family there is a willingness to recommend Jesus Christ 'as a good man, with a lot of the right ideas'. But if he was that and no more than that, how does he differ from the Reverend Jones of Jonestown, who also said he was God, claimed to do healing miracles, drew the love of his followers to him with promises of complete spiritual, emotional and temporal satisfaction, and led his followers finally to accompany him in a mass suicide that was a 'revolutionary protest' against a selfish, evil and unbelieving world? 'By their fruit you will recognize them' (Matthew 7: 16, 7: 20) is a criterion applied throughout the Gospels.

The whole 'package' that Archbishop Gibran believed it necessary to accept will certainly confirm Jesus Christ as 'a good man with a lot of the right ideas'; but it also requires Christians to believe that Jesus Christ was both fully man and fully God, an expression of the Creator made flesh, all-knowing, so that a single utterance (if reported correctly) must be taken as absolute truth. Hence, the saying of Christ in the Gospel according to Luke 10: 18, 'I saw Satan fall like lightning', has to be taken as Christ's divine experience of the origin of evil in a rebellion by a God-created Power who led other powers astray. Since that rebellion is not yet put down, we must expect continuing assaults from the Evil Powers, which have to be endured both by men and women and even by Christ himself, since he was both God and fully man – and this is evidenced from what in the gospels can only derive from Christ's own account of being tempted by Satan in the wilderness.

A substantial number of people in six different countries who see themselves as agnostic or atheist nevertheless believe there is a conflict between good and evil, one that may continue to the end of time. Fortified by Gibran's insistence on the 'full package' of the Christian gospel, I am emboldened to reverse my question: not 'Why do I feel so ill when writing in defence of what I believe to be gospel-truth?' but 'Why do the passionate proponents of atheistic neo-Darwinism seem to remain so apparently self-confident and gleeful?'

CONCLUSION

'To See Things as They Are':
The Consequences of Observation

To parody the opening of one of Jane Austen's finest novels, *Pride and Prejudice*: 'It is a truth universally acknowledged' that, in an age where deductive reason from observable fact is increasingly held to be the final arbiter of truth, and hence of appropriate human behaviour, any well-entrenched system of belief, especially the Christian faith in 'Immanuel', which means – "God with us" (Matthew 1: 23), must be in want of a rational defence.

Near the inception of what we now call 'the Age of Enlightenment', which offered to liberate western thought from the entanglement of religious preconceptions, one Thomas Sherlock (1678-1761), a lawyer and a divine who succeeded his father as Master of the Temple, realised that the best defence of Christianity against its critics might be to rely on the accuracy and truthfulness of the New Testament record.

Sherlock had been educated at St Catharine's College, Cambridge in the time-honoured techniques of disputation[1], with its emphasis on the principles of logic and the proper evaluation of evidence – a training

---

1. See Alex J. Novikoff, *The Medieval Culture of Disputation: Pedagogy, Practice and Performance* (Philadelphia, PA: University of Pennsylvania Press, 2013); and Olga Weijers, *In Search of the Truth: A History of Disputation Techniques from Antiquity to Early Modern Times* (Turnhout, Belgium: Brepols Publishers, 2013).

sadly omitted, so it would seem, from many of our modern university induction courses, if the increasing number of complaints against even peer-reviewed scientific papers are to be believed.

The tract Sherlock published in 1728, *The Tryal of the Witnesses of the Resurrection of Jesus*,[2] was wildly popular, and is said to have gone through 'up to a dozen' editions in its first year. It continued in print through subsequent centuries, even to an edition in the twentieth century. Its strategy was to present an imaginary group of lawyers from both sides of the religious debate, who agree to entertain themselves and us by staging a mock-trial, for which they appoint a judge and jury, with prosecuting and defending counsel, so as to try the New Testament witnesses to Christ's Resurrection on a charge of deceit.

Sherlock, who had served as Master of St Catharine's and subsequently was also Vice-Chancellor of the University of Cambridge, became Bishop of Bangor in 1728, of Salisbury in 1734, and finally Bishop of London and a Member of the Privy Council in 1748. A friend and supporter of the Prime Minister Walpole in Parliament, his work received the highest accolades from University, Church and State.

It is alleged that David Hume had *The Trial* in mind when he published his attack on belief in miracles in 1748.[3] However, it is noticeable that Hume sticks to the generalities of unbelief and evades discussion of New Testament evidence entirely – perhaps because his reputation for 'atheism' had already damaged his candidature for posts for which he had applied. Despite its reputation, the Hume tract is a rather lame riposte, if that is what it was intended to be, and includes in its 'Notes' a collection of more up-to-date reports of miracles, which are relayed rather than examined or interrogated.

The core-tenet of Christianity is that the Creator God, otherwise accessible only through Vision or 'spiritual intelligence', presented himself for observation in a single human being, Jesus Christ, at a known point in time, and with explicit claims, teachings, actions and miraculous powers that attested he was indeed God incarnate. According to the New Testament record, this same Jesus taught his followers to expect his judicial murder and his rising from the dead 'on the third day' as validation of his claim. His resurrection was immediately reported, by a range of testimonies verbal and written, which spread within a few

---

2. *The Trial of the Witnesses to the Resurrection of Jesus* (1729 edition), typescript converted to computer file by Lee Dunbar, July 2002, to be found at: https://classicapologetics.com/s/shertrial.pdf.

3. David Hume, *An Enquiry Concerning Human Understanding*, Section X, 'Of Miracles', PART I, at: https://davidhume.org/texts/e/10.

decades through much of the known world. These were further supported by the willingness from earliest days of large numbers of believers to suffer displacement, discomfort and death, rather than deny what they now held to be a fundamental truth of existence.

Some degree of anxiety as to what we as human beings understand ourselves to be might be appropriate in any modern enquirer, since (as I have endeavoured to demonstrate throughout this study) questions as to the beginning, development and destiny of the universe, disputes about the origin, evolution and possible uniqueness of life on earth, whether animal or human, and the likelihood (perhaps even the necessity) of some Originating Power, are by no means settled. Yet anxiety appears to be not evenly distributed amongst all parties to the dispute: why should expression of belief in a divine being who supposedly has the good of each one of us as his prime concern cause me, as a believer, such strain and stress to attest – whereas a thorough-going sceptic such as David Friedrich Strauss (1808-74), who wrote *The Life of Jesus Critically Examined* (1835-6) and who dismissed the New Testament records as perhaps little more than imaginative fantasy, does not seem, any more than Richard Dawkins in the twenty-first century, to have lost even a night's sleep over the matter?

A further oddity is that the collection of key evidence that constitutes the Christian New Testament is no more than 257 pages in my pocket edition – of no greater length than the average popular novel, and in editions readily available in most Western countries – and yet, in what has now been my very extended career in teaching literature and religion at university level, I can recall many students who admitted they had merely 'dipped into' the text, but not a single one who claimed to have read the New Testament through in its entirety, and yet was able to dismiss it as so much balderdash. It seems also that a majority in our Western populations prefer not to take the risk of direct enquiry, instead relying on hearsay – and not even, it would seem, on those now largely neglected 784 pages of Strauss' *The Life of Jesus Critically Examined*[4] that looked to nineteenth-century English intellectuals such as George Eliot to be worthy of translation, chiefly because Strauss, with enormous learning and meticulous examination of detail, explained the Gospel as a collection of pious fictions that had accumulated over an extended period of time.

The problem for neo-Darwinists when they consider the origins of life, as for the New Atheists with whom they are allied, and also for any remaining followers of those nineteenth-century Germanic revisionists

---

4. David Friedrich Strauss, *The Life of Jesus, Critically Examined,* trans. of the fourth edition by George Eliot in 1843 (New York, NY: Cosimo Books, 2009).

of the New Testament, is that when it comes to assembling evidence that might withstand scrutiny in a court of law, they all of them look to be on a hiding to nothing. I have indicated at length the extent of scientific observations that neo-Darwinism has proved inadequate to explain and the increasing tendency of current proponents of the doctrine to refuse further discussion. In contrast, the Christian faith, with its extraordinary claim that the Creator of all things opened himself to scientific scrutiny by being born as a human being, presents me with a wealth of evidence for what I have always felt to be preposterous – preposterous and yet true.

The grounds on which David Friedrich Strauss challenged the truth of the New Testament witness are evident from his Introduction to *The Life of Jesus Critically Examined*, as translated by George Eliot:

> Wherever a religion, resting upon written records, prolongs and extends the sphere of its dominion . . . a discrepancy between the representations of those ancient records, referred to as sacred, and the notions of more advanced periods of mental development will inevitably sooner or later arise . . . by degrees it manifests itself also in regard to that which is essential: the fundamental ideas and opinions in these early writings fail to be commensurate with a more advanced civilisation. (p. 39)

Time has been brutal to David Friedrich Strauss' criteria for judgement: faith in 'a more advanced civilisation' and its 'notions of more advanced periods of mental development' led, in less than fifty years after Strauss died, to the horrors of Nazi Germany and the Hitler regime.

Here, though, it is necessary to insert a caveat. Even if Strauss had a naively optimistic belief in the onward march of civilisation, that is irrelevant to the question whether his assessment of the New Testament evidence for Christ's resurrection is, or is not, reliable. Similarly, the suggestion that Darwin's theory of evolution by natural selection inspired development of a theory of eugenics that encouraged western imperialists to devalue their subject races and would result finally in horrendous Nazi atrocities against the Jews is not a reason to dismiss Darwin's original theory as untrue: the rules of admissible evidence do not permit guilt by association.

Nevertheless, when it comes to the three main ways by which David Friedrich Strauss sought to undermine the credibility of the New Testament as to the life, death and resurrection of Jesus Christ, all three of his approaches would be inadmissible in a court of law.

His first argument, which we have already considered, was to dismiss each and every account of miraculous events simply by an appeal to a supposed consensus in modern society that miracles cannot happen. However, the legal truth of any proposition cannot be established beforehand simply by a majority vote.

Strauss' second method was to impugn the reliability of New Testament historians by claiming that they were not who they claimed to be and had not been direct witnesses of events or accurate reporters of those who were. For this charge to bear maximum weight, every supposed witness would have to be discredited.

The third method, applied by Strauss with what a reader might feel to be an excessive if not mono-maniac obsession, was to trawl through every account of a New Testament event for instances of discrepancy and contradiction. But as all courts of law are aware, where there have been sixteen witnesses to an event, there will be sixteen accounts as to what happened that will differ, sometimes quite markedly, one from another– yet none of that will be proof that the event itself did not take place. Indeed, too obvious a concurrence between different accounts might be taken as indicative of a possible conspiracy to deceive.

In the end, all considerations of the truth of the Christian religion come down to a personal decision as to who, as well as what, we will trust. I am therefore forced back to something I had hoped to avoid: a personal testimony.

I can recall in most vivid detail the day, a full sixty years ago, when I conceded, on the evidence presented to me, that Christianity was true. It was a bright afternoon in May 1959, after I had completed my first-year undergraduate examinations preliminary to Part One of the Cambridge English Tripos – examinations that required little preparation, since the literature on which we were to be examined had been extensively covered in the sixth-form school syllabus for A level and Scholarship examinations. Instead, I had occupied much of my preparation-time in critically assessing the books of the New Testament, and especially the letters of St Paul in a modern English translation by J.B. Phillips, *Letters to Young Churches*.[5]

I was relaxing that afternoon in the set of rooms allotted to me as a first-year undergraduate at the top of Chapel Court, St John's College, and had before me my prize purchase, a portable gramophone, on which – much to my mother's alarm – I had expended a considerable portion of my student maintenance grant for the year. I was listening to one of the few records I had been able to afford: a collection of Negro spirituals sung by Paul Robeson,

---

5. J.B. Phillips, *Letters to Young Churches* (London: Collins/Fontana Books, 1955; or London: Geoffrey Bles, 1957).

who was then attracting vast audiences to his London recitals. He got to the spiritual, 'Were you there when they crucified my Lord?' – and I burst into tumultuous and prolonged sobbing. That was it. I have repeated the experiment once again before writing this – so far as I remember, for the first time in sixty years – and the impact and my own tumultuous response remain the same. To comprehend the emotional upheaval that accompanied – and still does accompany – my acceptance that Christianity was true and that Jesus Christ had indeed risen from the dead, it is necessary to understand how intense in the late 1950s was the pressure on students, old and young, from the Tübingen School of so-called 'higher biblical criticism'. 'Higher Criticism' was then widely believed to have demonstrated that New Testament evidence was inherently unreliable, the reports of Christ's life, death and resurrection being characteristic of similar mythic distortions in ancient cultures where information was initially conveyed by word of mouth, and only written down long after the events they purported to describe.

Tübingen University in Baden-Wirtemberg, Germany, has, since its foundation in 1477, been renowned as one of the most formative intellectual influences on western culture. Through the centuries up to the present day it has had a succession of international luminaries – amongst whom was David Friedrich Strauss. It is only now, after consulting Wikipedia, that I am fully aware of Tübingen's darker side: the tragic consequences of a Strauss-like faith in progress and in the opinions of 'a more enlightened age'. I quote from Wikipedia, verbatim:

Nazi period

The university played a leading role in efforts to legitimize the policies of the Third Reich as 'scientific'. Even before the victory of the Nazi party in the general election in March 1933, there were hardly any Jewish faculty [academic staff] and a few Jewish students. Physicist Hans Bethe was dismissed on 20 April 1933 because of 'non-Aryan' origin. Religion professor Traugott Konstantin Oesterreich and the mathematician Erich Kamke were forced to take early retirement, probably in both cases [because of] the 'non-Aryan' origin of their wives. At least 1,158 people were sterilized at the University Hospital.[6]

Even if it had been widely known in the spring of 1959 that 'Higher Biblical Criticism' kept bad company, neither that, nor any report from the writers of the four Gospels as to Christ's life, death and supposed

6. https://en.wikipedia.org/wiki/University_of_Tübingen#Nazi_period, accessed 3 March 2020.

resurrection, could be treated as evidence in a modern court of law – and in the case of the authors of the gospel narratives, whether Matthew, Mark, Luke or John, or any supposed later reviser, simply because they had never had a way to register their copyright!

Faced with an absence of first-hand evidence, a modern court of law is forced on occasion to rely on the testimony of expert witnesses: if it is a road accident, to call in investigators who can reasonably surmise what took place, and who may even have heard the reports of victims before they died. In the spring of 1959, weighing evidence for the Christian faith, I resolved to call in as my expert witness one Saul of Tarsus.

Since that decision, it has always seemed to me that to read the New Testament through and, especially, to admit Saul of Tarsus as your expert witness, is akin to committing yourself to a round of Russian Roulette: the odds are so stacked against an unbeliever that you stand to lose not only control of your life but also the shirt off your back. A sensible person might well choose to avoid the experience altogether.

But if it were a court of law that was attempting to settle, say, rights of inheritance to the estate of a deceased person – in this instance, to the legacy of a certain Jesus of Nazareth – it would need to take evidence, spoken or written, from anyone who claimed to have been his companion or to know his wishes, and also to seek help from someone who could assist over what might prove to be the most thorny of inheritance problems – whether this Jesus had in fact risen from the dead, and whether or not his current wishes had been consulted.

What then is the evidential status of the four Gospels, the Acts of the Apostles, the collection of twenty-one Letters allegedly by contemporary witnesses, and also of that late arrival in the canon of Scripture, the Book of Revelation, which all together make up the New Testament?

The Gospel of John claims to be the record of 'the disciple whom Jesus loved' (John 13: 23, 19: 26-27, 20: 2, 21: 7, 21: 20-24). Clement of Alexandria (c.150-c.215 CE) is reported by Eusebius in his *Ecclesiastical History* 6.14.7 (around 323 C.E.) as attesting that John wrote it when an old man serving at Ephesus (a major Greek city in what is now Turkey) – John's intention being to supplement accounts by the three earlier gospel writers, Mark, Matthew and Luke, whose 'synoptic' view (i.e. their 'looking from a common standpoint') John sought to amplify and adjust.

It is clear from Paul's letters, and also from those whom we now call 'the Early Church Fathers', that what was, in those initial centuries, effectively a new religion was beset by disputes with potential yet dissident adherents. Challenges came not just from those who wished to align faith in Jesus Christ more fully with the Judaism from which it sprang: there were also' many who had alternative creeds, new and old, classical or pagan, who sought to assimilate Christianity to their own position (a situation not so different from today). Hence, the question as to who had written what became of major importance to Christians, not least because of the number of alternative 'gospels' circulating, produced by sects such as the Gnostics. Irenaeus (c.140-203 C.E.) in his *Adversus Haereses* ('Against the Heretics') at 1.31.1 condemns a 'Gospel of Judas', and again, at 3.11.9, he rejects 'the followers of Valentinian's recent composition', *The Gospel of Truth*. Tertullian (c.155-240 C.E.), in *Against Praxeas*, when seeking to defend what was emerging as the standard understanding of the relation between the three persons of the Trinity, Father, Son and Holy Spirit, points to key passages in the Gospel of John, especially John 14: 9-10, as being his most reliable evidence.

Because the Gospel of John seems to claim explicitly that it is an account by an eye-witness, and has also had its authorship attested by early Church historians, it has attracted a particular scepticism from successors to the Tübingen School, in what has now become a vast and internationally competitive industry for biblical scholarship. The modern university is increasingly a place where appointments, promotions and the social and financial rewards that go with them require not just adequate knowledge and the skill to teach, but a good record also in research – research that is increasingly modelled on the procedures of the natural sciences, in challenging old suppositions with repeated observational evidence from which more accurate underlying principles might be derived. The academic disciplines that deal with history and literature have well-established techniques for discussing ancient texts – though not the religious assumptions that may underlie them. A plausible challenge to authorship or dating becomes big news – especially if, as in the case of scripture, it is also a chance to challenge with fashionable scepticism any underlying beliefs. Hence, the crack that was current about academic departments of religion when I first hit Cambridge in the 1950's, and is still current today: 'What does the Divinity Faculty teach?' – 'The Cambridge Divinity Faculty teaches you to doubt whatever you believe.'

A preference for regarding the Gospel of John in its current form as composed well into the second century of the Christian era has been somewhat qualified by the discovery of Rylands Library Papyrus P52. This is an early New Testament fragment in Greek of St John's Gospel, that had got by that time as far as Egypt and has been dated by its handwriting to around 125 C.E. the content of which I had already chosen before writing this, either by chance or providentially, to be the epigraph for my previous chapter. Some more modern estimates of when the Gospel of John was first composed would now put its date of writing as early as the fifties of the first Christian Era or, at the latest, to before 70 C.E., and we shall look shortly at the evidence for so definite a claim.

But as someone who can claim some expertise in the techniques for dating ancient literary and historical texts, arguments for dating the composition of New Testament documents often seem to me a case of seeking evidence for what you already want to find: I am impressed by the protest of Brent Nongbri, a papyrologist who examined that fragment from St John's Gospel, Rylands Library Papyrus P52, and who observes: 'The real problem is the way scholars have used and abused papyrological evidence.'[7]

That said, the degree of personal affirmation and of proximity to key events may vary markedly between different New Testament writers. At one extreme is the author of the Epistle to the Hebrews, who never gives his name but is clearly knowledgeable about Jewish traditions and customs, and chiefly concerned with what recent events imply for believers from the old faith. Only because the authors' stance is so similar did later Church historians attribute the Epistle to the Hebrews to St Paul – though whether Paul was actually the author was questioned at a very early stage.

At the other extreme is the author of the Gospel attributed to St John, who both directly and indirectly through his amanuensis appears to present himself as 'the disciple whom Jesus loved', and hence (if somewhat coyly) a privileged eye-witness to all that Jesus said or did and also to his resurrection. John's semi-anonymity may be because, as Clement of Alexandria attested, he wrote in old age to amplify, adjust and even correct the previous gospels known to him, but was (or so I surmise) reluctant to 'pull rank' or to seem to be gainsaying his predecessors. As someone who has been required to give evidence to a Royal Commission thirty or more years after the events I was asked to report on, I also understand how edgy one becomes at relying on one's memory for precise details, however memorable, after such a lapse of time.

The three earlier 'synoptic' Gospels, those attributed to Matthew, Mark and Luke, all have their authorship unanimously attested by the early Church Fathers. All three have substantial material in common, and all three depend on both written and oral traditions. The circumstances of writing can best be understood from Luke's own prefaces, the preface to his Gospel and that to the 'Acts of the Apostles', both of them dedicated

---

7. Brent Nongbri, 'The Use and Abuse of P52: Papyrological Pitfalls in the Dating of the Fourth Gospel, *Harvard Theological Review,* Vol. 98, no. 1 (2005), pp. 23-48.

to the same literary patron, probably a local dignitary, 'Most Excellent Theophilus' – unless we take this patron to be imaginary, in which case the dedication might be translated: 'To a Dedicated Lover of God'. Luke's Gospel begins:

> Many have undertaken to draw up an account of the things that have been fulfilled among us, just as they were handed down to us by those who from the first were eyewitnesses and servants of the word. Therefore, since I myself have carefully investigated everything from the beginning, it seemed good also to me to write an orderly account for you, most excellent Theophilus, so that you may know the certainty of the things you have been taught.
> (Luke 1: 1-4)

Luke's two prefaces, to his Gospel and to his 'Acts of the Apostles', give us a very plausible insight into how the writers of the New Testament put together their accounts: from personal reminiscences, from traditions oral and written, and probably from established collections of Christ's sayings and parables, which bear the hallmark of a single and unique voice. However, there is, throughout the writings of the New Testament, and with only one exception, a general reluctance to let the personal intrude too much into what was seen as universal, transnational and cosmic.

The Gospel of Matthew, agreed by all the early Church Fathers to be from Matthew the Apostle, offers nothing that explicitly invokes Matthew's apostolic authority or even claims to be evidence from a first-hand witness.

As for the Gospel of Mark, universally attested by the Church Fathers to be by John Mark, subsequently a fellow-worker with Paul, Luke and Barnabas, the author seems to have slipped in, but only as a reminder for those who already knew, that he himself was complicit in the momentous events he records. Mark tells us that the chief priests, the teachers of the law and the elders sent an armed mob to arrest Jesus, and Judas identified Christ for them with a kiss. At that point 'everyone deserted him and fled'. But the gospel-writer adds:

> A young man, wearing nothing but a linen garment, was following Jesus.
>   When they seized him, he fled naked, leaving his garment behind'.
> (Mark 14: 50-52)

This reads like a personal recollection, admissible perhaps because Mark was confessing to having shared in the great betrayal. Otherwise, it is left to Papias (c.95-c.120 CE), a first century Bishop of Hierapolis (now Pamukkale in modern Turkey), in his five-volume study, *Explanation of the Sayings of the Lord* (now lost except for fragments quoted by later writers), to report what to us is so important: that Mark, 'the companion and Greek translator of St Peter', wrote the earliest Gospel after having listened to Peter relate accounts of Jesus' life and teachings during their travels together.'[8]

When it comes to evaluating New Testament accounts of the miraculous, some modern biblical scholars, in what is now an international academic forum, advocate avoiding discussion altogether, claiming that it is only open to students of the past to decide between probabilities and miracles are, by definition, improbable.

Such evasion, presumably to avoid offending a prevailing zeitgeist, reminds me of Basil Fawlty of *Fawlty Towers*, when instructing staff on the prudent handling of paying guests from Germany: 'Don't mention the War!'

The spectacular if ambiguous advances of modern science, with its capacity to modify for good or ill the circumstances of all life, depend on an accurate understanding of *what is*, achieved through repeated observation and the deduction of underlying principles from what has been observed. Even the laws of physics must be revised to accommodate reports of waves and particles that behave contrary to expectation. But when it comes to conclusions drawn from those observations recorded by New Testament writers, the accounts that seem most persuasive to a modern enquirer are often those where the writer seems unaware of the full significance of what he is reporting.

I have myself received reports of miraculous events from two close friends whom I would trust with my life. One was the Cambridge Anglican priest who prepared my Indian wife for baptism, who was also chaplain to a Cambridge group of enquirers, the Epiphany Philosophers, and who drew our attention to a journal which investigated, for instance, a nomadic tribe whose whole life depended on a shaman who could accurately intuit where wild game was to be found. The same priest would also ring us to report on his prayer group for the sick whenever they had sought relief for a cancer sufferer whose tumour had then miraculously disappeared.

The second friend, whom I met when we were both members of the Church of England Liturgical Commission, and who is now a retired Bishop, gave me two accounts of abnormal occurrences where he had

8. https://www.newworldencyclopedia.org/entry/Papias.

been a direct participant. The first event was a 'laying on of hands', where he had been engaged in group prayer for a man who had been born with one leg shorter than the other. As they prayed and laid on hands, he felt a heat run through the defective limb, there was a shuddering sensation and the leg lengthened to match the other.

His second account of supernatural events was more disturbing. Being then on the staff of a theological college, he had been approached by a recently ordained student who celebrated the communion service on weekdays in a local church. The student asked my friend for advice on how to cope with a repeated disturbance, by which the communion vessels and accompanying instruments would bounce about on the holy table whenever he began to celebrate. My friend thought he should see for himself – and confirmed that everything did indeed 'bob about like crazy'.

I have not named my informants: in the first case because the witness is dead and I cannot ask his permission to quote him; in the second, because I share a general reluctance to expose such testimony to a prevailing scepticism that would group such accounts with the claims of fraudulent faith-healers. My third reason is that I have a certain preference for witnesses who tell me more than they are consciously aware of telling.

A prime instance is the 'we' passages in the Acts of the Apostles[9], the second volume of a record traditionally attributed to Luke, the companion of Paul, where use of the first person plural is generally understood to indicate episodes where the writer himself was a participant in the events described and may even be drawing on notes or a diary entry made at the time of the incident.

The first passage that uses the first person plural is worth repeating in full:

> Once when we were going to the place of prayer, we were met by a slave girl who had a spirit by which she predicted the future. She earned a great deal of money for her owners by fortune-telling. This girl followed Paul and the rest of us, shouting, "These men are servants of the Most High God, who are telling you the way to be saved." She kept this up for many days. Finally Paul became so troubled that he turned around and said to the spirit, "In the name of Jesus Christ I command you to come out of her!" At that moment the spirit left her. When the owners of the slave girl realized that their hope of making money was gone, they seized Paul and Silas and dragged them into the marketplace to face the authorities. (*Acts* 16: 16-19)

9. Acts of the Apostles 16:10-18, 20:5-21:18, 27:1-28:16.

What this first-hand witness tells us as modern readers is that Paul was perhaps 'on a short fuse' (as we might have deduced from his surviving letters) – but also that the slave girl was a *pythona*, involuntarily possessed by a demonic power analogous to that of the oracle at Delphi, which enabled her to predict the future with sufficient accuracy as to be of financial benefit to her owners. It gave her access to the same knowledge as that of the demons, so she was able accurately to identify the role and mission of the apostles in the divine plan. But though she tells truth, she does it under demonic control, so needs to be treated as a victim rather than as someone inherently evil.

Where a passage in Acts next uses 'we' to indicate that this is the testimony of an eyewitness, we find Luke displaying an understandable irritation at Paul's tendency to 'spin things out a bit':

> On the first day of the week we came together to break bread. Paul spoke to the people and, because he intended to leave the next day, kept on talking until midnight. There were many lamps in the upstairs room where we were meeting. Seated in a window was a young man named Eutychus, who was sinking into a deep sleep as Paul talked on and on. When he was sound asleep, he fell to the ground from the third story and was picked up dead. Paul went down, threw himself on the young man and put his arms around him. 'Don't be alarmed,' he said. 'He's alive!' Then he went upstairs again and broke bread and ate. After talking until daylight, he left. The people took the young man home alive and were greatly comforted.
> (*Acts of the Apostles* 20: 7-12)

What reading this, almost two thousand years after it was written, authenticates it for me as an eye-witness account, is that Luke never troubles to clarify whether this was a resuscitation or a resurrection: when Paul picks the boy up, the Greek translates literally, 'Don't be alarmed: for his spirit is in him'. Paul, as a follower of Christ, might both revive people and raise them from the dead, and there was no need to specify which. But a fabricator or a mere re-teller of the story would be likely to go for the more miraculous claim.

In subsequent passages in Acts where the writer uses the first person plural, he is a witness to a whole culture of Christians who believe in the power of prophecy to predict the future. Most commonly, they give warnings as to the imminent approach of evil, as when Paul and his companions are at Caesarea on the way to Jerusalem:

After we had been there a number of days, a prophet named Agabus came down from Judea. Coming over to us, he took Paul's belt, tied his own hands and feet with it and said, 'The Holy Spirit says, "In this way the Jews of Jerusalem will bind the owner of this belt and will hand him over to the Gentiles."'
(*Acts of the Apostles*, 21: 10-11)

Where Paul and his fellow-Christians are shown to be distinct from the pagan cultures around them is in their response to any evil foretold. Like the Jews before them, they believe that, whether it can be avoided or not, evil remains within the knowledge and control of a benevolent Providence that can frustrate any malign purpose and turn evil to good.

The last and most lengthy of the 'we' passages, in Acts, 27: 1-44 and 28: 1-16, gives us an extended portrait of Paul in action, from an observer and fellow-worker. After all the hostility, attacks, legal hearings, delays, further enquiries, prolonged imprisonment, and Paul's eventual exercise of his legal right as a Roman citizen to appeal to Caesar, Luke and Paul are together on the hazardous journey to Rome, under military supervision.

After a change of ship and 'slow headway for many days' (Acts 27: 7), they arrive at 'a place called Fair Havens, near the town of Lasea' (27: 8). There Paul gives a warning based on a reasonable presumption of adverse weather, yet with a suggestion of fore-knowledge: 'Men, I can see that our voyage is going to be disastrous and bring great loss to ship and cargo, and to our own lives also' (27: 10). But expert opinion, that of the pilot and of the owner of the vessel, wins the day and they decide to sail on. Then follows one of the most vivid accounts in world literature of a disaster at sea – even if it tells us much more than that:

When a gentle south wind began to blow, they thought they had obtained what they wanted; so they weighed anchor and sailed along the shore of Crete. Before very long, a wind of hurricane force, called the 'northeaster', swept down from the island. The ship was caught by the storm, and could not head into the wind; so we gave way to it and were driven along. As we passed in the lee of a small island called Cauda, we were hardly able to make the lifeboat secure. When the men had hoisted it aboard, they passed ropes under the ship to hold it together. Fearing that they would run aground on the sandbars of Syrtis, they lowered the sea anchor and let the ship be driven along. We took such a violent battering from the storm that the next day they began to throw the cargo overboard. On the third day, they threw the ship's

tackle overboard with their own hands. When neither sun nor stars appeared for many days and the storm continued raging, we finally gave up all hope of being saved.
(*Acts of the Apostles*, 27: 13-20)

At this point, the new although prophesied incursion into history asserts itself, and Paul as spokesman for the risen Christ takes control:

After the men had gone for a long time without food, Paul stood up before them and said: 'Men, you should have taken my advice not to sail from Crete; then you would have spared yourselves this damage and loss. But now I urge you to keep up your courage, because not one of you will be lost; only the ship will be destroyed. Last night an angel of the God whose I am and whom I serve stood beside me and said, "Do not be afraid, Paul. You must stand trial before Caesar; and God has graciously given you the lives of all who sail with you." So keep up your courage, men, for I have faith in God that it will happen just as he told me. Nevertheless, we must run aground on some island'.
(*Acts of the Apostles*, 27: 21-26)

Paul, with his newly recognized authority, intervenes again later, when the ship's crew attempt to abandon the vessel and all in it by launching the lifeboat, ostensibly so as to lower some anchors from the bow:

Then Paul said to the centurion and the sailors, 'Unless these men stay with the ship, you cannot be saved.' So the soldiers cut the ropes that held the lifeboat and let it fall away.
(*Acts of the Apostles*, 27: 31-32)

The sense that there is a new unrecognized power in control, whose standards must be met if you hope to benefit from his benign provision, extends even to the military:

The soldiers planned to kill the prisoners to prevent any of them from swimming away and escaping. But the centurion wanted to spare Paul's life and kept them from carrying out their plan. He ordered those who could swim to jump overboard first and get to land. The rest were to get there on planks or pieces of the ship. In this way everyone reached land in safety.
(*Acts of the Apostles*, 27: 42-44)

Thus is fulfilled the promise of the angel to Paul that 'God has graciously given you the lives of all who sail with you', as attested by the personal records that the writer of Acts presents himself as having to hand. The author cannot have been unaware, when composing his account, that he is claiming a unique authority, and he makes use of it in Chapter 28, when retailing what seems initially to be just a personal reminiscence:

> Once safely on shore, we found out that the island was called Malta. The islanders showed us unusual kindness. They built a fire and welcomed us all because it was raining and cold. Paul gathered a pile of brushwood and, as he put it on the fire, a viper, driven out by the heat, fastened itself on his hand. When the islanders saw the snake hanging from his hand, they said to each other, 'This man must be a murderer, for though he escaped from the sea, Justice has not allowed him to live.' But Paul shook the snake off into the fire and suffered no ill effects. The people expected him to swell up or suddenly fall dead, but after waiting a long time and seeing nothing unusual happen to him, they changed their minds and said he was a god.
> (*Acts of the Apostles,* 28: 1-6)

The author is, of course, not unaware that he is making the case as an apparent eyewitness for subsequent claims that are similarly established by his special authority. We are told that 'Publius, the chief official of the island . . . welcomed us to his home and for three days entertained us hospitably':

> His father was sick in bed, suffering from fever and dysentery. Paul went in to see him and, after prayer, placed his hands on him and healed him. When this had happened, the rest of the sick on the island came and were cured. They honoured us in many ways and when we were ready to sail, they furnished us with the supplies we needed.
> (*Acts of the Apostles,* 28: 8-10)

As a twenty-first century reader, I find myself viewing this evidence, both for a malignity in the animal kingdom from which some may be given immunity and for the capacity of certain believers to heal by prayer, as being akin to those reports from certain of my friends of known honesty and reliability, who also attest to the reality of unusual powers, whether maleficent or benign.

But as I suggested earlier, it is the eye-witness evidence that the author of the 'we' passages in Acts gives incidentally and without obvious intent that I find most valuable – especially in countering a corroding, if unfounded, cynicism in Departments of Religion which panders to the modern taste for confrontation. It is undeniable that Paul contested vehemently any attempt by the Christian Church to effect a reconciliation with Jewish custom as regards complete compliance with Mosaic Law. However, it is a violation of truth to present Paul as leader of a dissident clique, when he had by his own account checked what he taught with senior figures in the Jerusalem Church, had been influential in a crucial debate of the early Church on the topic, the so-called 'Council of Jerusalem', and had rebuked even Simon Peter at Antioch for compromising for the sake of goodwill. That this was understood and not resented can be established by a passing remark in Acts, at the commencement of Paul's final visit:

After this, we got ready and went up to Jerusalem. Some of the disciples from Caesarea accompanied us and brought us to the home of Mnason, where we were to stay. He was a man from Cyprus and one of the early disciples. When we arrived at Jerusalem, the brothers received us warmly. The next day Paul and the rest of us went to see James, and all the elders were present. Paul greeted them and reported in detail what God had done among the Gentiles through his ministry.
(*Acts of the Apostles,* 21: 15-20)

The Jerusalem Christians, after their 'warm reception' of the visitors and after praising God for Paul's work among the Gentiles, then raise a difficulty which had arisen among the 'many thousands' of Jewish converts – one created by an allegation that Paul taught Jews 'who live among the Gentiles to turn away from Moses, telling them not to circumcise their children or live according to our customs'. The Jerusalem elders repeat their own minimal instructions to Gentile believers, that they should 'abstain from food sacrificed to idols, from blood, from the meat of strangled animals and from sexual immorality'. Paul is then advised to assist four men who have undertaken a vow, to 'join in their purification rites and pay their expenses' at the Temple, as an indication of Paul's 'obedience to the law' – and Paul consents (Acts 21: 17-26). None of this suggests anything more than a genuine difficulty and a willingness on Paul's part to help defuse an awkward misunderstanding – a long way from any modern myth of two hostile camps.

To turn back now from ancient texts to more modern writings, it is difficult and perhaps unwise of me to admit this openly, but though I have had extensive experience in discussing the content and dating of literary texts from the past, neither William Shakespeare nor Thomas Middleton ever gave me one fraction of the trouble that my enquiries into the authorship and dating of New Testament records have occasioned. Admittedly, the pens and pencils on my desk do not, as yet, bob about uninvited. But the contrast with my past experience is now bizarre – and not least because I am at present merely gathering evidence in support of what have been my long-term beliefs. I am racked with pain in every nerve and muscle, yet without any obvious medical causation. There is a consequent lack of sleep, appalling nightmares if I do doze off, and an unremitting pressure day and night to desist from what I am doing. I would like to think that defenders of atheistic neo-Darwinism are similarly troubled – but somehow I doubt it.

It is perhaps more than time to bring in once again my expert witness, one Saul of Tarsus, in Greek calling himself Paul, who on behalf of the religious authorities in Jerusalem journeyed to Damascus to make enquiries into the beliefs and practices of a dissident sect that based themselves on the life, teachings, death and supposed resurrection of one Jesus of Nazareth, whom they took to have been the promised Messiah. By Paul's own admission, he himself persecuted the nascent Christian Church 'beyond measure' (Galatians 1: 13-14) – something he also owned up to when writing to the Philippians (3: 5-6) and which is further confirmed by his companion Luke's reports, both on Paul's youthful complicity in the mob-stoning of Stephen and also on his enthusiastic involvement in the house-to-house persecution of Jerusalem Christians that followed (*Acts of the Apostles* 8: 1-3).

Yet however aggressive Paul may have been, he had done what I could never do: he had made enquiries on the spot, no more than one to six years after Christ's crucifixion and alleged resurrection. And what is more, though he had been commissioned to round up supposedly dissident fanatics, his first-hand investigations turned him into that delight of court reporters: a Crown investigator whose fidelity to truth has compelled him to become a prime witness for the defence.

Saul (who seems to have preferred the more cosmopolitan version of his name, Paul) was someone the writers of *Upstart Crow* might see as most likely to appeal to the equivalent of the 'Oxbridge poshboys'. He hailed from Tarsus, a small but decently prosperous city in Asia Minor at the north-east corner of the Mediterranean – which even had a quite reputable university. He came from a well-heeled family who had some possible connection to royalty and could afford to send him to complete his studies in the big city. Once in Jerusalem, he became a pupil of Gamaliel, a leading scholar amongst the Pharisees of the Hillel school, where he studied further in Jewish traditions but was also able to pick up more than a smattering of the dominant international culture of Greece and Rome, its classics of literature, history, philosophy and ethics.

Once the established authorities – an uneasy combination of imposed Roman governor with traditional royal and religious leadership – got to hear about Paul, he was employed in a semi-official capacity to investigate a recent, disruptive sect and, if possible, to bring it to heel. What intrigues me about this 'Oxbridge poshboy' is that Paul was in a position to do what I cannot: face to face he interrogated witnesses to what had only recently taken place: the alleged judicial murder of one Jesus of Nazareth, who 'on the third day', and bearing the marks of his crucifixion, had risen from the dead.

Paul, on his conversion to that faith, seems to have had from the social and intellectual establishment much the same reception as a modern media-figure might, if he or she were to start wearing a caftan and then declare allegiance to some Asian cult. Though it may be acceptable to mock them and make their life more difficult where you can – they remain 'one of us', despite their oddities, and there are limits to the degree of persecution.

As a consequence, Paul was at liberty, for a period of some thirty years between the probable date of his conversion by a vision on the road to Damascus around 33 to 36 CE and up until his death, reportedly by beheading under the Emperor Nero between 64 and 67 CE, to propagate his strange but well-researched beliefs. He did so from Antioch in the east to Rome in the west, and at suitable points between – and possibly, after what is the supposed success of his appeal to Caesar, even as far as Spain. Though we do not have any surviving transcript of Paul's initial interrogations of Christians, Paul's First Letter to the Corinthians summarizes what he termed his 'gospel', the εὐαγγέλιον or 'good news':

> For what I received I passed on to you as of first importance: that Christ died for our sins according to the Scriptures, that he was buried, that he was raised on the third day according to the Scriptures, and that he appeared to Peter, and then to the Twelve. After that, he appeared to more than five hundred of the brothers at the same time, most of whom are still living, though some have fallen asleep. Then he appeared to James, then to all the apostles, and last of all he appeared to me also, as to one abnormally born.
> (1 Corinthians 15: 3-8)

Paul's personal researches, reported in his Letters, serve to corroborate and amplify details that appear in Luke's 'Acts of the Apostles', which was clearly intended as a record of the early Church. Where Luke tells us in Acts I: 15-26 that the eleven remaining Apostles determined to elect a successor to the traitor Judas and set as a basic condition that the new Apostle must have been an eye-witness to Christ's resurrection, Paul in his first Letter to the Corinthians gives us an idea of just how many could potentially have met that criterion.

Then, as now, there was no escaping the bright young man from Tarsus. Within thirty years of his first enquiry into Christianity's foundational events, Paul had formulated its essential doctrines, set up its organizational structures and propagated internationally what was, in effect, a new world religion. If he felt you or your community could be getting out of touch, he might well send you a letter:

An early fragment of the Second Epistle of Paul to the Corinthians.

Above is a page from a papyrus manuscript, most of it in the Chester Beatty Library, Dublin, but with some portions in the University of

Michigan[10], The manuscript contains the whole or a part of nine of the letters attributed to Paul, including Hebrews. The manuscript is judged to have been written at a point between 175 and 225 C.E., though dating of documents by their style of handwriting is not an exact science. But as a consequence of the subsequent discovery of an additional one hundred and forty Biblical papyri up until this present time of writing, November 2019, the old nineteenth-century style of sceptical criticism in the Tübingen mode has suffered the death of a thousand sheets, smothered beneath a mountain of Biblical papyri.

Why should this be so?

Nineteenth and early twentieth-century Biblical scholars such as David Friedrich Strauss, viewing the past from the standpoint of 'a more advanced civilisation', followed the practice of scientific disciplines that faced a parallel problem, and examined whatever might have survived from an age that was itself not directly observable. From classical myths and legends of the Gods, through Nordic sagas, legendary histories and fables, ancient Indian and other Asiatic sources, they surmised a process whereby primitive religious notions were transmitted, first by word of mouth, then by bardic elaboration, then finally in more sophisticated written interpretations – and therefore concluded that anything which presented itself in the Old and New Testaments as miraculous could not have been observed fact but was in reality the product of human imagination and an extended evolutionary process.

Such comfortable scepticism received a massive blow from the translation of a curiosity purchased on the Egyptian antiquities market in 1920. A fragment of writing on papyrus – a poor quality paper later superseded in Europe by more durable materials such as parchment or vellum – it had waited fourteen years to be translated by Colin H. Roberts in 1934: when it turned out to be a fragment of St John's Gospel in Greek: John, chapter 18: verses 31-33.

Till then, the earliest known copies of the Christian scriptures were the finely written codices on vellum or parchment, of which the most famous were the Codex Sinaiticus, written not before 325 C.E., the Codex Vaticanus, widely known to nineteenth-century Biblical scholars and dated to the fourth century of the Christian era, and also the Codex Alexandrinus, given to Charles I of England in 1627, and thought to have been written in the fourth to fifth centuries of the Christian era but not before 373 C.E.

---

10. The photograph, from Wikipedia Commons, is of one side of a double-sided papyrus sheet from P46 in the Chester Beatty Library, Dublin, containing 2 Corinthians 11:33-12:9.

Putting it bluntly, to commit your most intimate thoughts, let alone sacred texts, to papyrus was akin to writing on toilet paper. Made from the pith of the papyrus plant, a wetland sedge, papyrus paper was a cheap alternative to vellum, simple to produce but fragile and easily damaged, both by moisture and over-much dryness. The coarser type was used only for wrappings. A better quality was widely used for professional records – contracts, accounts, receipts and the like. Papyrus paper clogged the rubbish-heaps of the ancient world, and easily decayed: but in a dry climate like that of Egypt it could be more stable and might survive.

Why should the survival of twenty-nine fragments from Paul's letters, on papyrus and from various locations, and dated between 200 and 400 C.E., be such a big deal? First, because Paul is our earliest and most plausibly independent investigator into the circumstances of Christ's death and supposed resurrection; second, because the appearance of fragments of his letters from various sites around the ancient world gives us some idea of the circulation of Paul's writings in the early centuries of the Christian era; and third (and most destructive of wilful scepticism) because the gap between Paul's on-the-spot researches and the first written evidence we have from him is, by the discovery of these papyrus fragments, reduced by several hundred years. There was simply not enough time between Paul writing down his researches and the world at large being enabled to read them for any superstitious nonsense to accumulate and distort the record. I therefore invite the Court of Human Understanding to accept Paul's depositions as from a reliable reporter who also was a first-hand interrogator of witnesses.

In the sands of Egypt, further fragments of papyrus have lain in wait to confound the sceptic. In 250 C.E. the Emperor Decius, after killing his predecessor in battle and establishing himself in Rome, had his 'John Major moment'[11] of nostalgia for 'those good old days' when the traditional gods of the Empire had been appropriately venerated. Decius is reported to have instituted a comprehensive persecution of dissident sects and, in particular, of Christians (the Jews being officially exempt, since they belonged to a religion recognized by the Roman state). Empire-wide, anyone who would not offer sacrifice to the Roman deities was to be executed or thrown to the wild beasts as a popular entertainment. The Roman historian Tacitus in his *Annals* (c. 116 C.E.) had reported much earlier that Nero had tried to shift the blame for the Great Fire of Rome

---

11. John Major, speech to the Conservative Group for Europe, 22 April 1973: 'Fifty years from now Britain will still be the country of long shadows on county grounds, warm beer, invincible green suburbs, dog lovers and pools fillers and – as George Orwell said – "old maids bicycling to Holy Communion through the morning mist" and, if we get our way – Shakespeare still read even in school'.

in July 64 on to 'a class of men loathed for their vices' called 'Chrestianos', founded by one 'Christus', and Church historians such as Tertullian in his *Apologeticus* (c.197 C.E.) recorded other early persecutions of Christians. Eusebius, Bishop of Caesarea, in his *Ecclesiastical History* (probably first published in 313 C.E. and in final form before 325 C.E.) witnesses to the particularly traumatic affliction of Christians under Decius in 250 C.E.: prominent leaders such as Pope Fabian in Rome and Alexander of Jerusalem chose to be executed rather than renounce their faith, Patriarch Babylas of Antioch died in prison from the tortures inflicted on him, and Bishop Cyprian of Carthage chose to go into hiding.

The Enlightenment historian Edward Gibbon, in his *History of the Decline and Fall of the Roman Empire* (published in six volumes between 1776 and 1789), inclined to see Decius' Edict as directed specifically against a Christian threat, even though Gibbon himself was hostile to the organized religions of his day and saw the collapse of his admired classical civilization as a direct consequence of its embracing of Christianity. Nevertheless, living through the genesis of the French Revolution and about to witness the horrors consequent on abandoning religious belief in favour of a reliance on human reason alone, Gibbon was anxious to minimize what was already by then a widespread anxiety as to the unknown evils that might ensue. But the long line of sceptics who succeeded Gibbon have been concerned to downplay any reports of a widespread, organized and maintained persecution of Christians: accounts are dismissed as much exaggerated, a consequence of the susceptibility of the pious to mass paranoia and to the fatal lure of victim-status. Denial finally reached the point of questioning whether the supposed Imperial persecution under Decius had in fact been Empire-wide, whether it was especially directed against Christians, or even if it had amounted to anything much at all.

Then, from the rubbish-heaps of the Roman Empire, there surfaced first a text probably found at Fayoum in Egypt in 1893, then four texts from an archaeological site at Oxyrhynchus (modern Bahnasa), a town some 160 kilometres south-west of Cairo, and since then some forty-six *libelli* on papyrus, all of them certificates dated from the year of Decius' edict, 250 C.E., witnessing that individuals had sacrificed to the pagan gods.

The nature of Emperor Decius' demand and its empire-wide application is now well-established. Whether it was aimed particularly at the Christians depends on an estimate as to how far Christianity had penetrated by 250 C.E. Given that these *libelli* are found in the company of fragments of papyrus containing portions of the Old and New Testaments, the earliest of those New Testament papyri being dated to the middle of the second century C.E., only a century after the original documents were first written, it is likely (as

Christians have always maintained) that Christianity soon expanded to all parts of the known world. The total number of New Testament fragments so far identified in papyrus, up until 20 November 2019, amounts to 140, with many papyri yet to be examined. Here is an example of a libellus from the Decian persecution of 250 C.E. that has survived[12]:

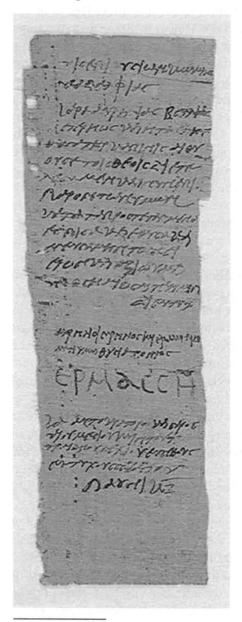

*To those in charge of the sacrifices of the village Theadelphia, from Aurelia Bellias,
daughter of Peteres, and her daughter, Karinis.*

We have always been constant in sacrificing to the gods, and now too in your presence, in accordance with the regulations, I have poured libations and sacrificed and tasted the offerings, and I ask you to certify this for us below. May you continue to prosper.

Under, written by another hand:

We, Aurelius Serenus and Aureius Hermas, saw you sacrificing.

A third hand,

I, Hermas, certify.

First hand:

The 1ˢᵗ year of the Emperor Caesar Gaius Messius Quintus Traianus Decius Pius Felix Augustus

---

12. Commons.wikimedia.org.wiki/Category: Libellus#/media/File: Libellus.jpg

Since my especial interest is in the letters of Paul, I note that there are thirty-eight segments from twelve of his Letters to be found among the papyri (excluding Hebrews from the count, since most modern scholars accept that epistle is not his), and only one is absent, the Second Letter to Timothy. This widespread representation, even in relatively obscure towns and villages of the Empire, suggests that by 250 C.E. Christian missions may well have infiltrated everywhere and so provoked an incoming Emperor to believe that their impiety toward the ancient Gods was at the root of all Rome's troubles.

The evidence is that from a very early date (as witnessed by the papyrus record) there were circulating nine authentic letters of Paul:

Letters of Paul to Various Recipients
(Hebrews is omitted as being by another author)

Letters	*Attested by Early Papyri* [13]
1 Thessalonians (c. 50 C.E.)	P30, P46, P65, P92
Galatians (c. 53)	P45, P46, P51, P135
1 Corinthians (c. 53-54 C.E.)	P15, P45, P46, P123, P129
Philippians (c. 55 C.E.)	P16, P45
Philemon (c. 56 C.E.)	P87, P139
2 Corinthians (c. 55 C.E.)	P45, P46
Romans (c. 57 C.E.)	P10, P27, P40, P45, P56, P113, P118, P131
Colossians (c. 62 C.E.)	P45
2 Thessalonians (c. 49-51 C.E.)	P30, P92

Letters attributed to Paul but held by some to be doubtfully his

Ephesians (c. 62 C.E.)	P45, P46, P47, P49, P92, P132
1 Timothy (c. 62-64 C.E.)	P133
2 Timothy (c. 62-64 C.E.)	(none)
Titus (c. 62-64 C.E.)	P32

Lost Epistles

There was an earlier letter to the Corinthians mentioned by Paul at 1 Corinthians 5: 9, a third letter to the Corinthians mentioned by Paul at 2 Corinthians 2: 4 and also at 7: 8-9 and an earlier letter to the Ephesians referred to at Ephesians 3: 3-4. There was also an 'Epistle to the Laodiceans' mentioned in Colossians 4: 16, one that, since it seemed to be missing,

---

13. See: https://en.wikipedia.org/wiki/List_of_New_Testament_papyri, accessed 29 November 2019.

some early forger was encouraged to supply! No Greek text of that forgery remains but what may be a Latin translation in the Codex Fuldensis, written between 541 and 546 C.E., found its way at the Reformation into a number of early printed Bibles. An 'Epistle to the Laodiceans' is mentioned in the Muratorian Canon (c. 180 C.E.) and that may be the same epistle of which St Jerome (c. 342-420 C.E.) said: 'It is rejected by all.'

Since I admit to having based my whole understanding of life and of my own place and direction in it on an enquirer who reached his conclusions nearly two thousand years ago, and since I have also been active for more than sixty years in persuading others to do the same, I need to be very sure that Paul's conclusions are reported as accurately as may be, that his methods of enquiry were as near perfect as possible and (most important of all) that his character and conduct were such as I would expect from my closest friend.

We have two written accounts in Letters from Paul that record his moment of decision, the First Letter to the Corinthians, 15: 3-8 and that to the Galatians, 1: 11-17. It is, however, the reports given by Paul's companion Luke in the Book of Acts that give the greater detail, the fullest being Luke's account of Paul's speech before King Agrippa II of Judea, when Agrippa, with his sister and supposed mistress, Berenice, entertained the new Roman Governor, Festus, by holding a formal hearing.

Since Paul, arrested at a public upheaval in Jerusalem, had exercised his right as a Roman citizen to appeal to Caesar, a written account for the Emperor of the evidence for and against Paul would have been necessary, though no record of that survives. But bear in mind that Luke, in reporting in Acts Paul's speech before King Agrippa, has elsewhere given us an indication that he liked to keep a private record, as witnessed by the 'we' passages in Acts. Paul, as reported by Luke, gives to Agrippa a detailed account of the process of his conversion:

> I too was convinced that I ought to do all that was possible to oppose the name of Jesus of Nazareth. And that is just what I did in Jerusalem. On the authority of the chief priests I put many of the saints in prison, and when they were put to death, I cast my vote against them. Many a time I went from one synagogue to another to have them punished, and I tried to force them to blaspheme. In my obsession against them, I even went to foreign cities to persecute them.
>
> On one of these journeys I was going to Damascus with the authority and commission of the chief priests. About noon, O king, as I was on the road, I saw a light from heaven, brighter than

the sun, blazing around me and my companions. We all fell to the ground, and I heard a voice saying to me in Aramaic, 'Saul, Saul, why do you persecute me? It is hard for you to kick against the goads.'

Then I asked, 'Who are you, Lord?' 'I am Jesus, whom you are persecuting', the Lord replied. 'Now get up and stand on your feet. I have appeared to appoint you as a servant and a witness of what you have seen of me and what I will show you. I will rescue you from your own people and from the Gentiles. I am sending you to them to open their eyes and turn them from darkness to light, and from the power of Satan to God, so that they may receive forgiveness of sins and a place among those who are sanctified by faith in me'.

(*Acts of the Apostles,* 26: 9-18)

I confess that I am sufficiently a product of my twentieth-century Oxbridge education as to become very edgy when anyone starts to talk about their 'visions'. I have heard Metropolitan Anthony of Sourozh speak of having a vision of Christ when he was a young man in Paris, and my Sydney doctor tells of walking alone on an Australian beach and feeling himself looked through to his inner core of selfishness by a Presence that surrounded him on every side. But though I do not question the truthfulness of both witnesses, I remain edgy. If one of my pupils were to claim a vision had converted him to jihadism, demanding that he murder the infidel even at the cost of his own life but with the expectation of paradise as an eternal reward, I would immediately call for a psychiatric investigation.

However, I have previously hailed the reliability of the test 'By their fruit you shall know them' (Matthew 7: 16), and the fruit of Paul's alleged vision was anything but malign. From violently persecuting a religious minority, he turned suddenly to promoting that same movement, which took as its fundamental premise the unique value of each individual in the universal fellowship of mankind. Moreover, the practical results for Paul were a lifetime of achievement in the face of many obstacles, a high level of personal satisfaction, and many centuries of gratitude from a large community (including myself) who attest to the profound benefits we have received from his work.

What were the phenomena that accompanied this alleged 'vision' of Paul's and how are they to be explained? As an amateur psychologist, I would point to one comment from the visionary Christ that I have not seen remarked on elsewhere but which would illuminate Paul's state of mind, whether the vision was self-induced or simply what Paul held it to be, a divine intervention. Christ in the vision observes 'It is hard for you to kick against the goads' (Acts 26: 14). Just what are these 'goads' that, like the whip used on a beast of burden, drive Paul in a direction that he does not wish to take? I suggest the 'goads' or 'pricks' can be only one thing: the reiterated testimony from those whom Paul has been persecuting, that one Jesus Christ of Nazareth was seen alive after he was put to death.

Now I must face a challenge that my dependence on Paul as a reliable witness compels me to accept. Was Paul's vision on the road to Damascus a true revelation, or some kind of delusion explainable by alternative means?

The facts as reported are not much contested. According to Acts 22: 1-11, Paul about noon, when nearing Damascus with authority from 'the high priest and all the council' to round up members of a dissident Jewish sect known as 'The Way' and to bring them back to Jerusalem for punishment, was struck by a 'bright light from heaven', 'fell to the ground and heard a voice say to me, "Saul! Saul! Why do you persecute me?"' Paul asks who is speaking, and the voice identifies itself as "Jesus of Nazareth, whom you are persecuting". Paul asks for instructions, and is then told what he must do.

There seem to be small discrepancies with parallel accounts from Acts, so that it is a question whether Paul's companions merely heard the sound of a voice or whether they actually understood what it was saying (compare Acts 9: 7 with Acts 22: 9). Amongst those intent on discrediting the whole episode, much is made of such differences – but it is likely that the problem arises from the same ambiguity in Greek as in English over the meanings of the verb 'to hear': if my wife tinkles the dinner-bell, I may shout 'I hear you'. If she rings again, I may shout 'I HEAR you!' – meaning 'I've got the message, I understand!'

The question of the truth of Paul's vision, or of any vision for that matter, is an acute problem for those of Richard Dawkins' persuasion: if observation seems to suggest a spiritual power underlying all existence, any such suggestion must be rejected as nonsense forthwith, or your whole sceptical edifice will collapse. When the neo-Darwinists were once again confronted by evidence for 'Intelligent Design', the new information presented by Michael Behe and his colleagues had to be denied discussion, since the facts could not be effectively challenged. If it comes to a question of the genuineness of spiritual Vision, a sceptic must immediately discount any supposed evidence by showing it to be fraudulent or caused by some serious mental disturbance.

But the difficulty there is that the evidence for Paul's physical or mental sickness is extremely thin and of limited duration, whilst the evidence for his mental health and physical endurance over several decades is very strong. Paul saw a bright light, fell to the ground, heard a voice speaking to him, got up – 'but when he opened his eyes, he could see nothing. So they led him by the hand into Damascus. For three days he was blind and did not eat or drink anything' (Acts 9: 8-9). Some medical journals have suggested that recurring epilepsy was the 'thorn in the flesh', otherwise 'the messenger of Satan', that Paul reports God as refusing to heal (2 Corinthians 12: 7-9), though there is no other record of Paul suffering any such disability. In my Boy Scout days, a scout guidebook judged Paul's ailment to be the habit of masturbation, which God did not treat as anything much to worry about! Yet the paucity of evidence for any major underlying sickness in Paul has not prevented a burst of academic papers beginning in the 1970s to 1980s, examples of which I list in no particular order of implausibility:

- In *Archives of Opthalmology*, by Manchester P. T. Jr., 'The Blindness of Saint Paul' (1978), Sept. 88 (3), 316-321;
- In *Opthalmology*, by J.D. Bullock, 'The Blindness of St Paul', (1978), October 85 (10): 1044-1053;
- In the *Journal of Neurology, Neurosurgery and Psychiatry*, by D. Landsborough, 'St Paul and Temporal Lobe Epilepsy', (1987), June 50 (6), 659-664.

I can understand that an ophthalmologist might wish to speculate on the physical mechanisms whereby a divine message might communicate itself. But I suspect that the underlying purpose of such papers was and is to present the capacity of science to explain so-called 'visions' as being well within the understanding of medical practitioners who, like their colleagues the neo-Darwinists in the natural sciences, can comprehend all things, whether in heaven or on earth.

It cannot be said that science by its time-honoured standards, or even in its more imaginative mode as 'scientism', is performing very well in accounting for Paul's 'vision'. Parallel events that seemed to require the agency of a Designer have been handled more persuasively. My former colleague Fred Hoyle objected that the conditions required for life on earth to emerge were so manifold and multifarious as to make the mathematical probability of their chance assembly on earth in the time available impossibly small. More imaginative minds were unable to accept Hoyle's preferred solution – that the spores of life were carried to earth on meteors from outer space – but posited the existence of parallel universes as yet undiscovered, sufficient in number and offering ample time during which life might develop by chance. How such a development might be communicated from a parallel universe to our own is yet to be resolved, transport by comet being currently out of favour!

But there does seem to me an alternative way to account for Paul's vision: one that accords better with current scientific thinking and has a considerable body of evidence to support it – even if the evidence offered might require a more stringent validation.

It is generally agreed by Dawkins and the neo-Darwinists that earth and its inhabitants are not a special creation, so the same mindless processes of blind evolution must, by universal necessity, produce life-forms elsewhere, which will inevitably over time develop intelligence, self-consciousness and a consequent curiosity and fear as to other possibly extant life forms in the universe that might be either a comfort or a challenge. Hence, our own widespread and constant monitoring of radio signals and other possible indications from all parts of the universe that might signal a sentient life like our own, which could turn out to be either an enhancement or a major threat to us as a species.

It is conceivable that Paul's so-called 'vision' was an incident like those widely reported in Great Britain and North America, and now a staple of popular entertainment world-wide – the account of a human being taken up by intruders from outer space, with the accompaniment of visual indicators such as lightning flashes and blinding lights, then interrogated by an unknown voice, subjected to brainwashing or similar intrusions into the mental processes and thus re-programmed, so that when he or she is re-inserted into their original environment they fulfil a programme not their own, and possibly one that is the exact opposite to any previous intention they may have had. Such accounts frequently report temporary blindness in the patient or inability to eat after such an ordeal, which fully accords with Paul's response to what was so obviously a violation.

I commend this explanation of Paul's 'vision' to Richard Dawkins and like thinkers for free, with the suggestion that it is likely to be more acceptable to the populace at large than any alternative, and conforms better with their expectations and those of that portion of the scientific community which Dawkins claims to represent. The only problem I foresee is that it is no more self-evidently true than any other neo-Darwinist doctrine.

If I were to re-visit now the grounds on which I took Paul of Tarsus to be my mentor for life, I would acknowledge more fully the witness of those other New Testament reports, the four Gospels and the eight

Letters from writers other than Paul, some of whom seem to have been eye-witnesses where Paul was not, because I would need to assure myself that there was no major contradiction in the record as a whole.

But there remain some questions that I would have liked to have put to Paul direct, if that were possible, but which I can now only answer on Paul's behalf from any evidence that survives.

1. **Did you, Paul, do all in your power to ensure that I and others would receive your opinions accurately?**
2. **Did you check with those who had first-hand experience the accuracy of what you have reported?**
3. (*a question that I can now only direct to myself*) **Are you the kind of person I should have trusted when determining the future direction of my life?**

To attempt an answer to my first question, there is evidence as early as Paul's Second Letter to the Thessalonians (c.49-53 C.E.) that he and one of his church communities had already suffered the consequences of a fake message:

> Concerning the coming of our Lord Jesus Christ and our being gathered to him, we ask you, brothers, not to become easily unsettled or alarmed, by some prophecy, report or letter supposed to have come from us, saying that the day of the Lord has already come.
> (*2 Thessalonians* 2: 1-12)

By the time Paul came to communicate a full account of his teachings and his experience of the Christian faith in a formal treatise to the congregations in Rome (around 57 C.E.), it is obvious that he had developed a battery of measures to ensure that his letters arrived exactly as he had composed them and could be proved to be such.

As he had done previously with similar letters, he concludes his Epistle to the Romans with a personal summary and greetings – though not this time in his own hand, as he had done some years earlier in his Letter to the Galatians: **'SEE WHAT LARGE LETTERS I USE AS I WRITE TO YOU WITH MY OWN HAND!'** (Galatians 6: 11). The problem with that as evidence of authorship is that, without the use of a photocopier, there is no way it could serve to authenticate further copies. When it comes to writing to the Romans, Paul is content to get his amanuensis to send his own greeting: 'I, Tertius, who wrote down this letter, greet you in the Lord' (Romans 16: 22).

What Paul had realized over many years is that the best way to validate communications and ensure that they are regarded as authentic is to rely on a network of personal contacts. As he had done previously when writing to other communities, Paul engages for the Romans a letter-bearer known to the Christian congregations at both ends – in this case, one Phoebe, 'a servant of the church in Cenchrea', a port six miles east of Corinth – whom Paul asks the Romans to receive 'in a way worthy of the saints and to give her any help she may need from you, for she has been a great help to many people, including me' (Romans 16: 1-2). Paul then follows that initial request with a list of some twenty-eight people, some of them Paul's working partners, close friends and even relatives in Rome, together with their families and communities, who are to receive through this current letter a personal salutation, and he adds for good measure greetings from his fellow-worker in Corinth, Timothy, along with 'Lucius and Jason and Sosipater, my relatives' (Romans 16: 21). Then, having encouraged 'Tertius, who wrote down this letter', to append his own greeting (16: 22), Paul adds for good measure salutations from a trio of Corinthian bigwigs: 'Gaius, whose hospitality I and the whole church here enjoy' (16: 23) and 'Erastus, who is the city's director of public works, and our brother Quartus send you their greetings' (16: 24).

Remember, remember, those tiny fragments that lie in the ground to confound the innocent sceptic: not this time a scrap of papyrus, but a large block of stone dug up north-east of the theatre of Corinth in 1929 bearing an inscription in Latin, 'ERASTVS. PRO. AED. S.P. STRAVIT': 'Erastus in return for his aedileship paved this at his own expense'. [14]

Erastus of Corinth inscription found North-East of the theatre of Corinth.

Of course, hope springs eternal in the sceptic breast. There are still scholars who would point out that an 'aedileship' may not necessarily involve responsibility for public works and that 'Erastus' is quite a common name . . .

14. Erastus of Corinth inscription, *read* holylandphotos, wordpress.com.

Nevertheless, there is no doubt that Paul's measures to protect the integrity of his text were inspired. A large number of people at both ends of the channel of communication had an interest in seeing that an accurate text was sent, received and circulated. Imagine the indignation if anyone heard that a letter had arrived with personal greetings to him or her, but they had not been permitted to see it. Worse still, if something had come, but what you were shown proved to have been copied slackly, so that sections were deleted or passages re-written. Imagine, too, if you dropped a line to thank your powerful friend Erastus and he denied all knowledge of being involved in the sending of any such greeting or letter. And if you had paid good money to the local church fund in Rome for a personal copy of what was said to be a complete summary of Paul's doctrine but had also carried a personal greeting to you, imagine if you discovered that Melania two doors down had commissioned a similar copy which had your name omitted and hers in big letters, and she had been given a full text, while you had only an inaccurate summary.

The second question that I would have liked to put directly to Paul – **Did you check with those who had first-hand experience the accuracy of what you have reported?** – is amply answered by the opening of Paul's Letter to the Galatians:

> For you have heard of my previous way of life in Judaism, how intensely I persecuted the church of God and tried to destroy it. I was advancing in Judaism beyond many Jews of my own age and was extremely zealous for the traditions of my fathers. But when God, who set me apart from birth and called me by his grace, was pleased to reveal his Son in me so that I might preach him among the Gentiles, I did not consult any man, nor did I go up to Jerusalem to see those who were apostles before I was, but I went immediately into Arabia and later returned to Damascus.
>
> Then after three years, I went up to Jerusalem to get acquainted with Peter and stayed with him fifteen days. I saw none of the other apostles – only James, the Lord's brother. I assure you before God that what I am writing to you is no lie. Later I went to Syria and Cilicia. I was personally unknown to the churches of Judea that are in Christ. They only heard the report: 'The man who formerly persecuted us is now preaching the faith he once tried to destroy.' And they praised God because of me.
>
> Fourteen years later I went up again to Jerusalem, this time with Barnabas. I took Titus along also. I went in response to a revelation and set before them the gospel that I preach among the Gentiles.

But I did this privately to those who seemed to be leaders, for fear lest I was running or had run my race in vain. Yet not even Titus, who was with me, was compelled to be circumcised, even though he was a Greek. This matter arose, because some false brothers had infiltrated our ranks to spy on the freedom we have in Christ Jesus and to make us slaves. We did not give in to them for a moment, so that the truth of the gospel might remain with you.

As for those who seemed to be important – whatever they were makes no difference to me; God does not judge by external appearance – those men added nothing to my message. On the contrary, they saw that I had been entrusted with the task of preaching the gospel to the Gentiles, just as Peter had been to the Jews. For God, who was at work in the ministry of Peter as an apostle to the Jews, was also at work in my ministry as an apostle to the Gentiles. James, Peter and John, those reputed to be pillars, gave me and Barnabas the right hand of fellowship when they recognized the grace given to me. They agreed that we should go to the Gentiles, and they to the Jews. All they asked was that we should continue to remember the poor, the very thing I was eager to do.
(Galatians 1: 13- 2: 10)

I have quoted Paul's letter at length, not just because it so fully answers my question as to whether Paul had checked his facts with accredited eye-witnesses, but because his self-defence is so revelatory as to the temperament of the man.

I come, then, to the third and most crucial of my questions. Is the character of Paul, as it emerges from his authenticated writings of nearly two thousand years ago, such that I should trust him when deciding the whole future direction of my life?

Undoubtedly, the characteristics and personal style of Paul in his Letters are as recognizable as that of Winston Churchill in those broadcasts and written speeches by which he rallied the British nation to a communal resistance to the Nazis in the Second World War – speeches which my parents followed avidly and which I heard and absorbed as a very young child. To a student of literature, Paul's mental set and his style of writing are as recognizable as a speech penned by Shakespeare or a passage from a novel by Jane Austen.

About both Winston and Paul one might have reservations. Winston remained an unrepentant Tory from the upper classes, and so my extended family universally rejected him as a leader once the war was over. As for Paul, he was anything but tactful: how productive was it to exclaim 'You foolish Galatians!' (Galatians 3: 1) – even if they undoubtedly were so? Paul's choice of phrase in describing his contact after fourteen years with 'those who seemed to be leaders' in the Jerusalem Church (Galatians 2: 2) betrays a personality that had little respect for authority and status, however well-founded that authority might be. 'As for those who seemed to be important – whatever they were makes no difference to me – God does not judge by external appearance – those men added nothing to my message' (Galatians 2: 6). The subsequent disputes that he reports with people who were apostles before him, and who had first-hand knowledge of Christ where he did not, could have been predicted from his own writings (Galatians 2: 11-21).

To be honest, were I still a University Professor in Newcastle NSW and Chairman of Religious Studies, I would think very hard about engaging Paul, despite his academic qualifications, his undoubted knowledge of his subject, and his intense personal commitment to the cause. I would anticipate passionate disputes with colleagues and challenges to my own leadership – though nothing would have prevented me from writing a wholehearted letter of support for any application to 'the Other Place'.

There is an outburst of exasperation that I have heard repeatedly in what has now been well over half a century of academic discussion, one as much from learned professors as from first-year undergraduates: 'For heaven's sake: get **real**!' My family ask me why I give such weight to the evidence of one Paul of Tarsus. My answer is that he was writing at intervals between twenty and a maximum of thirty-eight years after Christ's crucifixion, yet concerning events still central to what we as individuals understand about the nature of the world in which we find ourselves and our own place in it. Whether we are trained in the natural sciences or in the disciplines of historical enquiry, in medicine or psychology, in sociology or the art of predicting human behaviour, in politics or religion, 'getting real' involves assessing the evidence offered by the Jew, Paul or Saul of Tarsus, in writings undoubtedly his, which record his enquiries among those who claimed to be first-hand witnesses to the life, teachings, death and alleged resurrection of Jesus Christ. Face Paul – and 'get **real**!'

It was only when I was well advanced into my assessment of Paul of Tarsus and the reliability of his account of happenings two thousand years distant from my own life and times that I was struck by a strange parallel. Both of us were drawn to participate in assessing criminal events where we had not been eyewitnesses but had a close involvement with those who were. The enquiry involved personal friends and acquaintances, and it drew on a range of persons still alive who could have corrected or even contradicted us. Paul distributed his testimony by a method of communication that was for him worldwide; I gave my evidence across hemispheres, by phone call, e-mail and letter, and the hearings were televised. In either case, the time between the alleged events and our personal testimony was much the same: if Christ's judicial murder and alleged resurrection is dated between 30 and 33 C.E., Paul wrote his letters at intervals from around 50 C.E. to his death under Nero in either 62 or 67 C.E. That means that Paul wrote between as little as twenty years and a maximum of thirty-seven years after those events whose life-changing consequences he reported. In my own case, I did less well; it took thirty-nine years for me to bear my witness and see the truth confirmed and exposed.

But the injunction 'Get real!' has an application much wider than just to Paul's preachings and writings. A whole civilisation was very quickly convulsed by the Christian message. Within a few years the Apostles and their accredited pupils and assistants had promoted the Christian Gospel in spoken and written form to most of the known world. Moreover, for fifty years at least from Christ's death, whether it be in Antioch in the east or Rome in the west or even as far as the coast of India, the dispersion of populations through war and commerce meant that any preacher of the Christian message ran the same hazard: the objection from that elderly lady in the back row (or from her husband who speaks for her) who says: 'My dear, I'm sure you are a very dear young man. But we were both there – and it didn't happen quite like that!' We have evidence that Stephen was stoned to death for what he said had occurred. But is there one record of a dissident old lady or gentleman being hung from a convenient lamp-post?

I have demonstrated, in my own case as well as in the far more significant instance of Saul of Tarsus, that a time-lapse of half a century does not prevent an accurate account of past events emerging, given the likely survival of first-hand witnesses for sixty years or more after the events in question. But the converse is equally true. If, for example, you could find no account from the last fifty years of the River Thames ever flooding the financial centres of the City of London and no one around you who recalled any such happening, you might safely dismiss such a story as no more than an anti-capitalist fantasy.

But genuine disasters infect the human imagination for a century or much longer. The nuclear accident at Chernobyl on 26 April 1986 alerted the whole world to the dangers of nuclear fission and brought down the Union of Soviet Socialist Republics. Skilled dramatizations have made it our nightly entertainment as well as a constant reminder as to the madness of nuclear conflict. But any writing on nuclear power that does not show knowledge of what happened at Chernobyl is either irresponsibly incompetent or must have been written before April 1986.

In the seventieth year of the Christian era, the Jewish nation, its time-honoured faith, and the cultic centre of its worship in Jerusalem suffered a catastrophe of more than Chernobyl proportions. It seems not to have been something foreseen by Paul, who had been executed by Nero at some point in the previous decade. It is possible that some Christians might have anticipated the event, for it happened around the time of that same festival of Passover when the Jews some thirty or so years previous had gathered in Jerusalem from home and abroad to celebrate God's declaration of especial favour to the Jewish race but had connived with their Roman masters to put their supposed and long-promised Messiah, Jesus of Nazareth, to death.

The second catastrophe exceeded all imaginings. After four years of a Jewish rebellion against Rome, the Roman armies under Titus, the future Emperor, broke down the outer wall that protected Israel's most sacred site, burned the Temple of Yahweh to the ground, and then moved south to sack the lower city, with the result that (according to the renegade Jewish historian Josephus) 1.1 million of the population died, 97,000 were enslaved, and thousands were forced to become gladiators and so died in the arenas of the Empire. Jews dispersed to the four corners of the earth, remaining until now, despite their many attainments and survival skills, an abused, exploited and oppressed remnant. Worse still for any of a religious inclination, the office of the High Priest, the governing body under him, the Sanhedrin, and the ritual of the Passover that celebrated the union of God with his 'Chosen People', together with the whole apparatus for maintaining the Jews' favoured relationship with God by sacrifices for sin, by repeated prayers, by thank-offerings and sin-offerings, had all ceased to be. Those objects central to Temple worship, the Menorah, a seven-branched candlestick made from gold (whose image has now been adopted as the emblem of a revived Jewish state), the Table for the Holy Bread, and the other instruments for cultic worship were all carried off to Rome for a formal Triumph that celebrated the humiliation of the Jews and the demonstrable impotence of their God. [15]

But what is undeniable is that nowhere in the New Testament is there any indication that Judaism had yet suffered so appalling a catastrophe. For this there can be only one explanation – unless there was some universal *Faulty Towers* agreement to spare Jewish feelings and 'not talk about the War!' The writers of the New Testament do not mention the fall of Jerusalem and the destruction of the Temple simply because, at the time each of them was writing, it had not happened.

15. See: http://shot.holycross.edu/Courses/ICA/F12/illustrations/historicalrelief.html.

*Sacred implements from the Temple at Jerusalem
carried in triumph to Rome (a bas-relief on the Arch of Titus).*

That is not to say that New Testament writers had no inkling of what was to come. Jesus Christ himself had prophesied that not one stone of the Temple would be left upon another (Matthew 24: 2, Luke 19: 37-43, 21: 5-6), and some forty years or more before the actual disaster Christ had given practical directions to his followers to leave Jerusalem before it was surrounded by armies, 'trampled on by the Gentiles', with its inhabitants falling 'by the sword', or 'taken as prisoners to all the nations' (Luke 21: 20-24). Yet no New Testament writer (with the possible exception of the author of the Book of Revelation) knows that the prophecy has been fulfilled, simply because they were all writing before the fall of Jerusalem and the burning to the ground of the Temple, the central place of Jewish worship. The whole New Testament, therefore, with the possible exception of the book of Revelation, must have been completed before year 70 of the Christian era.

That is by no means a novel assertion. My Cambridge colleague John Robinson, at that time Dean of Trinity College, Cambridge, then subsequently the pastor for my home area as Suffragan Bishop of Southwark, published in 1976 his *Redating the New Testament*[16], where by the assiduous application of the most up-to-date and sophisticated historical methods for handling ancient texts he demonstrated how implausible it was that any New Testament writing, save perhaps the Book of Revelation, could have been put together after the Fall of Jerusalem.

---

16. J.A.T. Robinson, *Redating the New Testament* (London: SCM Press, 1976).

I was surprised therefore, when five years later and on leave from my Australian Chair I called in on John Robinson in his Trinity rooms, intending to congratulate him on a *magnum opus* that any student of ancient literature would be bound to take very seriously, to find him sour and disappointed. Admittedly, most reviewers had picked up on his image of the supposed dates for New Testament writers as being akin to a line of drunks staggering home after a party, each supporting themselves by an arm around their neighbour's neck, but with the inevitable consequence that if one went down, the whole line would collapse. However, when it came to John's effect on New Testament studies, he felt his colleagues had largely ignored him.

I might have said to John Robinson, though it would surely have distressed him yet further, that in the modern university it would seem to be more in the interest of ourselves and of our academic colleagues to keep the pot boiling and so avoid any too definite a conclusion. In the academy as now constituted, to silence opposition is bad for our corporate business. A modern university rewards innovative thought and unconventional practice, as against the bolstering and dissemination of established truth. Yet we need those established truths both as a basis for our scientific advances and for the avoidance of personal and corporate disaster. Over many centuries and in every corner of the world, thousands upon thousands of our fellow human beings have founded their lives and gone to their deaths, trusting in the essential truthfulness and reliability of the gospel narratives. 'Gospel truth' remains our gold standard.

What I can do, in support of John Robinson's dating of the whole New Testament before the year 70 of the Christian Era, is to point to a radical shift in the focus of Christian polemics after that date, as witnessed by the writings of Justin Martyr, born only thirty years later. In some ways nothing had changed, then or now: Christianity will always be a challenge to the absolute authority of the secular state and will, by the stringency of its moral demands, be unavoidably an irritant to any popular culture. It offers also a certainty of opinion that must always run counter to the multiplicity of philosophical theories and is bound to be felt as cramping both to intellectual style and distinctive invention, as Justin realized during his youthful encounters with the philosophical schools of his day.

Justin Martyr failed in his attempt to persuade the Emperor Antoninus Pius (138-161 C.E.) that Christianity was not a threat to the Roman Empire, and both he and his pupils followed the regular path of Christian witness after Antoninus' death, being first cross-examined by the Prefect Junius Rusticus (Prefect between 163 and 167) and then beheaded by the Roman state.

But what did change – and very markedly – was the tone and temper of the Christian approach to the Jews. The argument had always been, in earlier Christian preachings such the Epistle to the Hebrews and throughout Paul's letters, that the Christian faith was simply the fulfilment of promises made by the prophets as to a new dispensation: one that would be introduced because of the failure of God's Chosen People to fully embrace the old. Christianity only expressed more completely what had always been the divine intention. It had been introduced, as foretold, by a long-anticipated Messiah of the Jews, born of King David's line, whose more perfect injunctions and requirements might render redundant some of those rules and regulations given by Moses in the past. Argument centred on whether Jesus of Nazareth had indeed been the expected Messiah or was an imposter and on how much of the old rules might still apply.

The author of the Epistle to the Hebrews, who addresses himself to Jews in particular, is especially knowledgeable about Jewish law and custom, and his main concern is to present Jesus as the promised Messiah, Son of David, but one who has experienced our weaknesses and understands them, 'who has been tempted in every way, just as we are – yet was without sin' (Hebrews 4: 15). He has penetrated the veil of the Temple and will take his followers with him into the Holy Place (Hebrews 6: 19-20). He is a priest not from the Aaronic line but in the order of Melchizedek (Hebrews 5: 10). Jesus Christ enables in us a more perfect fulfilment of the Law, and as our Great High Priest he makes of himself the perfect atoning sacrifice for all our sins. It is understandable that the Epistle to the Hebrews was for many centuries (though there were some objections) attributed to Paul, for both writers were Jews themselves, and both had much the same stance toward the 'People of God'.

The Fall of Jerusalem and the destruction of the Temple changed all that. As is clear from Justin Martyr's *Dialogue with Trypho* the Jew and his Jewish associates, it is no longer a question of 'Which High Priest?', the High Priest of the Jews or the High Priesthood of Jesus Christ. Christ may have been crucified but the Jewish High Priest is no more. God has emphatically declared his utter rejection of those who still think of themselves as his Chosen People.

In Chapter 16 of the *Dialogue with Trypho*,[17] Justin Martyr argues that circumcision 'according to the flesh is from Abraham and was given for a sign . . . that you alone may suffer that which you now justly suffer; and

---

17. Chapter references are to the online edition of Justin Martyr, *Dialogue with Trypho*, in the Early Church Theology Series, Fig Classics, Electronic Edition, August 2012.

that your land may be desolate, and your cities burned with fire; and that strangers may eat your fruit in your presence and not one of you may go up to Jerusalem.' In Chapter 24, Justin again cites Isaiah: 'The city of your holiness has become desolate, Zion has become as a wilderness, Jerusalem a curse; the house, our holiness, and the glory which our fathers blessed, has been burned with fire.'

In Chapter 40, Justin, teaching that the Mosaic laws were 'figures of the things that pertain to Christ', suggests that the Passover regulations were temporary until the true sacrificial Lamb that was Christ could be offered – so such arrangements were necessarily provisional.

> God does not permit the lamb of the Passover to be sacrificed in any other place than where His name was named; knowing that the days will come, after the suffering of Christ, when even the place in Jerusalem shall be given over to your enemies, and all the offerings, in short, shall cease; and that lamb which was commanded to be wholly roasted was a symbol of the suffering of the cross which Christ would undergo. For the lamb, which is roasted, is roasted and dressed up in the form of a cross.

Justin reminds the Jews once again of their loss:

> And further, you are aware that the two goats, which were enjoined to be sacrificed at the fast, was not permitted to take place similarly anywhere else, but only in Jerusalem.

So the Jews after 70 C.E. can never be purified by sacrifice, nor can the selection of them as a favoured nation be memorialized in the Passover sacrifice. That opportunity has been closed, as have all avenues to God save that established eternally through submission to Jesus Christ.

Epilogue

In my beginning is my end . . . In my end is my beginning.
The first and last lines from the second
of T.S. Eliot's *Four Quartets*, 'East Coker'

As I settled to the task of writing an Epilogue to this book, I was reminded once more that I had still done little to address directly the problem with which it all began: the problem (now fifty years back) of what to say to a colleague whose young daughter, when crossing the street to her home, had been knocked down by a passing car and killed outright.

My writing was interrupted by a tap on the door to our bedroom-cum-study in the loft extension of our Cambridge house: our youngest grandson, Daniel, home from his primary school after the last day before the Christmas holidays, and ready for his dunking ceremony. This, a custom recently introduced by my wife, is a shared dunking of hard ginger biscuits into tea, coffee or fruit-juice, strongly restorative when badgered by siblings or in trouble with parents, powerful even against matrimonial disputes.

After the customary ritual, Daniel asked what I had been doing for so long. I explained that I had been writing about a man called Richard Dawkins, who had said that all life was accidental and meaningless – though I was using him as an example of a range of opinions that made some people very unhappy.

I then reminded Daniel that I had asked permission from all five of my grandchildren to dedicate my book to them. Not only was his name there with the others at the front, but there was a picture of him and his elder brother Matthew, in the first chapter, where I explained how much they meant to me.

Then flashed into my mind – though I didn't think it opportune to mention it to Daniel – an image of my last meeting with my own grandfather, when I and my cousin-brother John must have been about Daniel's age. Totally contrary to the wishes of my mother and of my aunt, and against fierce opposition from our grandmother, John and I were summoned together, on our own, to attend our grandfather's deathbed.

Grandfather had always been someone who alarmed me. Every time I met him, he insisted on being kissed – and this meant negotiating his unkempt but luxuriant beard, dotted with remnants of his most recent meal. There had always been some odd tension in the family over Aunt Ivy's hair, and only after Grandfather's death did I learn why. In the trenches of the First World War, Grandfather had had a bosom-friend, with the most striking ginger hair, who had made him promise, in the event that the friend was killed, that Grandfather would look after his widow, Bella. Grandfather had honoured his promise to his dead friend by marrying her – but the daughter of that second marriage was born with the most luxuriant auburn hair.

Grandfather in his youth had been something of a Bible-basher – though that faded after his marriage. But my last memory is of him drawing the attention of Cousin John and myself to the copy of the New Testament lying open across his bare chest, putting a hand on its pages and then saying to us both: 'I want you both to know: if people had paid more attention to this, the world would be a much better place.'

I am aware, naturally, that it is likely that within the next decade I shall know finally, or not know eternally, the truth or otherwise of what I have believed for the last sixty years. So I took the opportunity to explain to Daniel some of the reasons why I had included in my book a picture of him and his brother, and I confessed that, whenever I felt miserable or depressed or that life was perhaps not worth living, I sat in the corner of the living room, watched him and his brother, and marvelled at their existence.

I asked Daniel how old he was. – 'Eight'. – 'I remember a time when I didn't know you. Where *were* you?' – Daniel, with a cheeky grin: 'In my mummy's tummy'. – 'But where were you before that?' – Silence and a grin of comprehension. – 'So how can you and your brother be so wonderful?' We fell silent, savouring a truth too great to be expressed:

'Where wast thou when I laid the foundations of the earth? . . . When the morning stars sang together, and all the sons of God shouted for joy?' (Job 38: 4-7, Authorized Version).

In one day's time, our extended family will celebrate, with the world at large, our corporate wonder and delight at the birth of a child: the recurrent marvel of creation *ex nihilo* – apparently, from nowhere. It will be almost as extraordinary as hearing a Richard Dawkins assert that life occurs blindly and without meaning: where was *he*, from the foundation of the earth?

But what we will celebrate as Christians, in an otherwise dark and terrifying world, is the incursion into our pained existence of the Supreme Commander of the Forces of Light. That is what I failed to say to my colleague fifty or more years ago, suffering the loss of his daughter simply because a stranger had been careless of her life: I was afraid of meeting blank incomprehension if I said what I believed, that death is not necessarily the end.

If I find myself inhibited this time from what I ought to say, it is not from fear that a consoling truth will be rejected, but by a sense, which seems shared by the world at large, that what I anticipate rationally will not be allowed to happen. Nuclear weapons were first used in this world when I was five years old. Their proliferation amongst competing nations and their ever-increasing destructive power, must mean, rationally, and given human nature, that through international power-struggles and our inability to control our own aggressive yet self-destructive inclinations, we are bound, sometime in the next seventy years, to destroy ourselves and the planet on which we live. If I did not wish to be around to see my grandchildren through that, I would want to be about to help them endure a climate change that even immediate action seems unlikely to mitigate sufficiently to make life as sustainable as it once was. In the meantime, an increasing concentration of the resources and riches of the world in the hands of one or two per cent of the population (now according to leading economists an undeniable fact in America, and in Great Britain a likely consequence of a Brexit that will take us out of cooperative interaction with the countries of Europe) is going to lead us further into worldwide exploitation of the many by the few.[1]

The problem for believers and unbelievers alike is that there is a war at present around us that none of us are keen to talk about – 'Don't talk about the War!' – that apparently eternal conflict within our own personalities

---

1. See, for example, the Nobel Prize winner Joseph Stiglitz, *The Price of Inequality* (New York, NY, and London: W.W. Norton & Co., 2012) and *The Great Divide: Unequal Societies and What We Can Do about Them* (New York, NY, and London: W.W. Norton & Co., 2015).

and in the world at large between the powers of good and evil. What I most fear from any reviewer of this current book is the derisive headline: 'Satan Rides Again!'

And yet the 'Understanding Unbelief' programme led by the University of Kent that I have referred to previously,[2] which interviewed thousands of people across six countries, Britain, the United States, Brazil, China, Denmark and Japan, found that almost a third of atheists and forty-five per cent of agnostics in Britain 'believe in underlying forces of good and evil, compared with almost 60 per cent of the general population'.

How then can it be that the Christian Churches and I myself are so nervous of rehearsing the truth of the matter as put out by the man whom we insist theoretically both to be fully human and also the Second Person of the Trinity and the Son of God – someone who unites in his personhood the relationship on offer: a unity of love between God and Man? Do we need to 'get real' not only about ourselves but about what we really believe about Jesus of Nazareth and his always fashionable and yet never entirely accepted message? The ministry of Jesus Christ began with an account which, if true, could only have come from Jesus himself: the story of his encounter with Satan in the wilderness (Matthew 4: 1-11; Luke 4: 1-13). From the outset, Christ faces the decision that is before all human beings, of which way to go. He rejects the offer of worldly power and possessions if achieved by Satanic means and refuses to test God's willingness to save him from a deliberate act of self-destruction, even if that might be something you could take to be a confirmation of status. In actual human circumstances, there are no guarantees, only a choice between attitudes, and maybe a decision 'for the work's sake'.

Nevertheless, Christ was always insistent that physical ailments and mental and spiritual malfunction were not accidental but are, like death itself and human wrongdoing, all the product of evil or more specifically of 'the Evil One', from whom the prayer he taught his followers pleads that we be delivered. Christ anticipated accurately his rejection by the Jews and his death at the hands of the Roman authorities and prophesied that he would 'rise again on the third day' – a promise understood by his followers to be a guarantee that physical death in this world would be followed by resurrection, and reported by them as a simple fact.

He also taught that evil would eventually be overthrown, but after the destruction of the current order, the putting down of the worldly powers and heavenly potentates and the institution of 'a new heaven and a new

---

2. Anna Behrmann, 'Atheists have belief in the supernatural', *The Times*, 3 June 2019, p. 11.

earth' as prophesied by the Jewish prophets, where the whole natural order, suffused with wonder yet inflamed by the horrors of cruelty, suffering and death, will at last be put to rights:

> A shoot will come up from the stump of Jesse;
> From his roots a Branch will bear fruit.
> The Spirit of the Lord will rest on him –
> the Spirit of wisdom and of understanding,
> the Spirit of counsel and of power,
> the Spirit of knowledge and of the fear of the Lord –
> and he will delight in the fear of the Lord.
>
> He will not judge by what he sees with his eyes,
> or decide by what he hears with his ears;
> but with righteousness he will judge the needy,
> with justice he will give decisions for the poor of the earth.
> He will strike the earth with the rod of his mouth;,
> with the breath of his lips he will slay the wicked.
> Righteousness will be his belt
> and faithfulness the sash around his waist.
>
> The wolf will live with the lamb,
> the leopard will lie down with the goat,
> the calf and the lion and the yearling together;
> and a little child will lead them.
>
> The cow will feed with the bear,
> their young will lie down together,
> and the lion will eat straw like the ox.
> The infant will play near the hole of the cobra,
> and the young child put his hand into the viper's nest.
> They will neither harm nor destroy on all my holy mountain,
> for the earth will be full of the knowledge of the Lord
> as the waters cover the sea.
> (Isaiah 11: 1-9)

The greatest threat to Christianity in its early centuries was the danger represented by the Gnostics – in modern English, 'Them as know'. How far there was any similarity with modern opponents of Christianity is hard to tell: the modern flowering of university departments for religious studies has resulted in so complex an account of supposedly Gnostic beliefs and their manifold sources that it is hard to detect any parallel between them and modern opponents of Christianity, save the confident if unjustified belief that they both have a special skill in determining what is and what is not.

It used to be said of the Gnostics that they believed in two, mutually opposed and eternally irreconcilable powers of good and evil, or that some believed in a God who had made a subordinate demi-urge who in creating the world had deviated from the divine intention. Both explanations are clearly alternative ways of explaining our experience of good and evil.

The Christian explanation of all our ills, then and now, is that God chose to give freedom to all his creation: first to the heavenly powers, then to his late and most cherished creation, Man. He would not compel love, nor any blind or automatic obedience: he gave to human beings and to angels the power to choose. Choice extended to the whole world of executive spirits, some of whom developed life-forms according to the appropriate divine blueprint and performed creative variations, whilst some – if they had refused divine direction – might engineer a range of malevolent variations on the divine plan, enticing (for instance) the creatures of the deep to prey on one another, and the whole developing world to be 'red in tooth and claw'. Even that, however, could not entirely preclude reversion to something nearer to the divine intention: our cat Pinkerton, identifying with his owners as his better angels, could learn to defend the birds that were his 'natural' prey: Christian the Lion could recall his first affection, restrain his 'killer instinct' and embrace the eatable young man who had nourished him as a cub.

Why we as a race should have been given freedom to choose to respond in love to God and to his manifold and multifarious creations – or to refuse – is something that cannot be easily explained. But when it comes to freedom to love or not love, to respond or not to respond, I have never read or met anyone who wanted it to be otherwise. We are repelled by killing in the natural world, unless there is something that appeals to our own aggressive inclinations. We flinch from anyone who appears to care for us just out of a sense of duty. Perhaps, if we were fully to recognize our own loveability as it should be recognized, we had first of all to be ourselves free to choose.

As for the Christmas that approaches, it marks (as I have said earlier) the irruption into our imperfect and broken world of the forces of light, an invasion by which the world will, in the fullness of time, be made new, where the earthly and heavenly oppressors will have been overthrown, where 'the lion shall eat straw like the ox' and 'the young child will put his hand into the viper's nest', 'where they shall neither hurt nor destroy in all my holy mountain', 'where the earth will be full of the knowledge of the Lord as the waters cover the sea', where our understanding will be complete, where vision and scientific knowledge are united, and what should be is what is.

Christmas Eve, 2019

Further Reading

As supportive of and supplementary to my discussion of the origin of life on earth and its subsequent development, I would direct the reader first to two comprehensive studies by Johnathan Wells of the evidence for and against the neo-Darwinist account of accidental and undirected evolution: Icons of Evolution, Science or Myth? (Regnery Publishing, Washington DC, 2000) and his follow-up study a decade later, Zombie Science: More Icons of Evolution (Discovery Institute Press, Seattle, WA, 2010).

Bibliography

Behe, Michael, *Darwin Devolves: The New Science About DNA That Challenges Evolution* (New York, NY: Harper One, 2019), accessed in the Kindle edition (Sydney, Australia: Harper Collins, 2019)

——*Darwin's Black Box: The Biochemical Challenge to Evolution* (New York, NY: Simon & Schuster, 1996, second edition 2006)

——*The Edge of Evolution: The Search for the Limits of Darwinism* (New York, NY: Free Press, 2006)

——Behe and the Mystery of Molecular Machines', Discovery Science: https://www.youtube.com.watch?v=7ToSEAj2VOs

Bunyan, John, *Grace Abounding to the Chief of Sinners* and *The Pilgrim's Progress*, ed. with an Introduction by Roger Sharrock (London: Oxford University Press, 1966)

Burnett, Bishop Gilbert: SOME PASSAGES ON THE Life and Death Of the Right Honourable JOHN Earl of *ROCHESTER,* Who died the 26th July 1680. Written by his own Direction on his Death Bed, By *Gilbert Burnet* D.D. *LONDON,* Printed for *Richard Chiswell,* at the *Rose* and *Crown* in St. *Paul's Church-Yard,* 1680. A facsimile is available in the Early English Books series, at: quod.lib. umich.edu/e/eebo/A30466.0001?view=toc

The Cambridge Liturgical Psalter (with Notes) (Cambridge: Aquila, 2012), first published as *The Psalms: A New Translation for Worship,* copyright David L. Frost, John A. Emerton, Andrew A. Macintosh (London: William Collins, 1976, 1977) and re-published in a number of national prayerbooks

Chrysostom, St John, *Homilies on the Gospel of Saint Matthew,* Vol. X, First Series (Grand Rapids, Michigan: W.B.Eerdmans Publishing Co., 1978)

Collins, Francis, *The Language of God: A Scientist Provides Evidence for Belief* (New York, NY: Free Press, 2006)

Crick, Francis, *Life Itself: Its Origin and Nature* (New York: Simon & Schuster, 1982)

Cyril of Alexandria, St., *Commentary on the Gospel of St Luke*, Homily 121, B#42 (Astoria, NY: Studion Publishers, 1983)

Darwin, Charles, Letters to Asa Gray, at: https: Biodiversitylibrary.org/ bibliography/130912#/summary

Darwin-Hooker Letters, Cambridge University Library, cudl.lib.cam.ac.uk/ collections/darwinhooker

Davies, Paul, *The Demon in the Machine: How Hidden Webs of Information Are Solving the Mystery of Life* (London: Allen Lane, 2019)

—— *The Goldilocks Enigma: Why Is the Universe Just Right for Life?* (London: Allen Lane, 2006)

Dawkins, Richard, *The God Delusion* (London: Bantam Press, 2006)

——*River out of Eden: A Darwinian View of Life* (Basic Books, a division of Harper Collins, New York NY, 1995 and Orion, an imprint of Weidenfeld & Nicholson, London, 1995)

Flew, Antony, with Roy Abraham Varghese, *There Is A God: How the World's Most Notorious Atheist Changed his Mind* (New York, NY: Harper Collins, 2007)

Harris, Stephen L., *The New Testament: A Student's Introduction*, fourth edition (Boston, MA: McGraw-Hill, 2002)

Hoyle, Fred and Wickramasinghe, Chandra, *Evolution from Space: A Theory of Cosmic Creationism* (New York, NY: Simon & Schuster, 1982)

—— 'The Universe: Past and Present Reflections', *Engineering and Science* (November 1981)

Hume, David, *An Enquiry Concerning Human Understanding*, Section X, 'Of Miracles', PART I, see:https://davidhume.org/texts/e/10

Jammer, Max, *Einstein and Religion* (Princeton, NJ: Princeton University Press, 1999)

Martyr, Justin, *Dialogue with Trypho,* Early Church Theology Series, Fig Classics, Electronic Edition, August 2012

Moreland, J.P., Stephen C. Meyer, Christopher Shaw, Ann K. Gauger and Wayne Grudem (eds), *Theistic Evolution: A Scientific, Philosophical, and Theological Critique* (Wheaton, IL: Crossway Books, 2017)

Nicholson, R.A., *Rūmī, Poet and Mystic* (London: Allen & Unwin, 1950)

Novikoff, Alex J., *The Medieval Culture of Disputation: Pedagogy, Practice and Performance* (Philadelphia, PA: University of Pennsylvania Press, 2013)

Phillips, J.B., *Your God is Too Small* (New York, NY: The Macmillan Company, 1953)

—— *Letters to Young Churches* (London: Collins/Fontana Books, 1955; also London: Geoffrey Bles, 1957)

Plato, *The Republic*, VI, translated by Benjamin Jowett, The Internet Classics Archive, classics.mit.edu/Plato/republic.7.vi.html

Psalms: a New Translation: see entry above for (The) *Cambridge Liturgical Psalter*

Robinson, J.A.T, *Redating the New Testament* (London: SCM Press, 1976)

Rochester, John, Earl of: for an account his opinions and dramatic conversion, see Burnett, Bishop Gilbert

Shapiro, Robert, *Origins: A Skeptic's Guide to the Creation of Life on Earth* (New York: Summit Books, 1986; 1987)

Sherlock, Thomas, *The Trial of the Witnesses to the Resurrection of Jesus* (1729 edition), typescript converted to computer file by Lee Dunbar, July 2002, to be found at: https://classicapologetics.com/s/shertrial.pdf

Strauss, David Friedrich, *The Life of Jesus, Critically Examined,* translation of the fourth edition, by George Eliot in 1843 (New York, NY: Cosimo Books, 2009)

Stiglitz, Joseph, *The Price of Inequality* (New York, NY, and London: W.W. Norton & Co., 2012)

—— *The Great Divide: Unequal Societies and What We Can Do about Them* (New York, NY, and London: W.W. Norton & Co., 2015)

Tennyson, Lord Alfred, 'Ulysses'; 'In Memoriam A.H.H. (Arthur Henry Hallam): see: poetryfoundation.org/poems/45392/Ulysses

Weijers, Olga, *In Search of the Truth: A History of Disputation Techniques from Antiquity to Early Modern Times* (Turnhout, Belgium: Brepols Publishers, 2013

Werner, Carl, *EVOLUTION: The Grand Experiment – The Quest for an Answer* (Green Forest, AR, New Leaf Press, third edition 2014)

Wilson, A.N. *Charles Darwin: Victorian Mythmaker* (London: John Murray, 2017)

Articles

Aubin, Henri-Jean, Ivan Berlin and Charles Kornreich, 'The Evolutionary Puzzle of Suicide', *International Journal of Environmental Research and Public Health,* Vol. 10, no. 12 (December 2013)

Behrmann, Anna, 'Atheists have belief in the supernatural', *The Times,* 3 June 2019,

Brown, Olen R., 'Enzymes Are Essential for Life; Did They Evolve?' at https://evolutionnews.org/author/olenbrown/), August 22, 2018

Coyne, Jerry A, Review of Michael Behe: 'Intelligent design gets even dumber', *The Washington Post,* 8 March 2019

Hugdahl, Kenneth, 'Auditory Hallucinations: A review of the ERC "Voice" Project, *World Journal of Psychiatry,* Vol. 5, no. 2 (June 2015), pp. 193-209, surveying 117 learned papers, available online at: https://www.ncbi.nlm.nih.gov/pmc/articles/PMC4473491/

Nongbri, Brent, 'The Use and Abuse of P52: Papyrological Pitfalls in the Dating of the Fourth Gospel, *Harvard Theological Review,* Vol. 98, no. 1 (2005), pp. 23-48

Thomson, William, 'The Sorting Demon of Maxwell', *Nature,* Vol. 20, no. 501 (1879)

Videoclips and Internet References

BBC One, 'The Human Body', Episode 2, www.bbc.co.uk/programmes/b096slbg.

BBC Two, 'Natural World: The Ant Factory'; also BBC Nature's 'Miniature Miracles', Episode 5, 'The Ant Factory', http://www.bbc.co.uk/news/business-44789823

Behe and the Mystery of Molecular Machines', Discovery Science: https://www.youtube.com.watch?v=7ToSEAj2VOs

'Capuchin monkey fairness experiment', https://www.youtube.com/watch? v=-KSryJXDpZo

Crear, Simon, 12 April 2013, approach to wild animals, *The Courier Mail (Australia)*

[Chimps] https:/www.bing.com/videos/search?q=Nature+Chimps+Keeping+a+Pet

[Crow] 'Causal understanding of water displacement by a crow' at youtube.com/watch?v=Zer4bHmuY0

Davies, Professor Nick: see 'Reed Warbler'

[Drongo]'Drongo bird tricks meerkats', BBC Earth (Africa), excerpt available at: https://www.youtube.com/watch?v=tEYCjJqr21A

[Elephants]'Rare Footage: Wild Elephants "Mourn" Their Dead', www.nationalgeographic.com, 31 August 2016

[Evolution] evolutionfaq.com/faq/have-scientists-ever-created-life-laboratory, accessed 27 August 2019

[Intelligent Design] https://evolutionnews.org/2017/06/brian-josephson-nobel-laureate-in-physics-is-80-percent-confident-in-intelligent-design/

[Lion, Christian] https://www.youtube/watch?v=hLHDp_dL5Uk

"Liquid water 'lake' revealed on Mars", – BBC News, 27 July 2018, at: https://www.bbc.co.uk/news/science-environment-44952710

[Mars] https://www.youtube.com/watch?v=Dfg1n7Lh62Q

Megalodon: Wikipedia Commons, https://en.wikipedia.org/wiki/FileVMNH_megalodon.jpg

'Molecular Machines', Discovery Science: https://www.youtube.com.watch?v=7ToSEAj2VOs

Musk, Elon, https://www.independent.co.uk/life-style/gadgets-and-tech/news/elon-musk-mars-launch-2019-bfr-spacex-next-year-sxsw-falcon-heavy-a8251081.html

Papavassiliou, Archimandrite Vassilios, 'Original Sin: Orthodox Doctrine or Heresy?', 25 February 2017, at: http://pemptousia.com/2017/02/original-sin-orthodox-doctrine-or-heresy, accessed 13 August 2019

['Playing possum"] (shamming dead): https://en.wiipedia.org/Apparent_death=media/File:Opossom2.jpg

—— [hognose snake] youtube.com/watch?v=ICPVGstdNjU

—— [surviving bear-attack] https://www.mnn.com/earth-matters/animals/stories/how-to-survive-a-bear-attack

'Pufferfish Love Explains Mysterious Underwater Circles', via Netflix, from BBC Four, 'Life Story', Episode 5

'Rabbit Rescue'. See among many: edition.cnn.com/2017/12/07/US/California-wildfires-rabbit-trnd/index.html

[Reed Warbler] Professor Nick Davies, 'The Reed Warbler and the Cuckoo: An Escalating Game of Trickery and Defence', available at https://www.cam.ac.uk/research/features, 22 February 2016

[Sealion] https://thedodo.com/sea-lion-mother-crying-1819338298.html

Spy in the Wild, DVD Disc 1, 'Love' (London: BBC Earth and Dazzler Media, 2017)

Spy in the Wild, DVD Disc 2, 'Mischief' (London: BBC Earth and Dazzler Media, 2017)

'Tanzanian lion nurses leopard cub', *The Guardian*, 14 July 2017, and www.livescience.com

[Tubingen# Nazi period] https://en.wikipedia.org/wiki/University_of_
    Tübingen#Nazi_period, accessed 3 March 2020
[Whales]'Humpback whales' attempt to stop killer whale attack' from BBC 1,
    'Planet Earth Live', 11 May 2012, available via You Tube
Tunmore, Karen, 'A killer with a conscience? Why murderer Karen Tunmore
    was devoted to good causes, *The Chronicle*, 4 October 2018, https://www.
    chroniclelive.co.uk/news/north-east-news/killer-conscience-murderer-karen-
    tunmore-15226714.
——https://www.thetimes.co.uk/edition/news/football-coach-hands-herself-in-to-
    police-14-years-after-killing-teen-6kcf6qlvt
——'Scott Pritchard murder: The full story behind Karen Tunmore's dark secret
    and dramatic confession', *The Chronicle*, 1 October 2018, https://www.
    chroniclelive.co.uk/news/north-east-news/scott-pritchard-murder-full-
    story-15220542

Index

Note: page references in **bold** are for illustrations.

You may also be interested in:

Creationism and the Conflict over Evolution
Tatha Wiley

A concise and accessible analysis of the controversy between evolutionism and creationism rejecting simplistic science-versus-religion stereotypes.

Creationism and the Conflict over Evolution attempts to move our understanding of the relationship between creation and evolution away from the biblical literalism of fundamentalism to a historically aware and scholarly framework in which each of the components involved – the Bible, Christian doctrine, evolutionary science, and creationism – can be intelligently understood.

Dr Wiley clarifies the theological notion of creation and the necessity of a historical-critical approach in understanding the Bible, and explains the nature of scientific enquiry and the scientific importance of Darwin's theory. In doing so, she rejects as illegitimate the idea that divine creation and biological evolution are incompatible.

She goes on to analyse modern creationism by tracing its historical development and discussing the religious concerns underlying creationist resistance to evolution. She concludes that these concerns lack adequate theological foundation, and defends the integrity of science education against creationist attempts to undermine the teaching of evolutionary biology in schools.

Dr Tatha Wiley is the author of *Original Sin: Origins, Developments, Contemporary Meaning* and *Paul and the Gentile Women: Reframing Galatians*. She has edited the volume *Thinking of Christ: Proclamation, Explanation, Meaning* and the series *Engaging Theology: Catholic Perspectives*, and teaches theology at the University of St Thomas and the College of St Catherine in St Paul, Minnesota.

Print Paperback ISBN: 978 0 227 17282 7 / PDF ISBN: 978 0 227 90303 2
Specifications: 203x127mm (8x5in), 164pp
Published: June 2009

Evolutionary Creation
A Christian Approach to Evolution
Denis O. Lamoureux

*An approach to origins trascending the traditional
'evolution-versus-creation' debate, providing a vision of evolution
as the unfolding of God's creative power.*

In this provocative book, evolutionist and evangelical Christian Denis O. Lamoureux proposes an approach to origins that moves beyond the 'evolution-versus-creation' debate. Arguing for an intimate relationship between the Book of God's Words and the Book of God's Works, he presents evolutionary creation – a position that asserts that the Father, Son, and Holy Spirit created the universe and life through an ordained and sustained evolutionary process. This view of origins affirms an evolutionary understanding of the concept of intelligent design and the belief that beauty, complexity, and functionality in nature reflect the mind of God.

Lamoureux also challenges the popular Christian assumption that the Holy Spirit revealed scientific and historical facts in the opening chapters of the Bible. He contends that Scripture features an ancient understanding of origins that functions as a vessel to deliver inerrant and infallible messages of faith.

The book closes with the two most important issues in the origins controversy – the pastoral and pedagogical implications. How should churches approach this volatile topic? And what should Christians teach their children about origins?

Denis O. Lamoureux is an assistant professor of science and religion at St. Joseph's College, University of Alberta, Canada. He holds three earned doctoral degrees – in dentistry, theology, and biology. He coauthored with Philip E. Johnson *Darwinism Defeated? The Johnson-Lamoureux Debate on Biological Origins.*

Print Paperback ISBN: 978 0 7188 9191 6 / PDF ISBN: 978 0 7188 4284 0
Specifications: 229x153mm (9x6in), 512pp
Published: February 2009

BV - #0026 - 241121 - C0 - 234/156/15 - PB - 9780227177112